THE NARRATIVE OF CARLOS FUENTES: FAMILY, TEXT, NATION

HM8

Copyright © Steven Boldy 2002

The right of Steven Boldy to be identified as the author of this work has been asserted by him in accordance with the Copyright, Designs and Patents Act 1988.

Published by Manchester University Press
Oxford Road, Manchester M13 9NR, UK
and Room 400, 175 Fifth Avenue, New York, NY 10010, USA
www.manchesteruniversitypress.co.uk

Distributed exclusively in the USA by
Palgrave, 175 Fifth Avenue, New York NY 10010, USA

Distributed exclusively in Canada by
UBC Press, University of British Columbia, 2029 West Mall, Vancouver, BC, Canada V6T 1Z2

British Library Cataloguing-in-Publication Data
A catalogue record for this book is available from the British Library

Library of Congress Cataloging-in-Publication Data
A catalog record for this book is available from the Library of Congress

ISBN 978 0 7190 8591 8 *paperback*

First published 2002 by Durham Modern Languages Series

This edition first published 2011 by Manchester University Press

Printed by Lightning Source

THE NARRATIVE OF CARLOS FUENTES: FAMILY, TEXT, NATION

Steven Boldy

Durham Modern Languages Series

University of Durham 2002

For Isabel and Emily

Contents

INTRODUCTION	1
I: FIRST NOVELS	7
La región más transparente, 1958: Mexico and Memory	11
Las buenas conciencias, 1959: Family Tradition and Individual Talent	53
La muerte de Artemio Cruz, 1962: Fathers and Sons, History and Myth	75
II: SERIOUS GAMES	105
Cambio de piel, 1967: Literature and Evil	107
Zona sagrada, 1967: Carnival Time	141
III: NATIONALISM UNWRITTEN	159
Una familia lejana, 1980: Ballet transatlántico, fandango en los sótanos de la muerte	161
Gringo viejo, 1985: Over the Río Grande	187
IV: NOVELLA CYCLES	203
Agua quemada, 1981: Violence and Impunity	205
Constancia y otras novelas para vírgenes, 1989: A Post-Modern Baroque	215
La frontera de cristal, 1995: Frontier Realism	231
BIBLIOGRAPHY	245

INTRODUCTION

This study analyses ten works of narrative by Carlos Fuentes written over almost forty years, from 1958 to 1995. It is closely based on twelve articles published in journals between 1984 and 2000 and one unpublished piece. The first, on *La muerte de Artemio Cruz*, was written in Liverpool as a presentation for a post at Tulane University, New Orleans, in 1983, and the latest, on *Una familia lejana*, a novel which has haunted me for a long time, made my brain ache for most of the summer and autumn of 2000.

The various chapters will carry the scars of their origin, as the pieces on which they are based were written for different purposes — conference papers, a memorial lecture, journal articles, some conceived as chapters. The time span over which they were written produces inevitably some divergence in approach and terminology, which I have opted not to iron out too obviously. Some were written in Spanish, which might also leave its mark. Some were written with enormous labour, which showed mainly in a laboured style. Others emerged relatively easily with results which displeased me less. On rereading or reworking some I have come across occasional flippancy or even improbability in interpretation. Mostly, however, they are the fruit of a continuing excitement and fascination with Fuentes's texts, some determination, and committed engagement with the complexities and challenges they offer. Beyond superficial differences, all my work on Fuentes was conceived in the same spirit, and follows a series of coherent concerns. The pieces were after all written on the same author, who, in an enormous range of styles and genres, which do not necessarily correspond to any chronology, returns to the same intellectual, existential and ethical issues. They were also written by the same person — yo, desgraciadamente ... no soy Borges.

In all of Fuentes's work, the individual is inseparable from others, is conceived within a family, and is part of patterns developing over generations, through historical periods, of which he may or may not be aware, or have memory. Children from Rodrigo Pola in *La región más transparente* to Bernabé Aparicio in *Agua quemada*, twenty-three years later, inherit dilemmas from their fathers which they have to face and rework, or may invert by choosing alternative father figures. Inseparable twins, *cuates*, of antithetical or complementary values, from Lorenzo Cruz and Jaime Ceballos in *La muerte de Artemio Cruz*, through Guillermo and Giancarlo in *Zona sagrada*, up to Dantón and Santiago in *Los años con Laura Díaz*, thirty-seven years later, play out parallel dramas: existential, intellectual, moral or concerned with representation.

The texts display a self-conscious, but passionate, sustained and often dramatic dialogue with literary and cultural tradition. This may be with the whole of the Medieval and Renaissance Spanish tradition, as in *Terra Nostra*, or an intertextual engagement with the life and works of a specific writer such as Ambrose Bierce in *Gringo viejo* or Alexandre Dumas in *Una familia lejana*. The range of cultural reference is breathtaking and demanding on the reader, liberating but at the same time questioning and problematised, highly cosmopolitan but ever focused on the realities of Mexico and Latin America, rerooted into its discourse. Originality, belatedness, significant process and decentred play, national identity and internationalist dialogue are not alternatives but a vital cultural project. The effect may be Oedipal or fantastic as Felipe Montero literally rewrites the memoirs of General Llorente in *Aura* and is seduced by his one-hundred-year-old wife; it may be comically inappropriate as when Baltasar Bustos in *La campaña*, a passionate disciple of the nature-loving Rousseau as a model for American Independence, loses the complete works of his master when surrounded to his horror by a rather natural herd of cattle.

Christianity is important. From the scruple-bound and tortured adolescent reading of Mounier and Kierkegaard in *Las buenas conciencias*, through the Nietzschean polemic and paradoxes of the Madness of the Cross in *Cambio de piel* and the emblematic struggle between dogma and heresy of *Terra Nostra*, to the post-modern virgins, saints and martyrs of *Constancia y otras novelas para vírgenes*, it is a recurring presence. In the early works, especially, the notion of Christian sacrifice and redemption is one thread in a complex fabric: Manuel in *La región*, shot in a *cantina*, Lorenzo Cruz playing out in the Spanish Pyrenees the story of redemption dramatised in the *Divina Commedia*.

National identity is central to Fuentes's project. In *La región* the debates of the *filosofía de lo mexicano* are dramatised by Ixca, Robles and Zamacona, telluric and racial essences are played off against the rapid capitalist modernisation of 1950s Mexico City, while in *Artemio Cruz*, the curse of *la chingada*, the violation inseparable from the birth of Mexico in the Conquest and repeated in alienating cruelty is challenged by an affirmation of freedom in writing and behaviour. Later, national identity is approached more as dialogue and exchange with others: the none-too-subtle exchange of U.S. and Mexican national clichés and their textual dissolution in *Gringo viejo*; the uncontrollably complex migration of texts, ideas, poets and families between France and Latin America in *Una familia lejana*: the hybrid, neon-light neo-realism of the Ciudad Juárez/El Paso border in *La frontera de cristal*.

Fuentes, like the Cuban Alejo Carpentier, is a key historical novelist in Spanish America. A highly detailed reference to the events, periods and personalities of Mexican history lends a powerful structure to novels from *La muerte de Artemio Cruz* through *Agua quemada* to *Los años con Laura Díaz*. But that history is also woven into different temporalities, alternative memories: cyclical, eschatological, mythical, reversible. In texts like *Artemio Cruz*, history is complex but seen as a grand, powerful scheme. Artemio has a direct experience and memory of the Mexican Revolution, even though one key episode is rewritten from a novel by Stephen Crane on the American Civil War. In *Gringo viejo* he chooses to emphasise the irremediably textual and mediated nature of history: the Revolution can be glimpsed only through multiple layers of ideology, fake propaganda movies from the U.S. and romanticising films from Mexico, the tradition of the *novela de la revolución*, extraneous texts on other historical realities, Bierce's stories of the American Civil War, which filter into the picture... But this is not a straightforward move from naive referentiality to post-modern scepticism, but a shifting focus, which can easily be reversed, as it is in *Los años con Laura Díaz*.

Representation, the being of language, is problematised but not fetichised in these novels. The language of the novel opens out to that of other media: architecture, film, painting. The concentration camp, the temple, the pyramid, and the church in *Cambio de piel* speak of narrative closure, foreshadowing the authoritarian, dogmatic structure of El Escorial in *Terra Nostra,* while the rooms of Mito and his mother Claudia in *Zona sagrada* are opposed like Diocletian's palace in Split and the castle of Capodimonti in *Cumpleaños*: layering, and palimpsest against absolute, original space. Such oppositions are undone in the dizzying games of *Constancia*, where inside and outside, unity and dispersion, in the shopping malls of Savannah, and in the labyrinthine echoes between the stories, are endlessly shuffled. Pre-war German films alluded to intertextually in *Cambio de piel*, even reproduced in stills, carry political meaning, and also, as in the case of *The Cabinet of Dr Caligari*, point to inversions and questionings of the authority of narrator and author, their power to control and neutralise the Other. In *Zona sagrada*, while the presence of Fellini's cinema points to the similarly self-conscious games in the novel itself, Mito at one point becomes a cinema director and turns the plot into a shoot.

My four sections are both thematic and largely chronological. The first examines the critical realism of the early novels of the late fifties and early sixties. Engagement with Mexican national identity and history, and with the intellectual traditions of Mexican national thinking, European realism and Anglo-American modernism, is focused through the prism of family dramas. The second studies two highly experimental novels from the late sixties. The question of the Other is approached through the notion of tragedy, madness, the undoing of narrative conventions and securities. The third analyses two novels from the eighties where national identities are playfully evoked and largely dismantled through intertextual games, migrations of people and ideas. The final section looks at three works where collections of short stories or novellas combine loosely to form a novel. They move from the sharply focused violence with impunity in the Mexico City of *Agua quemada*, through the postmodern virgins of *Constancia* to the neo-realism of *La frontera de cristal*.

Fuentes's life has been told elsewhere. Maarten Van Delden has very usefully charted his public, political and intellectual stance through essays and journalism; Raymond Williams in *The Writings of Carlos Fuentes* has gathered a lot of biographical detail; Fuentes himself in his 'Cronología personal' offers a fascinating account of his life and publications. The person Carlos Fuentes is as warm, intelligent and generous as his books. I first met Fuentes in Cambridge in 1978, when I asked him to sign my copy of *Terra Nostra*, got to know him much better when he returned here for a year as Simón Bolívar Professor in 1986–1987, and since then, usually with his wife Sylvia, in Cambridge and London, Spain, and in Providence, R.I. with our common friend Julio Ortega. I have much valued his readiness to talk freely about his work, but especially his loyal friendship.

INTRODUCTION 5

Over the time I have worked on this material I have received financial assistance from the Welford-Thompson fund of Emmanuel College, from Cambridge University and from the British Academy. This has allowed me to visit Mexico, take up the hospitality of my friend since postgraduate days in Cambridge, Sealtiel Alatriste, now Fuentes's editor at Alfaguara, and through Sealtiel and Edna, and other friends such as Hernán Lara Zavala, Margo Glantz, and Gonzalo Celorio, peep into the life of that country. My wife Isabel has read everything I have written, as I wrote it, and has always been the ultimate arbiter of whether it made any sense.

Original publications on which this study is based

'Fathers and Sons in Fuentes's *La muerte de Artemio Cruz*', *Bulletin of Hispanic Studies*, 65:1 (1984), 31–40.
'De Fuentes y de Dante y de Gorostiza, ¡siempre tres!', *Iberoromania*, 25 (1987), 103–19.
'*Cambio de piel*: Literature and Evil', *Bulletin of Hispanic Studies*, 66 (1989), 55–72.
'Carlos Fuentes: *Gringo viejo*', *Literatura Mexicana*, 2:1 (1991), 57–71; in English as 'Intertextuality in Carlos Fuentes's *Gringo viejo*', *Romance Quarterly*, 39:4 (1992), 489–500.
'Family Tradition and the Individual Talent in Fuentes's *Las buenas conciencias*', *Bulletin of Hispanic Studies*, 71 (1994), 359–80.
'*Cambio de piel* de Carlos Fuentes; El poder de la contradicción', *Revista Canadiense de Estudios Hispánicos*, 19:2 (1995), 401–6.
'Towards *Zona sagrada*', *Inti*, 45 (Primavera 1997), 181–95.
'On memory and Mexico in Carlos Fuentes's *La región más transparente*', *Antípodas*, 8–9 (1997), 13–43.
'Cuento y cuarteto: *Agua quemada* de Carlos Fuentes', *América (Cahiers du CRICCAL)*, 18 (1997), I, 203–11.
'Lo real fronterizo en *La frontera de cristal* de Carlos Fuentes', *América (Cahiers du CRICCAL)*, 25 (2000), 83–93.
'De *Constancia y otras novelas para vírgenes*', *Inti*, 51 (Primavera 2000), 17–29.

I: FIRST NOVELS

La región más transparente, 1958; *Las buenas conciencias*, 1959; *La muerte de Artemio Cruz*, 1962

In 1958, just three years after Mexico's most brilliant rural novel, Juan Rulfo's 120-page *Pedro Páramo*, came the publication of the most brilliant novel of Mexico City, the 550 pages of Carlos Fuentes's *La región más transparente*. Whereas Rulfo's only novel is concentrated, haunted, marked by lacunae and silences, Fuentes's novel, published when he was twenty-nine, is an exuberant explosion and celebration of all the voices of Mexico: the rural poor, emigrant workers, dense poetical pieces, society chat, precious intellectual exchanges, epic battle scenes. Its inverted mirror image from the Southern Cone is Juan Carlos Onetti's 1949 *Tierra de nadie*, also influenced by John Dos Passos, but while Onetti gradually divests his characters of all attributes and sense in a sort of despairing mysticism, Fuentes finds layer after layer of signification which he orchestrates on a grand scale. His revolutionary articulation of the many voices of Mexico with the multilingual jargons of cosmopolitan literary modernity is echoed five years later in Cortázar's *Rayuela*, while his all-encompassing depiction of the functioning of a whole society is only really matched by the ambition of the late-sixties novels of the Peruvian Mario Vargas Llosa, such as *Conversación en la Catedral*, 1969.

Fuentes's second masterpiece, *La muerte de Artemio Cruz*, appeared four years later, in 1962. Shorter than the first novel, parallel in theme if not in technique, it gained wider resonance outside Mexico and Latin America, becoming one of the emblematic examples of the new Latin American 'boom' novel. This is perhaps because it is less overwhelmingly Mexican in its language and reference, though in its probing of issues of revolution, national autonomy, and the recurring cycles of cruelty and betrayal of Mexican life, it is certainly no less passionately Mexican. The clever use of literary novelties such as the splitting of the narrative into YO, TÚ, and ÉL voices, radical chronological disordering, and the complex delving into classical themes of existence, destiny and freedom attracted wide international attention.

Between these two landmark novels came *Las buenas conciencias*, a shorter novel written in a conventionally realist style, which might strike the reader as something of an anomaly, seemingly written by an apprentice Carlos Fuentes. There is perhaps a parallel with the publication in 1978, which Fuentes has suggested was possibly a mistake, of the thriller *La cabeza de la hidra* after his most ambitious and largest novel *Terra Nostra*. I find that both offer an interest and attraction of their own. *Las buenas conciencias* quaintly mimics the atmosphere of provincial Guanajuato in its Galdosian realism, and offers a curiously, but probably deceptively, unguarded, unelaborated insight into the Christian interest and the Oedipal scenes developed more obliquely or with greater sophistication elsewhere.

All three novels are based very firmly on family structures, the dynamics of inheritance; all are marked by a fluidity or reversibility within these structures, which seems to underlie many of Fuentes's much later works also, such as *Una familia lejana* or *Agua quemada*. *La región más transparente* follows the complex relationships between fathers and sons in two families from about the time of the Revolution until the 1950s; *Las buenas conciencias* follows the intense story of adolescent rebellion and conformity over a year or so, while *La muerte de Artemio Cruz* shows the involvement of Artemio Cruz in three families, in Veracruz, Puebla and Mexico City, and the generations which unfolded within the cycles of Mexican history from the time of Santa Anna to that of López Mateos.

While the second novel captures a moment of adolescence, the first and third each follow the largely similar pattern of the life of a powerful capitalist entrepreneur, Federico Robles and Artemio Cruz: Robles within a teeming cast of characters, Cruz with overbearing physical and psychic intensity on his death bed. Both characters share humble rural origins, Robles from a loving family, Cruz the fruit of rape; both distinguish themselves in the Revolution, begin to gain political favour and financial success by betrayal (of the syndicalist Feliciano Sánchez, of the priest padre Páez), build a powerful economic empire based in Mexico City, are destroyed by financial ruin or illness, and look back on their lives and the social and historical processes they embodied in order to search for some coherent pattern, personal meaning, transcendental or historical purpose within the chaos and fall. These novels show an acute and angry awareness of the social injustices and inequalities of Mexican society, consistent with Fuentes's admiration for the person and politics of Lázaro Cárdenas, and his enthusiastic adhesion to the 1959 Cuban Revolution. They are intensely concerned with the question of the nature and destiny of Mexico. In *La región más transparente*, intellectual characters such as Ixca, Rodrigo Pola and Manuel Zamacona often eloquently, but interminably, debate propositions and theories of the sort developed by Samuel Ramos and Octavio Paz. In *Artemio Cruz*, the issues clearly present in the social and political action of the novel are sublimated and personalised in the tortured thoughts of the dying man, revolving around themes of betrayal, abuse of power with impunity, *la chingada*, and allegorised in the symbolic schemes of the work.

La región más transparente, 1958: Mexico and Memory

Rapid characterisation

Fuentes's first novel, *La región más transparente*, offers a vivid portrayal of the Mexico City of the late forties and early fifties, during the rapid capitalist development under President Miguel Alemán and the confident rise of a new energetic bourgeoisie. The characters also recall and narrate vital episodes of their rural origins and industrial strife before the Revolution, key events of the Revolution, and politics and trades-unionism in its aftermath. It is a large, overflowing and polyphonic work. The immediate impression it makes is high modernist, with the aggressive Anglo-Saxon presence of John Dos Passos, William Faulkner and D.H. Lawrence. Fuentes talks of the works of these writers as narrative in the past, present and future, in a way which prefigures the three narrative voices and tenses of *La muerte de Artemio Cruz*.[1]

---

[1] 'Yo estaba haciendo un juego de tiempos, y me interesaban mucho esos tres modos de verlos. (...) En Dos Passos todo fue. Aun cuando él escribe en presente una cosa, sabemos que fue. En Faulkner todo está siendo siempre. Aun el pasado más remoto es un presente. Y en D.H. Lawrence, lo que hay es ese tono profético, de inminencia.' Luis Harss, *Los nuestros* (Buenos Aires: Sudamericana, 1973), 361.

From Dos Passos, Fuentes derives the large number of characters in short fragmented passages, the poetic vignettes in italics, ubiquitous fires and fire-engines. There are also direct little homages, such as the accounts and reports of the deaths of taxi driver Juan Morales and milkman Gus. Fires, however, are translated into an altogether more sacramental dialect in the 'hundred fires' of Fuentes's character-narrator Cienfuegos, and when Robles accidentally sets fire to his house there are resonances of Aztec sacrifice.

Joseph Sommers gives a nice example of the intertextual working of the novel in the rewriting of the bullfight scene from *The Plumed Serpent*. Fuentes's celebration of the vitality of the language and horseplay of the migrant workers Gabriel and his friends is a rectification of the rather racist and classist reaction of D.H. Lawrence's Kate. See his essay 'La búsqueda de la identidad' in Giacoman, ed., *Homenaje a Carlos Fuentes* (New York: Las

The second striking feature is interminable debate among the characters about the nature and fate of Mexico. Fuentes was writing at the end of the decade of the fifties which saw the outpourings of the Hyperión group of thinkers on the 'filosofía de lo mexicano', which he reproduces 'sin ser mis tesis ni mucho menos' (Harss, 258), and at the end of a half century which also saw the thinking of Ateneo de la Juventud members such as Reyes and Vasconcelos, and later contributions from writers close to the Contemporáneo group such as Salvador Novo's *Nueva grandeza mexicana*. Though the arguments are often elegantly expounded, the effect is that of pastiche.

The wide-ranging, complexly structured and dramatic nature of the plot, however, is far more akin to the scale and spirit of the classical nineteenth-century novel of Balzac or Stendhal. The dramatic vicissitudes of social classes through the Revolution and its aftermath are plotted out over generations and from province to capital city; ambitious individuals make meteoric rises to power and often to disaster. Rodrigo Pola, torn between the pure intellectuals of the Círculo and the easy money of the commercial cinema, is a latter-day Lucien de Rubempré torn between the *cénacle* of d'Arthez and the cynical Lousteau in *Illusions perdues*, while Cienfuegos, able to make and break fortunes with a superhuman power of intrigue, is a tropical avatar of Vautrin / Carlos Herrera. The magical energy of Robles stems

Americas, 1971), 275–326, esp. 307. Similarly, the life-promoting and semi-fascist Aztec mysticism of don Ramón and his followers, which fascinated Lawrence, becomes a cruel throwback in Fuentes's account of the sorceress Teódula Moctezuma and her tyrannical hold on Ixca Cienfuegos.

Mexico shares with the South of the USA the feeling of defeat. The ever-present ghostly weight of the defeat is nowhere heavier than in *Absalom, Absalom!:* 'a kind of vacuum filled with wraithlike and indomitable anger [...], a kind of entailed birthright father and son and father and son of never forgiving General Sherman [...] you won't be anything but a descendent of a long line of colonels killed in Pickett's charge at Manassas' (Harmondsworth: Penguin, 1987), 296. As Fuentes puts it: 'el ser, en el mundo de Faulkner, es lo que se *lega*: sólo lo legado será *legible*' (*Casa con dos puertas* (Mexico City: Joaquín Mortiz, 1970), 54). Faulkner's texts are also linked with Fuentes's first novel by the narration of a dim but traumatic family past through conversation, interview and reported speech. It seems to be impossible to overcome the presence of this past: 'not only a man never outlives his father but not even his friends and acquaintances do' (*Absalom*, 228).

from a rural Michoacán equivalent of the *Peau de chagrin*, and his epic battles in banking reproduce those of Nucingen. Incredible, even flaunted coincidences in the past of the main characters also have a wryly anachronistic Balzacian flavour: a forebear of Pimpinela de Ovando raped Robles's mother; Mercedes Zamacona's brother delivered the coup de grâce to Gervasio Pola; Manuel Zamacona is introduced ostensibly by chance to his father, Federico Robles, etc.

The dispositional structure of the novel is diverse in that it contains many different generic strands, but there is a generally smooth alternation between chapter types. There are three parts of uneven length, of which the short third section is a coda which brings the reader up to date and introduces the new generation. There are three basic chapter types. About half are given the name of a character and his or her key dates, and usually take the form of the characters reminiscing about their history, to Ixca Cienfuegos. The second chapter type is more panoramic and moves quickly from one character or group to another in the narrative present, using the convention of parties, conversations in bars, even essays written by the characters. The titles of two of these are names for Mexico, while another four take lines from a popular Mexican song.[2] A third type, intercalated regularly in the long second part consists of short vignettes in italics, which hover between pathos and satire, featuring socially representative characters at key moments.

To this structure of the body of the novel are added elements which present two significantly divergent ways of reading history. The novel begins and ends with two extraordinarily intense and difficult prose poems, based on oxymoron and antithesis and with a large mythical Nahua element, woven around the contradictory figure of Ixca Cienfuegos. In stark contrast to this highly symbolic discourse, the first

---

[2] Georgina García Gutiérrez provides this information in her excellent introduction to the novel. 'El lugar del ombligo de la luna' is the nahuatl name for Mexico: *Metl, xictli, co*, while 'La Ciudad de los Palacios' was the name given to Mexico City by an eighteenth-century traveller, perhaps Baron von Humboldt. The relevant part of the song is: 'México en una laguna / Guadalajara en un llano / Me he de comer esa tuna / aunque me espine la mano./ L'águila siendo animal / se retrató en el dinero / para subir al nopal / pidió permiso primero.' See García Gutiérrez, ed., *La región más transparente*, (Madrid: Cátedra, 1982), 155, 281, 359.

text of which verges on the indecipherable, since the 1972 second edition, the novel has included a preliminary 'Cuadro cronológico' and list of 'Personajes'. I attempt in my analysis of the novel to develop a series of terms, antitheses and structures which will allow a single account of the intertwined conflicting narratives of modern Mexico which make up the text, while respecting their difference.[3]

Oxymorons, Mexicanness, family

The introductory prose poem, which begins with the reassuring and deceptively conventional 'Mi nombre es Ixca Cienfuegos', is built around a tight sequence of oxymora, antitheses, contradictions, and offers an impression of Mexico characterised by rupture, loss of coherence, suffering. Later in the novel, in various of the ideological or essayistic pieces there are variations on the basic notion exemplified by Octavio Paz in *El laberinto de la soledad* that Mexican identity is based on a negation of the country's own past, its own past self or selves: 'Es pasmoso que un país con un pasado tan vivo [...] sólo se conciba como negación de su origen.'[4] This negation is repeated over time, so that the Reforma, for example, is a 'triple negación' (*El laberinto* 113). Mexico and Mexicans are thus seen as split from themselves. In *La región más transparente*, the main vehicle which Fuentes uses to articulate, resolve and repropose the contradictions and splits hinted at here is the family, in the complex dynamics of the inheritance of such dilemmas over the generations. The culminating moment of this process in the novel is perhaps the scene of anagnorisis or recognition, when Federico Robles recognises himself in all those others from whom he has derived his being and has negated or forgotten.

Most of the symbolic antitheses important for the novel will emerge in a reading of the prose poem. They include day and night, life and

[3] A significant body of essays on *La región más transparente* can be consulted in *Écrire le Mexique, América (Cahiers du CRICCAL)*, 25, 1999. It includes pieces by Claude Fell, Jacqueline Covo, Jean Franco, Maryse Gachie Pineda, Florence Olivier, Julio Ortega, Elizabeth Pagnoux, and Daniel Vives.

[4] *El laberinto de la soledad* (Mexico City: Fondo de Cultura Económica, 1973), 79. Manuel Zamacona talks of the 'negación del pasado como supuesto inicial de todo proyecto salvador' (69).

death, self and other, together and alone, memory and forgetfulness. The relation between the two terms is far from stable and ranges from fertile duality, rhythm and cosmic harmony, to stark contradiction and stalemate or stagnation. To offer a tentative summary of the play within the two main family groups: the two main fathers or patriarchs of the novel, Gervasio Pola and Federico Robles, are set in an opposition which is reworked in *La muerte de Artemio Cruz*: one dies in the Revolution while the other survives at any cost. Both in turn are marked or defined even in their relation with others by a basic duality in their origin, or at the origin of their power. In the case of Pola, communality and individualism, usually posted by the words *solo* and *juntos*. In that of Robles, the tension is between light and dark, day and night. These dualities seem to imply or articulate most of the other splits around which the question of identity, national or individual, is posed. The dualities are formed, transmitted (perhaps in a distorted form) or imposed as a curse by a woman: Rosenda Pola and Mercedes Zamacona. They may be projected almost magically, or transmitted through the family in a psychologically realistic manner. In both cases the pair of man and woman are separated by death or other circumstances. Both men have a son whom they never meet: Rodrigo Pola and Manuel Zamacona, who have to take up a problematical inheritance of which they know little or nothing. In the case of Gervasio Pola, the duality inherited by his son is projected onto two alternative and rival father figures: the dead father and the powerful, successful businessman Federico Robles. In the case of Federico Robles, the day / night option is projected onto two women in his later life: his wife Norma associated with the sun, and his blind lover Hortensia associated with the darkness. The separation of Robles from his original mythical unity with Mercedes, embodied in the two women, is to an extent broken symbolically by the death of his son Manuel, which seems magically to release Robles's memory of his past selves inseparable from a whole series of men now long dead. Rodrigo Pola chooses and is granted great immediate success in films, and thus forms with the martyred Manuel a mythical pair which is to be found in much of Fuentes's work.[5] Each member of the pair repeats the lot of the other's father.

[5] These include Artemio Cruz and Ignacio Bernal in *La muerte de Artemio Cruz*,

'Mi nombre es Ixca Cienfuegos'

The poem offers an essential insight into the rhetorical functioning of *La región más transparente*, especially the figures of splitting, separation, duality and oxymoron. It is instructive to examine it at some length, looking in detail at the language, while taking some phrases together with relevant passages from the main text to develop key concepts and relations, and teasing out the intertextual resonances on which the poem depends for its wider meaning. The rather chaotic presentation of issues in this choice of analysis has the advantage of avoiding the impression that *La región más transparente* is a novel of ideas. It uses ideas not as one does in an essay, but rather as one might words in a poem or quotations in a novel, where their value is shifting, ambiguous and plural, different from their literal or original meaning.[6]

It is Ixca Cienfuegos who introduces the poem, the book and himself in the first person: 'Mi nombre es Ixca Cienfuegos. Nací y vivo en México, D.F. Esto no es grave.' A seemingly simple beginning, but already the expected is undermined by echoes of English phrasing in the first sentence, and the French 'c'est pas grave' in the third. The name already contains two languages: Nahuatl and Spanish. The mixture is later shown to indicate not the *mestizo*, but an alternation or contradiction between the European and native American.[7] Both words

> Mito and Giancarlo in *Zona sagrada*, Franz and Javier in *Cambio de piel*, and in a somewhat different way, Víctor and André in *Una familia lejana*. The associated notion of alternative parents, of choosing one's own father, is explored in *Artemio Cruz*, *Las buenas conciencias*, *Una familia lejana*, and *La campaña*.

[6] Some critics have tended to take the 'ideological content' of the novel and contrast it with the characters and action, or 'reality' of Mexico City in the novel. Hence Ernest Lewald in an early study concludes: 'En *La región más transparente* Fuentes se lanza a la búsqueda de *su* México debajo de las capas de asfalto de la capital rodeada de nubes de gasolina y luces de neón. Al no encontrar otra cosa que una parodia de lo que, para él, debiera ser *lo nuestro*, vuelca en sus páginas una ironía ácida y mordaz, el resultado de la distancia aristotélica entre la historia y la poesía; o sea, lo que es y lo que debiera ser.' 'El pensamiento cultural mexicano en *La región más transparente* de Carlos Fuentes', in *Revista Hispánica Moderna*, 33:4, 216–23, 219.

[7] His features are described as 'alternativamente indígenas en pureza, pura y oscuramente europeos' (131–2).

indicate fire,[8] and later in the passage Ixca seems to be associated with the 'Duende de Anahuac', probably the sun god Huitzilopochtli.[9] There is also possibly an echo of the devil Cienllamas whose task is to take the Diablo Cojuelo to hell in Vélez de Guevara's *El diablo Cojuelo*. He is constantly seen lighting cigarettes, and is associated with the sacrifice of Norma by fire. On the other hand, he is often seen in the rain, and is associated with the sea against the sun of Norma when they are shipwrecked: his mother says to him, 'como que has peleado con el sol' (340). He is also seen on high with the sun-god Robles, in his sixth-floor office, thus forming the Tlaloc or rain god of the pair Huitzilopochtli-Tlaloc which dominated the Templo Mayor in Tenochtitlan, the Aztec Mexico City. Ixca is thus a contradictory and split figure, Indian and European, fire and water. On the other hand, 'Burnt Water', 'agua quemada', is another name for Mexico City-Tenochtitlan, the title of the 1981 collection of novellas by Fuentes, and a cipher of the union of contradictions, or dynamic coexistence of opposites in Nahua cosmology and poetry.[10] Duality itself is a highly unstable relation in the text, and subject to very complex ideological, moral, textual and intertextual processing throughout the novel.

Ixca is a Protean figure, and the first in a line of such characters, who include Freddy Lambert from *Cambio de piel* and Baltasar Bustos from *La campaña,* and prefigures similar semi-characters in Julio Cortázar such as *mi paredro*, from *62. Modelo para armar* and *el que te dije* from *Libro de Manuel*. Ixca is an embodiment of Mexico and Mexico City, inseparable from the plot of the novel which he magically creates;[11] he is a confessor figure whose very presence causes the most

[8] 'Ixca' apparently means 'to roast'. See María A. Salgado, 'El mito azteca en *La región más transparente*', in Giacoman, ed., *Homenaje*, 229–40, 234.
[9] See Oscar Montero, 'The Role of Ixca Cienfuegos in the Thematic Fabric of *La región más transparente*', in *Hispanófila*, 20:58, 1976, 61-83, 62; Elsa Aida Ramírez Mattei, *La narrativa de Carlos Fuentes* (Río Piedras: Universidad de Puerto Rico, 1983), 66.
[10] See Laurette Séjournée, *Burnt Water. Thought and Religion in Ancient Mexico* (London: Thames and Hudson, 1957), and especially the chapter 'Union of Heaven and Hell', 99–119.
[11] When, for example, Rodrigo opts for success, against Ixca's expectations, Ixca nevertheless declares that he has already spoken to some film producers, and Rodrigo's rise is meteoric. His role in the downfall of Robles and thus in the resolution of the novel is no less dramatic: he advises Robles on a financial

intimate memories of the characters to appear in italics on the page, an anthropologist after the style of the Oscar Lewis of *The Children of Sanchez*, who irritates Gabriel by his intrusive curiosity: 'Qué buena gente ni qué la pinga. A poco cree que así nomás suelta uno lo que trae dentro?' (192). He is a dangerous Aztec fundamentalist who actively promotes blood-sacrifice for his mother Teódula; he is the slavish double of the characters who has to mimic their actions in order to make them happen.[12] This radical lack of fixity is played out in the poem in the shifting of pronouns and possessive adjectives. Ixca opens the poem in the first person: 'mi nombre [...]', and goes on to talk about the Duende de Anáhuac in the third person, but then the hand of the latter belongs to an 'us' who would include him: 'flagelado por su propia (por nuestra) mano'. The 'se caza a sí mismo' of the Duende is translated into the first person singular 'dañarme'. As the difference between Ixca and the Duende is elided, Ixca addresses first figures from Mexican history and then ordinary Mexicans as 'tú' ('¡No te rajes manito!'' though the sentiment here is a parody of the Mexican closedness described by Paz), before finally joining those Mexicans in a final 'nosotros': 'jamás nos hemos hincado juntos'. Ixca simply dissolves into, and becomes the places, people and even literary techniques he approaches.

In intertextual terms, he seems to be a conscious reworking of many important literary archetypes: Mephistopheles, the Devil of Dostoyevsky's Ivan Karamazov, Melmoth the Wanderer, Balzac's Vautrin, D.H. Lawrence's Ramón from *The Plumed Serpent*, Tezcatlipoca as 'The Burning Mirror' or the 'He Who Is At The Shoulder'.[13] The very provisional nature and heterogeneity of such identifications has a curiously post-modern and eclectic ring to it, but perhaps 'baroque' would be a better term for this sort of decentred Mexican hero.

manoeuvre, and then suggests to Pimpinela that Robles is in financial trouble, which starts the run on his bank. He seduces and transforms Norma so that she will not support Robles to restore his fortune.

[12] He reluctantly marries the maid Rosa, just as the main character Robles marries the low-class Hortensia Chacón. In the fantastic novella *Aura*, the young Aura is seen to repeat the movements of the witch Consuelo in a similar fashion.

[13] See C.A. Burland, *The Gods of Mexico* (London: Eyre & Spottiswoode, 1967), 131.

Ixca follows his 'Esto no es grave' with: 'En México no hay tragedia: todo se vuelve afrenta'. Tragedy, the highest point in Greek civilisation, is opposed to Mexican insult or offence. The grand and sacramental has become petty and mediocre. Ixca-Fuentes's phrase echoes at least two more well known declarations. D.H. Lawrence's *Lady Chatterley's Lover* begins 'Ours is essentially a tragic age, so we refuse to take it tragically.' In the England following the Great War, life was rebuilt timidly: 'The cataclysm has happened, we are among the ruins, we start to build up new little habitats.'[14] The gamekeeper Mellors has Constance Chatterley break out of the timidity to affirm her freedom and sexuality in much the same way as Ixca, through words and sex, that brings about the self-affirmation (and death) of Norma Larragoiti. Indeed, one of Ixca's roles is to demand existential intensity, and the choice between opposites from the characters rather than the compromise of 'chingaqueditos' like Rodrigo Pola. Octavio Paz, himself given to a dense, dialectical approach to identity in *El laberinto de la soledad*, clearly recognises this attitude in Fuentes, who ruffled so many Mexican feathers with his first novel: 'espíritu exaltado en el introvertido país del medio tono [...] paradójico en el país de los lugares comunes, irreverente en un país que ha convertido su historia trágica y maravillosa en un sermón laico'.[15]

The second echo of Ixca's phrase 'En México no hay tragedia: todo se vuelve afrenta' is Marx's dictum from *The Eighteenth Brumaire of Louis Bonaparte*: 'Hegel remarks somewhere that all facts and personages of great importance in world history occur, as it were, twice. He forgot to add: the first time as tragedy, the second as farce.'[16] Marx's title and his opposition tragedy / farce refer to the date of the coup d'état of Napoleon Bonaparte. His satirical pamphlet against the 1851 regime of Louis Napoleon and the latter's attempt to emulate his uncle shows how it is 'possible for a grotesque mediocrity to play a hero's part'.[17] The phrase is important in at least two ways in a novel much concerned with belatedness. The first belatedness is that of the

[14] *Lady Chatterley's Lover* (Harmondsworth: Penguin, 1972), 5.
[15] 'La pregunta de Carlos Fuentes' in *Plural*, 14, 1972, p. 8, cit., Ramírez Mattei, 42.
[16] Karl Marx, *Selected Writings*, ed. by David McLellan (Oxford: OUP, 1877), 300.
[17] Ibid.

two young men in the novel, Rodrigo Pola and Manuel Zamacona, vis-à-vis their fathers who took a more or less heroic role in the epic action of the 1910 Mexican Revolution, and have no real arena in which to take up the challenge of emulating them. A second belatedness is that of the Mexican middle class vis-à-vis the nineteenth-century European bourgeoisie. Natasha puts it crudely: 'son una aproximación a la burguesía, son toujours les singes' (177); 'Me da risa estar viviendo aquí lo que pasó en Europa hace más de un siglo. [...] Les Révolutions ont toujours son Empire; les Robespierre devient Napoléons ... [sic]' (399). A third, taken up in *Las buenas conciencias*, is that of the Mexican writer who must portray these belated phenomena vis-à-vis writers like Balzac and Stendhal.

Marx goes on to expand his point in a way which both Rodrigo and Manuel could well make their own: 'Men make their own history, but they do not make it just as they please; they do not make it under circumstances chosen by themselves, but under circumstances directly encountered, given, and transmitted from the past. The tradition of all the dead generations weighs like a nightmare on the brain of the living.'[18] Memory, on the other hand, is shot through in this novel with amnesia, and not of the positive, liberating sort discussed by Nietzsche in 'On the Uses and Disadvantages of History for Life'. Rosenda Pola has an even more extreme formulation. The unresolved conflicts of the past, whether individuals are aware of them or not, turn these individuals into ghosts and puppets:

> no hay triunfos ni derrotas en este país, que no hay memoria para el paso de los hombres sobre la tierra, que todos fueron y serán fantasmas antes de nacer, sin proponérselo, porque sólo los fantasmas rondan en la verdadera vida de México, y ellos traen sus batallas muy hechas, muy sólidas, para que sean reales nuestros ejercicios de polvo, nuestras individualidades aplastadas por esa otra batalla permanente de fantasmas y sus luchas que no se han resuelto. (232-3)

---

[18] Kristine Ibsen in *Author, Text and Reader in the Novels of Carlos Fuentes* (New York: Peter Lang, 1993), 102, points out that Fuentes uses the last sentence of this passage as the epigraph to the second part of *Cristóbal Nonato*.

Marx suggests elsewhere that the movement from tragedy to comedy in drama and in history serves the purpose of allowing man to say farewell to his past joyfully.[19] If this does not happen in Fuentes's novel, it seems to be because the tragedy of Mexico was somehow suppressed, though it was no less powerful for that. Later in the poem, Ixca expands on the defeat he had assumed personally and laments: 'ciudad de la derrota violada (la que no pudimos amantar a la luz, la derrota secreta)'. It is perhaps that in a country fatally split into two ethnic groups, the defeat of the subordinate group in the Conquest, the loss or flight of their gods, never became part of the official consciousness, and thus could never be really assimilated.[20] Later in the novel Ixca says: 'Noche de los dioses que huyeron despavoridos [...] no ha habido dolor, ni derrota ni traición comparables a los de México' (378).

The 'afrenta' felt by Ixca pricks him like a 'filo de maguey', like the cactus thorn with which Quetzalcoatl, the Plumed Serpent, made offerings of his own blood. More characteristically, he adds that his 'afrenta' is 'mi parálisis desenfrenada', the oxymoronic 'unleashed paralysis'. The words are important to Fuentes because in *La muerte de Artemio Cruz* he writes: 'entre la parálisis y el desenfreno está la línea de la vida'.[21] Life is conserved when there is a balance or dialectic between paralysis and frenzy (which in other terms may be seen as stasis and movement, structure and pluralty) but for Ixca the two terms seem to cancel each other out, and lead to a sullen stagnation. Given the preceding lament of the loss of the tragic spirit, it may be useful to associate the duality of the terms 'parálisis' and 'desenfreno' with the

[19] 'The struggle against the German political present is the struggle against the past of modern peoples [...]. It is instructive for them to see the *ancien régime*, that played tragedy in their history, play comedy as a German ghost. [...] The last stage of a world-historical form is its comedy. The gods of Greece who had already been mortally wounded in the *Prometheus Bound* tragedy of Aeschylus, had to die once more a comic death in the dialogues of Lucian. Why does history follow this course? So that mankind may take leave of its past joyfully' ('Introduction' to *Towards a Critique of Hegel's Philosophy of Right*, in *Selected Writings*, 66).

[20] *Visión de los vencidos: relaciones indígenas de la conquista*, edited by Miguel León Portilla and translated by Angel María Garibay, was published in 1959.

[21] *La muerte de Artemio Cruz* (México: Fondo de Cultura Económica, 1972), 206.

two principles which Nietzsche in *The Birth of Tragedy* saw as reaching a supreme balance in Greek tragic art: the Apollonian and the Dionysiac. The Apollonian is associated with dream, illusion, form, the scene and individual hero, and the Dionysiac with drunkennness, orgy, dissolution, the destruction of the individual, the collective chorus:

> Thus we have come to interpret Greek tragedy as a Dionysiac chorus which again and again discharges itself in Apollonian images. These choric portions with which the tragedy is interlaced constitute, as it were, the matrix of the *dialogue*, that is to say, of the entire stage-world of the actual drama. This substratum of tragedy irradiates, in several consecutive discharges, the vision of the drama—a vision on the one hand completely of the nature of Apollonian dream-illusion and therefore epic, but on the other hand, as the objectification of a Dionysiac condition, tending towards the shattering of the individual and his fusion with the original Onenness.[22]

Nietzsche saw the Apollonian and Dionysiac in cultural and political terms. The extreme manifestation of the affirmation of individuality in the former was the Roman Empire, while the second led to eastern mysticism and quietism. Greece, in its brief tragic period, he claimed, was able to strike a balance between the two: 'Placed between India and Rome, and tempted to choose one solution or the other, the Greeks managed a classically pure mode of existence'.[23] Without wishing to draw too strict a parallel, it is certainly true that in the novel, the Indian and white races or, in terms of class, the *pueblo* and the oligarchy, are seen respectively in terms of anonymity and of the collective against individualism. Manuel talks of the 'esencia, la sustancia informe, morena, oscura, indígena del padre' (69), while the image of the flowing river, alien to history or thought, is often used to describe the ordinary people: 'como un río subterráneo, indiferente y oscuro, que corría por debajo de cualquier cambio o idea' (275). Rodrigo, on the other hand, tries to see his ego as a rock set against this alien torrent: 'su persona, sería como la roca — lo nombrable, lo singular — que,

[22] Friedrich Nietzsche, in *The Birth of Tragedy and The Genealogy of Morals* (New York: Doubleday, 1956), 56. See also 97, 108. For an excellent explication of Nietzsche's ideas see M. S. Silk and J. P. Stern, *Nietzsche on Tragedy* (Cambridge: CUP, 1983), esp. 62-89.
[23] Nietzsche, 125.

ahogada por la torrente de la inundación, no deja de ser roca, no deja de ser singular aunque la arrase esa catarata anónima, central, pero sin núcleo' (254). In the case of Mercedes, individualism or egoism is seen as a loss of origin or a curse. After being scolded by the priest, Mercedes 'quiso asirse al yo–soy y dejó de ser lo que era' (421) and goes on to curse her lover Federico Robles, condemning him to 'vivir presa del yo–soy, a condenar su poder maltratado' (424). The masses are seen as an empowering collectivity and origin or a terrifying dionysian abyss. The loss of a tragic vision in Mexican terms, however, does seem to be related to the loss of a consciousness of duality or of the Other as a necessary complement to the self, in Nietzschean terms, the serene contemplation of suffering and the abyss: 'the marvelous naïveté of the older Greeks — flower of an Apollonian culture blossoming over a somber abyss, in token of the victory of the Greek will over suffering, and of the wisdom of suffering.'[24]

In slightly different terms, those of more conventional religion, but no less relevant to the notion of identity in the novel, Octavio Paz contrasts the collective dimension of death and salvation in the Ancient Mexican with the notion of the individual soul in the Christian: 'Para el cristiano se trata de salvar el alma individual, desprendida del grupo y del cuerpo. El cristianismo condena al mundo; el indio sólo concibe la salvación personal como parte de la del cosmos y de la sociedad.'[25]

Following his reference to 'parálisis desenfrenada', Ixca seems to offer another aspect of his 'afrenta': 'Y mi eterno salto mortal hacia mañana.' Just as the difference between paralysis and frenzy is elided, the continuity of day and night is broken. The cosmic rhythm whereby the sun descends into the underworld of Mictlan at night and is reborn each morning after a struggle with the darkness has become precarious. The image is taken up later in the poem and associated with nostalgia and memory: 'Deja que toda tu nostalgia emigre, todos tus cabos sueltos; comienza, todos los días, en el parto.' Each day is a new birth, there is no memory or continuity with the past. If Mexican history is a series of masks and negations of the past as Paz suggests, this will be the case for the whole country. This forgetfulness is emphasised in the final litany to the city: 'ciudad presencia de todos nuestros olvidos [...]

---

[24] Nietzsche, 108.
[25] *El laberinto de la soledad*, 97–8.

ciudad tejida en la amnesia'. Memory and forgetfulness are inseparable from self and others. Ixca's voice goes on to talk of a memory, but a memory of the evanescent, the urban and the subjective, to be recovered by the individual, in the absence of any 'heroes', presumably with the meaning of stable tradition and archetypes:

> Y recobra la llama en el momento del rasgueo contenido, imperceptible, en el momento del organillo callejero, cuando parecería que todas tus memorias se hicieran más claras, se ciñeran. Recóbrala solo. Tus héroes no regresarán a ayudarte.

Ixca himself has the role in the narrative of unlocking the forgotten or suppressed memory of key characters, and yet he himself remembers nothing of his own personal life. His face is a 'rostro como la lluvia, el rostro sin fijeza ni memoria' (260-1), and when Rodrigo asks about his past life, he answers: '¿Mis recuerdos? [...] Crees que recuerdo mi propia cara? Mi vida comienza todos los días [...] y nunca tengo el recuerdo de lo que pasó antes' (452).

Memory and forgetfulness, tradition and cultural orphanhood are further evoked in a couple of oxymoronic phrases playing on life and death: 'Al nacer, muerto, quemaste tus naves para que otros fabricaran la epopeya con tu carroña; al morir, vivo, desterraste una palabra, la que nos hubiera ligado las lenguas en las semejanzas.' The reference to burning one's boats and to the epic would seem to evoke the figure of Hernán Cortés and the Conquest: the Modern Mexico was born, but with death in its soul, bringing genocide and the dark Catholicism of the Counter-Reformation. By contrast, the second stanza would refer perhaps to Aztec martyrs such as Moctezuma or Cuauhtemoc, whose living culture was destroyed and banished. These are the heroes who will not return. The living 'palabra' is set against the dead letter of the 'epopeya', and evokes the lines from 'Himno entre ruinas': '¿Qué yerba, qué agua de vida ha de darnos la vida, / dónde desenterrar la palabra, / la proporción que rige al himno y al discurso, / al baile, a la ciudad y a la balanza?'[26]

---

[26] Octavio Paz, *La estación violenta*, in *Poemas (1935-1975)* (Barcelona: Seix Barral, 1981), 233.

Near the beginning of the poem, Ixca-Fuentes fuses periods and incompatible dimensions of life in an extraordinarily difficult sequence. The voice is that of a deity stranded in modernity, or a modern urban man somehow crippled by orders or a trauma in a past, both real and mythical. Positive action or belief has been forbidden from the depths of the bed of the lake on which Tenochtitlan was built and over which Mexico City was built: 'Juego, acción, fe [...] sé que me lo vedaron abajo, abajo, en el fondo del lecho del valle.'[27] The Duende de Anahuac, the fierce sun deity of the Aztecs, Huitzilopochtli, no longer, he continues, drinks blood, that is, accepts sacrifices of prisoners taken in the sporting battles of the *guerra florida* to ensure the continuity of life. That life-giving violence is turned inwards, onto himself, in the same way as the very language of the poem is: 'se caza a sí mismo en una licuación negra de piedras torturadas'. The sacred language of the ancient culture is predicated on the same verbs as the expressions of the most banal urban mediocrity in a sort of zeugma or oxymoronic disjunction or apposition: 'suspendido de un asta de plumas, o de la defensa de un camión, muerto en la guerra florida, en la riña de cantina'. The disjunction foretells one of the basic questions of the novel: can any sense or transcendental meaning be attributed to seemingly senseless, random deaths, such as that of Juan Morales against the bumper of a lorry, or of Gabriel in a brawl in a *cantina*? In answer to this question, Ixca becomes the poet, but a typically dual one: 'lépero cortés, ladino ingenuo', 'courteous coarse-tongued, naive cunning character'. His language veers, in a move similar to that between 'palabra' and 'epopeya', from prayer to obscene insult: 'mi plegaria desarticulada se pierde, albur, relajo'.

The two languages here, of salvation and despair, in dialogic alternation,[28] seem to be translated in the poem into the language of the Chilean poet Pablo Neruda at two different periods of his career: the tortured, disjointed poems of urban alienation of *Residencia en la tierra* (1935), and the optimistic, socialist and messianic poem 'Alturas de Macchu Picchu' from the 1950 collection *Canto general*.[29] The voice of

[27] This is the muddy lake bed that Federico Silva from *Agua quemada* could still smell in his youth.
[28] Óscar Montero, 82, rather nicely describes the only possible vision of the coexistence of the mythic and satyric in the novel as 'stabismatic'.
[29] In 'El hijo de Andrés Aparicio' from the 1981 collection of novellas *Agua*

the poet as a martyr and suffering witness resounds from Neruda's earlier collection to Fuentes's poem. Ixca complains that the gods witheld their pity from him and 'me exigieron apurarla hasta el fin para saber de mí y de mis semejantes'. Neruda is similarly obliged to bear witness; he speaks of a 'párpado atrozmente levantado a la fuerza' ('Agua sexual')[30] and describes himself as a 'blind watchman': 'un vigía tornado insensible y ciego' ('Sistema sombrío'). His style is similarly based on contradiction, catachresis and oxymoron: 'Acecho, pues, lo inanimado y lo doliente, / y el testimonio extraño que sostengo, / con eficiencia cruel y escrito en cenizas, / es la forma de olvido que prefiero' ('Sonata y destrucciones'). Ixca expresses his vision of disintegration in language reminiscent of that of Neruda: 'cuerpo fracturado, de trozos centrífugos, gimientes de enajenación, ciego a las invasiones'. Neruda writes, for example: 'Yo lloro en medio de lo invadido' ('Débil del alma') and 'cortando el tiempo en mitades inaccesibles' ('Lamento lento'). In the later Neruda poem, however, when the poet was a convinced Marxist, his poetic persona is that of a redeemer, who invites the whole Latin American people, past and present, to rise up and be born with him in a new, socialist communion: 'Sube a nacer conmigo, hermano. / Dame la mano desde la profunda / zona de tu dolor diseminado.'[31] Towards the end of the poem, when Ixca declares his common citizenship with the ordinary inhabitants of Mexico City, his exhortation has clear echoes of that of the Chilean: 'A ver si algún día mis dedos tocan los tuyos. Ven, déjate caer conmigo en la cicatriz lunar de nuestra ciudad.' The possible degree of irony in the reversal of the 'sube' to 'déjate caer' is difficult to gauge.[32]

The poem ends with an evocation of well known icons of Mexicanness. The first is the national emblem of an eagle on a nopal cactus with a serpent in its beak, said to have been the sign to the

[30] quemada, Ureñita, the older Emilio Uranga, a key member of the Hyperión group, many of whose ideas are mouthed by Manuel Zamacona and to a lesser extent Rodrigo Pola and Ixca, reads from the 'Alturas de Macchu Picchu' to the young neo-fascist recruit Bernabé.
I quote from the Losada edition, Buenos Aires, 1959.
[31] *Canto general*, vol. 1 (Buenos Aires: Losada, 1970), 38.
[32] See from *Residencia en la tierra*: 'Rodad conmigo a las oficinas, al incierto / olor de ministerios, y tumbas, y estampillas. / Venid conmigo al día blanco que se muere / dando gritos de novia asesinada' ('Desespediente').

wandering Aztecs that they should settle on the spot where they saw this: in what became Tenochtitlan. Here the elements are strangely separate, on the one hand charged with positive energy and on the other belittled: 'Tuna incandescente. Águila sin alas. Serpiente de estrellas.' The eagle is wingless: flight, fall and crawling are recurring images in the novel. The eagle in a sense has become a serpent, but has not reached that synthesis of eagle and snake, earth and air in the god Quetzalcoatl, the Plumed Serpent. The resignation of 'Aquí nos tocó. Qué le vamos a hacer' is at the same time an ironic parody of the Mexican apathy or 'nimodismo'. The final line is no less ironic: 'En la región más transparente del aire'. It is at once a homage to Alfonso Reyes, who used this description of the light of the Central Valley of Mexico, attributed to von Humboldt, as the epigraph to his *Visión de Anáhuac,* and a recognition that Mexico no longer deserved that epithet.

The poem, then, is an intricate, paradoxical and rich web of oppositions, not a system so much as a kaleidoscope and a world. To mention the main dualities distinguished here: Aztec / Spanish, fire / water, tragedy / insult, America / Europe, memory / forgetfulness, paralysis / frenzy, anonymity / ego, collective / individual, day / night, life / death, epic / word, prayer / insult, mythical / modern urban, salvation / despair, eagle / serpent. Duality may be a sign of simple alienation of one from the other, a fatal split, or it may be the necessary complementarity of the cosmos, expressed in the dual nature of most Nahua deities and in the whole Ancient Mexican cosmology, and also in Nietzsche's notion of tragedy. Origin, death, and truth itself are dual and ambiguous. Ixca explains to Rodrigo that man 'en la muerte se reintegra a la dualidad original' (264). When Robles feels that he is approaching his final truth, it is also ambiguous: 'Ahora los recuerdos se detendrían y caerían en su verdadero orden, en su explicación original y ambigua' (433). The play of inheritance in the novel seems to have the function of keeping this duality open, or proposing and renewing the original ambiguity.

Towards the end of the poem a couple of lines articulate combinations of oppositions which will serve in the novel as the basic pattern of ambiguity to motivate the characters and forms the plot. The first is that of solitude and communion, key terms for Froilán Reyero, Gervasio Pola and Federico Robles: 'Jamás nos hemos hincado juntos, tú y yo, a recibir la misma hostia; desgarrados juntos, creados juntos, sólo morimos para nosotros, aislados.' Inseparable from this basic moral and human split is the almost absolute economic and social split (which is also of course partly racial) in Mexico City and in the nation between the rich and the poor, the haves and have-nots: 'ciudad famélica, suntuosa villa'. The complex mythical and philosophical elements of this novel should not obscure its social and socialist problematics. The abysmal class differences in Mexico are foregrounded as the novel opens with a raw but affectionate account of the whore Gladys García going about her business, and enviously encountering the rich social set of Norma Larragoiti off to a party, and with the taxi driver Juan Morales being abused by the socialite Bobó. The main part of the novel also ends with Gladys. Gladys, whose special Friday customer enjoys shouting 'cabrona raza de bronce' (23), is linked with the waiter at the party, to whom Bobó refers with chilling indifference in the same breath as he quotes the trendy *Illuminations*: 'Por ahí anda un indígena con charola y bebestibles. Voici, oh Rimbaud!; le temps des assassins' (28). He does, of course, in the context of the novel, say more than he means. The waiter turns out to be Fidelio, the brother of the migrant worker Gabriel, whose murder at the end of the novel precipitates a series of recognitions on the part of Robles which go some way to reverse the radical 'desconocimiento' or social blindness which we see here.

The social split in the novel is also a political split: between the policies and general ideology of President Lázaro Cárdenas (1934–1940) and that of Miguel Alemán (1946–1952), two alternative political father figures.[33] There is a series of characters in the novel who could be loosely associated with the attitudes of *cardenismo*: Gervasio Pola, Librado Ibarra, Froilán Reyero, Feliciano Sánchez. Fuentes sums up the alternatives in an interview with Luis Harss:

> Había [en 1950] perspectivas ideológicas tajantes: una, la perspectiva que políticamente representó en México el gobierno de Lázaro Cárdenas, la posibilidad de un gobierno de tipo popular, un socialismo mexicano construido desde la base con la participación del pueblo y con todo el pensamiento marxista vigente en cada uno de los actos del gobierno; y por otro lado, la tesis política de Miguel Alemán, que respresentó la reacción contrarrevolucionaria en el año 46 con la tesis del hamiltonismo: la riqueza

---

[33] Ramírez Mattei, 46, also stresses the portrayal of Mexico as a 'país escindido'.

se acumula arriba, se concentra arriba, y luego se desparrama hacia abajo. Política y económicamente, estas eran las alternativas. (Harrs, 357-8)

Two Mexicos

The split between rich and poor Mexicans is perceived strongly, but in slightly different ways, by three characters: Ixca, Rodrigo Pola, and Federico Robles. In the prose poem which ends the novel, there is a very effective juxtaposition of two enormous lists, one of humble, suffering Mexicans addressed as *tú* ('tú sin nombre, tú que fuiste marcado con el hierro rojo [...] tú que no tienes zapatos, que te llenas de fritangas y aguardiente'), and another of those who are safe and comfortable and middle-class, addressed as *ustedes*: 'y en la otra orilla ustedes que esperan el bienestar y la fama —yo, nosotros, ustedes, nunca tú, nunca el tercero— y ustedes que [...] poseen un nombre y un destino claro [...] y ustedes que se barnizan la cara y se joden a maxfactor y se arreglan las chichis' (456-8). Sandwiched between these castes is Ixca: 'y en el centro vacío mi corazón que delira'.

Ixca tends to see the split in mythico-historical terms, instituted by the Conquest. In one hallucinatory scene he sees, looking down Avenida Juárez, the whole of Mexican history rolling back until he reaches

> el lejano día de agosto en que las aguas se dividen y todo es confusión y escudos y silbos y penachos y y estruendo de arcabuces y bergantines y el Señor Malinche [Cortés] se asoma a la azotea de una casa de Amaxac y ve aproximarse la canoa del vencido [Moctezuma]. Y desde entonces son dos [...], el del origen y el del destino, los dos plantados sobre la misma avenida, fuese de agua o de cemento. Del Yei Calli al 1951. Siempre dos, el águila reptante, el sol nocturno. (269-70)

The two sides perpetuate the rivalry between Quetzalcoatl and Tezcatlipoca, the Plumed Serpent and the Smoking Mirror.

Rodrigo Pola is in the middle like Ixca, but the focus is that of social class. His distaste for the common people is expressed in extreme animal imagery:

> Y los cuerpos pequeños, las eternas caras mongólicas, de especie olvidada, como ictiosaurios comprimidos, jorobados sobre las comidas ardientes, escondidos detrás de todas sus máscaras. Y él anclado en el centro, el único hombre con conciencia de la zona intermedia, de estar entre dos mundos que lo rechazaban. [...] Él entre las dos zonas, en la ciudad de fronteras imperceptibles en la materia, pero altas, alambradas, férreas en el espíritu. ¿Creaba la ciudad esos abismos, o eran obra de sus hombres? (255-6)

The case of Federico Robles is slightly different, and in terms of plot more crucial: he is not between the two worlds, but the two worlds are within him, as he realises in the following vision:

> Robles se restregó la cara; un mundo blanquecino, con bordes niquelados y ojos de gas neón, cruzó velozmente por sus pulpilas; detrás de él, otro mundo, horizontal, rojizo, poblado de canciones y nombres y colores enarbolados y corceles furiosos. En el centro de cada uno de estos mundos, se plantaba su propia figura: transparente y pálida en uno, renegrida y quemada en el otro. (287)

Two families. I: the Polas

All the dramas of the novel are played out through two families, the Polas and the Robles-Zamacona. Indeed the dilemma (associated with the split described above) seems to be passed from one family to the other by Ixca Cienfuegos. Both families have a son, Rodrigo Pola and Manuel Zamacona, whose life is determined by his past, the heritage of the father, and yet this past is not immediately available to either of them, but mediated by the language or silence of others. One son dies while the other survives, which is an inverted reflexion of the fate of their respective fathers. Both mothers, Rosenda Pola and Mercedes Zamacona, are abandoned by the father, and strongly influence the son. The case of Robles is more complex because he survives to have a wife and lover, Norma and Hortensia, who embody dualities engendered at the beginning of his career.

Rodrigo Pola accepts that he is a prolongation of his father: 'yo sólo quería ser su prolongación, de alguna manera, y creía que esa prolongación era moral' (133). He also realises that his heritage is problematical in various ways. The first reason seems to be that death, violent death, breaks any sort of continuity or memory in Mexico: 'pero él vivió en otro país, en otra ciudad: México y México mueren radicalmente cada vez que un hombre vuelve a manar sangre con pasión' (133). In a way the whole question asked by the novel is whether all those deaths can be given a meaning, written into some coherent historical narrative. ('¿No es el nuestro un sacrificio más, en balde?' (85), asks Pedro, Gervasio Pola's companion.) The second reason is the sense of belatedness, in that the Revolution in which his father Gervasio dies, was a unique event, and that the father had robbed him of one major possibility in his life, lived it out for him: 'Hay tantas cosas que pesan sobre nosotros [...] que es como sentir que otros cumplieron ya con esa parte de nuestra vida. Sólo mi padre, ¿ves?, pudo vivir lo que vivió, pero no sólo para él; para mi madre y para mí, también. Es como si esa posibilidad mía ya hubiera sido vivida por él, en la Revolución, fusilado' (264). The other reason is that he depends on the memory of his mother, but realises that she has an interest in distorting his image: 'desde que tengo memoria, trato de encontrar algo que me ayude a recrear su verdadera imagen; [...] y mi madre nunca quiso recrear la imagen que yo deseaba, que no era la de ella [...], un rencor reiterado' (133).

The heritage of Gervasio, like the origin of Federico Robles, is reduced to one crucial episode.[34] That episode is, moreover, dual and highly ambiguous. Gervasio Pola had been a syndicalist before the Revolution, a fund-raiser for the Zapatista cause (103), and involved with the Círculo de Obreros at the Río Blanco textile works in Veracruz State at the time of the highly significant strike there in June 1906 (104). He is described as 'de letras', presumably an arts graduate. He had married the middle-class Rosenda Zurbarán as a *maderista* officer, and fought against Huerta on the side of Zapata. The episode in the War, when he escapes from the prison at Belén with three other prisoners, is recaptured and shot, revolves around a series of choices concerning the two terms *solo* and *juntos*. Though they clearly involve a choice between the individual and the communal, the combinations of

---

[34] Borges, for example in 'Biografía de Tadeo Isidoro Cruz', similarly tends to reduce a whole life to a symbolic moment: 'Bien entendida, esa noche agota su historia; mejor dicho, un instante de esa noche, un acto de esa noche, porque los actos son nuestro símbolo' (*El Aleph, Obras completas* (Buenos Aires: Emecé, 1974), 562).

the concepts are often far more complex. Both terms can be positive and negative, solitude signifying either egoism or the sort of awareness of isolation and suffering which is the first step towards solidarity, or even its consequence. 'Together', on the other hand, can signify both true communion or a superficial belonging to a privileged group and social conformity. Ixca makes this clear in the choice for Rodrigo between being 'único y solo en medio de la compañía y la igualdad y la pertenencia' and being 'hermano de todos en la soledad' (76-7).[35] Froilán Reyero, another syndicalist, who dies with Gervasio, expands on this paradox. Froilán forms an important link between Gervasio Pola and Federico Robles, who is his cousin and who remembers being impressed by his phrase about the hunger of the Río Blanco strikers: 'Si usted los hubiera visto, ya sabría a estas horas que no está solo. Y también que no estar solo es como morirse de pena' (105). Not being alone means sharing the sufferings of others.

The episode in the Revolution is not so much one of paradox, as in these phrases, but of contradiction and ambiguity. After seeing General Gabriel Hernández shot and burnt by the *huertistas*, Gervasio Pola escapes from the prison with Froilán and two others and they make for the nearest *zapatista* camp. Gervasio proposes that they should split into two groups, and then perhaps go it alone: 'Más vale que uno viva solo y no que los cuatro mueran juntos' (81). The others, like Pedro, prefer to share their fate: 'Pero que no me dejen solo. Juntos aguantamos. Juntos nos pescaron y nos volverán a pescar' (82). One of them tells a story about an old man in his village who had wanted to die alone, but at the last moment had crawled out to share his experience with the others. Gervasio, however, whether out of conviction or as a justification for his lack of solidarity, argues to himself that he can save others only if he survives personally, that he can relate to the undifferenciated mass, to the collectivity, only from his own individuality:

---

[35] Following the same sort of paradox, though it is the 'pueblo' which is normally associated with anonymity, the togetherness of the Mexican oligarchy is seen as dissolving their expensive individualities into a jelly: 'ahora circula el mismo alcohol, la misma sange diluida [...] ahora las singularidades tan buscadas en el corte de los trajes, en las citas, en las puntas del pañuelo [...] caen al pozo de la gelatina común: agarrarse juntos, emblema del señorío mexicano' (60).

percibió en ese instante que, lejos de las heridas de sus compañeros, lejos de la imagen encadenada de la tierra triste [...] —en la otra orilla del mundo indiferenciado, masivo, de México— cabía la salvación de un hombre como él, [...] ausente de la memoria de los demás hombres mexicanos, pero fiel, sólo fiel a ellos cuando era fiel a sí mismo. Salvarme hoy, a mí, a mi piel, para salvar mañana a los demás. Ellos quieren que muera con ellos; esta muerte impersonal, de todos, sería reconfortante para mis hombres. [...] Estoy dispuesto a salvarlos, si se dejan salvar. Pero sólo salvándome puedo salvarlos hoy a ellos y mañana a otros. (83-84)

He abandons the sick Pedro and reaches the camp of General Inés Llanos, declaring that he had escaped alone: 'Yo solo me escapé y crucé el monte en un día [...] Me salvé solito' (87). Here, despite his survival to fight for the wider cause, there seems to be some personal betrayal. When it transpires that Llanos has joined the forces of Huerta and Gervasio is returned to the *solitaria* in Belén, he cannot face death alone: 'Quiero contársela a mis camaradas, para que callemos juntos y muramos juntos, juntos, juntos' (89). He tells the officer Felipe Zamacona (the brother of Mercedes) the whereabouts of his companions, believing that they would be caught sooner or later, and they are executed together. Before they die, he murmurs to them 'Nos salvamos juntos', and they defiantly face death hand in hand, as Froilán shouts '¡Viva Madero!'. The text offers no evaluation of this collective salvation in death. The solidarity and oneness are made even more problematic when Gervasio closes his eyes so as not to see death in those of his companions. Betrayal and solidarity, communion and individuality are inseparable in this strange episode. This is the inheritance of Rodrigo Pola.

There is in a way no alternative to the action of Gervasio, but rather alternative conclusions to be drawn from it, dual and inseparable strands for Rodrigo to take from it: 'los dos hilos de vida que se cruzaban y entretejían en la sangre de Rodrigo, que partían de una mañana gris y un paredón acribillado en Belén' (400). Characteristically, however, there is in the novel a short episode, belonging to the vignettes, which are generally not linked to the main plot though they reflect social trends and attitudes, that is a stark and almost parodic alternative to the version of Gervasio's story which would have him simply as a coward: 'El rostro catalán, de hachazos'. The story is that of the Spanish militiaman Pablo told by his companions to a woman who is possibly his widow, now living for the last thirteen years in Mexico and tending a 'tienda de dulces'. The messenger had escaped from a Francoist prison camp with other companions. Pablo was killed as he saved their lives by covering their backs and giving the impression that he was the only escapee. It is difficult to know how to take the description of the Spanish Civil War as 'la única historia honrada y pura hasta la raíz, [...] la única prueba absoluta del hombre concreto' (303). In *La muerte de Artemio Cruz*, the Spanish Civil War is similarly contrasted with an episode from the Mexican Revolution. Robles's heroic action at the battle of Celaya is only an alternative to this episode in so far as he survives whereas Gervasio dies.

Gervasio's death leaves Rosenda alone, hardly having known her husband, with a child who in many ways comes to replace the husband. Rosenda's case is analogous to that of many other women in Fuentes's work: Mercedes in this novel, Asunción in *Las buenas conciencias*, Catalina in *La muerte de Artemio Cruz*, Claudia in *Zona sagrada*, Consuelo in *Aura*.[36] Spurned by her family after her father dies intestate, she lives in a dingy house 'del mal lado del sol' (230), with only memories of her 'palacio' in the Colonia Roma, earns her living in a haberdasher's, while Rodrigo stays at home or is later scorned at the *Preparatoria*. Like Mercedes and Claudia, Rosenda comes to look on her son as a product of parthenogenesis, to believe that she had fertilised herself: 'que Gervasio no había existido, que el niño había sido engendrado por mi voluntad y mi designio, que yo mismo me había fecundado con el sueño de un hombre que sólo dormida conocí' (229). Like other witch figures, Rosenda tries unsuccessfully to cast a spell on Rodrigo while he is asleep: 'mis palabras se repetían en un sonsonete bajo dentro de su sueño. Era un encantamiento, un encantamiento más que no supo surtir efectos' (235). She wishes to retain Rodrigo in a sort of never-ending birth, reduced to an elementrary nature set against history, action, the city, associated with the masculine: 'un eterno parto parlante que le dijera lo que ella quería saber siempre, alzada sobre las placentas como un monumento, viva en su espeso anhelo de ser siempre la madre, de encarnar a la naturaleza ya que lo demás —la vida de los

[36] Gloria Durán also notes some of these parallels: 'In all three cases the young man-child replaces the older one in the heart of the woman, almost as a reincarnation'(*The Archetypes of Carlos Fuentes: from Witch to Androgyne* (Hamden, Conn: Archon, 1980), 70).

hombres, lo urbano, lo que se resuelve en proyectos y papeles— nunca la tocaría' (145). Rodrigo's writing, his 'papeles', is a direct attack on Rosenda's world: it is a revolt and a defence against nature, the home, the maternal. As in Nietzsche it is the necessary lie against the original truth which is death.

Rodrigo is not able to respond to Rosenda's asphyxiating demand for affection and eventually leaves home. His defensive lack of generosity for his mother, which leaves Rodrigo emotionally crippled, is seen by Ixca to be the image of the separation and alienation of the city. Rosenda's striking out the figure of the father, distorting his memory, is linked to the dirty urban rain which rather than 'confundirse, bienhechora y momentánea, en la tierra que bañaba' remains 'intermedia, en el lodo y el regurgitar de alcantarillas'. The term 'intermedio' is often associated with the emotional mediocrity and stagnation of Rodrigo. The rhythm of the generations has been broken like the link between the rain and the land or the concatenation of day and night in nature: 'el día jamás se encadenaba a los días ni las noches a las noches'. From the 'amor exigido e indiferencia personal y sacrificios gratuitos' of the truncated relationship of Rosenda and Rodrigo-Gervasio, Ixca jumps to an image of all the inhabitants of Mexico City who, unlike Gervasio and his men, do not hold hands as they face their daily death: 'Cuatro millones se alineaban, sin tocarse las manos, cada uno rígido al lado de los otros, a lo largo de un muro coronado de pólvora' (241).

Rodrigo, too, extrapolates from his own incapacity to open out to others. The barriers between the two classes in the city ('ciudad de fronteras imperceptibles en la materia, pero altas, alambradas, férreas en el espíritu') are the same barriers of words and forms with which he had defended himself against the love of Norma, even though he had tried to take up her challenge to love without intermediaries:

> Rodrigo creyó que sólo una vez había intuido esa necesidad —que jamás dicta la inteligencia— de no presentar defensas, cuando conoció a Norma. Había querido abrirse por entero y dejar que de él corriera todo y que en él penetrara todo lo que ella hubiese querido entregarle. Era la forma, el estilo, lo que construía la barrera que cada nuevo encuentro, cada nuevo beso, iba levantando. [...] Ella había planteado el reto, él no lo había aceptado. Había

amado más sus ecos, sus palabras, que a la mujer que pudo quererlo a él, desnudo, sin palabras. (256)[37]

The hardening of the individuality, the ego, and the incapacity to relate dynamically to the other, to see the other in oneself, seem to be linked to the breaking of memory, the continuity with the past which makes up the present self. It is also perhaps the consequence of the fear of being absorbed by the mother. Rodrigo's haunted, almost Dostoyevskian self-punishment also seems to derive from his guilt-ridden relationship with Rosenda: he more or less intentionally makes a fool of himself twice at parties, and abstains from going to the toilet until he develops peritonitis. The self-punishment alternates with excessive pride, which makes him move from one extreme position to another: to pure art when faced with the contamination of domestic closeness; to political activism when his poems are rejected by the Círculo, etc. Rodrigo joins a group of poets dominated by Tomás Mediana, who seem to have much in common with the group of the Contemporáneos. They are a group dedicated to lasting works of art as an expression of the self, ('salvarnos individualmente' (148)) and yet the contradictions which they express echo those lived by Gervasio. They form a 'comunidad de poetas [...] determinada [...] por la divergencia y soledad de individuos que ejercen un oficio cada día más ajeno al interés colectivo'. Poetry, says Mediana, starting from a phrase of Cocteau, is inseparable from both communion and the unique and individual: 'La poesía de nuestro tiempo conservará la belleza del martirio. Poesía: afán de comunión. Martirio: experiencia única, intransferible, aunque los leones del Coliseo digan otra cosa' (150).

Two people fight for the future and soul of Rodrigo: Ixca Cienfuegos and his mother Rosenda. They both do so by presenting a different view of his father and the model he should thus follow. Rosenda develops a view of her husband which is the fruit of her resentment at not sharing his life or even his death, and of what she sees as the vulgarity of the

---

[37] Paz links the Mexican's fear of opening out, 'abrirse', to his love of form: 'La preeminencia de lo cerrado frente a lo abierto no se manifiesta sólo como impasibilidad y desconfianza, sino como amor a la Forma' (*El laberinto*, 28).

new classes who come to occupy the privileged position she once enjoyed with her family, and whom she now serves in the shop:

> en esas horas vulgares sólo aprendí a reprochar a Gervasio, a reprocharle otras cosas que nada tenían que ver con el origen de nuestras vidas y nuestras cópulas y su fruto, que sólo tenían que ver con la nueva vida, la nueva ciudad que crecía a mi alrededor y sus nuevas gentes, las que habían llegado a ocupar los puestos abandonados, y de esa falsedad [...] salió el nuevo Gervasio. (231)

Rosenda clearly sees an essential, original truth in relationships, which can be falsified by language and memory. She realises at the end of her life, on her death-bed as she talks to Ixca, that Gervasio had been kind and generous, but that she had tried to change that:

> él sí; era bueno, lo sé ahora, muy tarde, bueno y generoso y éstas son las cosas que se nos escapan porque complicamos el pensamiento y la carne también y queremos que las cosas sean otra cosa, y no lo que realmente son, al principio, y sin progreso posible, incanjeables y dignas de la mayor protección, de la única protección: bondad, generosidad. (231-2)

Rosenda, however, uses the new, false image to dictate the future of Rodrigo: 'de esa nueva imagen salió también el destino que tracé para Rodrigo' (231). Her decision is to mould him to the new capitalist values she sees around her, to the pursuit of success and conformity: 'Pero haré (ésta era la mentira, ésta era la mentira nacida de mi reproche [...]) que tu hijo triunfe, como se triunfa aquí. Lo torceré pero le daré su carrera, le enseñaré a buscar a los poderosos y a ser sumiso con ellos' (232-3).

At two key moments of Rodrigo's youth, Rosenda opts to lie to him. When he asks whether his father was good to her, she answers: 'Tu padre fue un cobarde que delató a sus compañeros y murió como un tonto, dejándonos en la miseria' (145). The second decisive moment comes when she discovers Rodrigo's manuscript, and decides to 'culminar la mentira' (235), by telling him that he had no destiny, even though she meant the opposite: 'quería contarle cómo quería que sí tuviera un destino pero que fuera prolongación del mío y del de su padre muerto' (236). What she actually says is that he is not an independent individual, but depends on others: 'No tienes ningún destino, sábelo ya. Tienes responsabilidades' (152). The sense of responsibility which he derives from this is not the positive sense of *juntos* as community, but a mediocre dependency and blurring of self: 'Acaso ella tenía razón y nadie tenía derecho a ser y la vida era un continuo desvanecerse en los deseos y actos de los demás' (153). Though Rosenda's lie loses her her son ('que el cordón se quebraba, que las piernas se cerraban' (151)), it marks his life, distorts his 'true', 'original' heritage and replaces it with one born of resentment and the social values of the moment, depriving Rodrigo of any continuity with his past.

Ixca has a different agenda. As a supernatural figure himself, as an Aztec fundamentalist or as an uncomprehending instrument of his 'mother' Teódula Moctezuma, a modern-day version of Tonantzin and Coatlicue,[38] Ixca demands a sacrifice from Rodrigo. Though the sacrifice may be one of attitude, there is also an element of real blood sacrifice. More significantly, Ixca constantly demands that Rodrigo should choose, that he should abandon compromise and mediocrity and fully assume one side of his dual destiny: 'asumir uno u otro plenamente, ya nunca más a medias' (76). Ixca misreads Rodrigo's situation on two significant occasions. On the first, he thinks Rodrigo had tried to commit suicide, whereas he had simply burned a leather belt. He demands that Rodrigo sacrifice himself to become one with the suffering of the anonymous masses and to transcend their solitude in fraternity. The other option is to choose success, a name, a different sort of solitude:

> Pero una [decisión] te traerá con nosotros, te abrirá los ojos al contacto de llantos más graves y desnudos que el tuyo, te clavará un pedernal en el centro del pecho. Y la otra te pondrá frente a nosotros, nítido y brillante, único y solo en medio de la compañía y la igualdad y la pertenencia. Acá serás anónimo, hermano de todos en la soledad. Allá tendrás tu nombre, y en la muchedumbre nadie te tocará, no tocarás a nadie. (76-77)

Ixca later takes advantage of the death of Rodrigo's mother, which he initially hides from him to increase his guilt, to propose the sacrifice

---

[38] Fuentes describes her as 'Tonantzin desplazada a las vecindades', cit. in Durán, 204.

again. Each man, he argues, 'feeds the creation' of a god until he is reintegrated into the 'original duality'. It depends on the intensity of a man's life whether he maintains that god: 'hay que saber, solamente, si ese tránsito entre la creación y la muerte, ese breve paso, se cumple con la intensidad propicia al alimento del creador, o si se gasta en el compromiso, en el simple transcurso inconsciente' (264). Ixca's language increases in religious intensity and violence until he proposes assuming 'la derrota y la humillación' (266) of his parents, becoming the moral prolongation of his father, who 'es el sacrificio, es la muerte enfrentada a solas' (267). Here Ixca is wrong again, and is beaten by the strategy of Rosenda. Gervasio for Rodrigo is (no longer) an heroic figure of sacrifice: '[mi padre] tuvo que delatar a esos tres hombres para poder morir. Hasta en la muerte quiso caer con otros, no solo... no solo. Hizo lo mismo que mi madre me pidió a mí: protegerme, no quedar solo. [...] Pertenencia. [...] ¡De eso me tienes que salvar! De la humillación, de la derrota ...' (267). Ixca is mortified by his mistake. He realises that Rodrigo has chosen an alternative father figure, rewritten his geneaology: 'Federico Robles era la imagen viva y prolongada de Gervasio Pola a los ojos de Rodrigo' (267).

Two consequences arise from this realisation. Ixca, in the true style of a Goethean Mephistopheles or Balzacian Vautrin, or their Hollywood counterpart, produces the success that Rodrigo wants instantaneously: he has *already* spoken to some producers about Rodrigo, whose success is enormous and literally diabolical. When his success is confirmed, Manuel cancels out the past: 'todo lo pensado o recordado por Rodrigo se canceló, en ese instante, para siempre' (400), and breaks the dual thread which linked him to his father. The other is that Ixca turns his attentions to Robles and his family. Robles is forced by Ixca's manipulation to face the dual inheritance of Gervasio Pola, which, as he remembers at the end of his life, was also his own.

Rodrigo's choosing an alternative father is a significant moment in Fuentes's work, which is echoed elsewhere. In ideological terms it signifies little more than the move from the ethics of Cárdenas to those of Miguel Alemán. In terms of freedom and destiny, choice and historical and cultural determinism, it is a significant tool against the tyranny of the past. Nietzsche returns frequently to this theme, for example in the formulation 'it would be the most extreme sign of vulgarity to be related to one's parents'.[39]

Two families. II: The Robles-Zamacona

In the case of the Pola family, the father dies early and the son survives to prolong his life in one way or another. Here the situation is different in that Robles survives the Revolution to become a successful and powerful businessman, while his son, Manuel Zamacona, dies. Whereas Rodrigo is cut off from his paternal origins and past by the manipulations of Rosenda, it is Robles who is cut off from his own past. His affirmation of his own individual power and his censoring the source of that power, which he has derived from others whom he has destroyed or conveniently forgotten ('Robles canceló, automáticamente, todos los momentos anteriores' (165)), is magically represented by a curse put on him by Mercedes Zamacona whereby his power and life are fatally split. The death of Robles's son Manuel breaks that split and alienation in two ways. He puts many ideological and personal questions to Robles, which make him doubt his own position. Symbolically, within the wider plot, Manuel dies as a representative of all those who had died for Robles, who constitute his self and his origin censored by Mercedes, but who also constitute the plurality and potential community on which his exclusive singularity is spuriously built.

Manuel Zamacona, though an important forerunner of Lorenzo Cruz, another martyr son of a powerful father, is not a terribly interesting character in himself, except symbolically as a link between Mercedes and Robles, in the meaningless manner of his death, and in his role of (often somewhat tedious) mouthpiece to many of the ideas of the Hyperión group, Paz, Reyes and other philosphers of 'lo mexicano'. Neither son nor father are aware of their consanguinity, though Ixca (usually omniscient, though he misinterprets key attitudes badly, as he

[39] *Ecce Homo* (Harmondsworth: Penguin, 1992), 12. In 'On the uses and disadvantages of history for life', he describes the struggle to free oneself from heredity and the past as 'an attempt to give oneself, as it were *a posteriori*, a past in which one would like to originate in opposition to that in which one did originate', *Untimely Meditations* (Cambridge: CUP, 1994), 76.

did with Rodrigo) seems to be aware.⁴⁰ Ideologically, Manuel is equidistant between Ixca, with his obsessive insistence on the origin and past as the only truth, and Robles who sees truth and self residing in the future and progress. From this point of view the three characters represent the three dimensions of time associated with the YO, TÚ and ÉL voices in *La muerte de Artemio Cruz* and the three Anglo-Saxon authors mentioned above. Robles affirms that 'Aquí hay que mirar hacia el futuro. Y los poetas son cosas del pasado. [...] El pasado es lo muerto, amigo' (275-6). Manuel rather sees the past as a dead, unresolved weight which is forever present and must be faced and purged: 'No podemos vivirnos y morirnos a ciegas, [...] tratando de olvidar todo y de nacer de nuevo todos los días sabiendo que todo está vivo y presente y aplastándonos el diafragma, por más que queramos olvidarlo: Quetzalcoatls y Corteses e Iturbides y Juárez y Porfirios y Zapatas, todos hechos un nudo en la garganta' (278). The past must be purged of the dross so that a new future can be built: 'No, no se trata de añorar nuestro pasado y regodearnos en él, sino de penetrar en el pasado, entenderlo, reducirlo a razón, cancelar lo muerto —que es lo estúpido, lo rencoroso—, rescatar lo vivo y saber, por fin, qué es México y qué se puede hacer con él' (279). He has a similar, if inverted disageement with Ixca: 'México debe alcanzar su originalidad viendo hacia adelante; no la encontrará atrás. Cienfuegos asegura que regresar, dejarse caer hasta el fondo, nos asegurará ese encuentro, esa revelación de lo que somos. No; hay que crearnos un origen y una originalidad' (68).

Another point of dissension between Ixca and Manuel is important for an understanding of the fate of Robles: that of the nature or even the possibility of the individual in Mexico. Manuel and Ixca fight ideologically over the fate of Robles, as did Rosenda and Ixca over that of Rodrigo. All three characters, at the time of the collapse of Robles's financial empire are, with no pretence to verisimilitude, sitting in a scruffy café discussing concepts of renunciation, sacrifice, and

---

⁴⁰ There is a curious, atavistic coincidence between Manuel and his grandfather Albano Robles. Albano is 'un viejo de pocas palabras, que las pocas que decía eran arrojadas [...] al centro del sol' (392), while his grandson Manuel fills various sheets of paper with the repeated word 'México' and then 'salió al balcón, fijó los ojos en el sol, apretó las cuartillas y con todas sus fuerzas las arrojó hacia el centro del astro' (67).

salvation. Manuel, whose position is basically that of the Christian, wonders whether Robles will renounce his power only to fall into nostalgia, or to transcend loss for solidarity with other Mexicans: 'Y usted, licenciado, ¿va a renunciar a todo para añorar lo perdido, o va a renunciar para acabar renunciando incluso a añorar, para arrancarse la piel de su individualidad falsificada y cubrirse con el llanto y la sangre desnudos de los otros mexicanos?' (375). Ixca counters that this demands the existence of a strong sense of individuality, which is nonexistent or has been destroyed in Mexico through betrayal and defeat: 'Toda esta tesis está bien cuando se apoya en una idea de personalidad capaz de recibir, y engendrar redención, culpa, etcétera. Pero no veo qué razón tenga en un país donde no hay persona, sino otra cosa —aire, sangre, sol, un tumulto sin nombre, una masa torcida de hueso y piedras y rencores, pero jamás una persona.' (376). For Zamacona, this dispersion and fragmentation of human unity constitutes the 'satanic'. For the suffering and deaths of Mexico to signify something, there must be a strong individual to take them on himself: 'por cada mexicano que murió en vano, sacrificado, hay un mexicano responsable. Y regreso a mi tesis: para que esa muerte no haya sido en vano, alguien debe asumir la culpa [...]. Entonces, sólo entonces, ese hombre singular de México será todos los mexicanos humillados. Pero ¿quién acarrea los pecados de México, Ixca, quién?' (378–9). He outlines two possible symbolic roles for death in Mexico. The land either demands vengeance for the deaths, or demands the deaths to keep itself alive, the Aztec vision: 'Lo espantoso, Cienfuegos, es que a veces no sabe uno si esta tierra, en vez de exigir venganza por tanta sangre que la ha manchado, exige esa sangre. Si esto fuera cierto, entonces sí acepto tus ideas: volcán anónimo, dispersión y muerte del hombre' (379). This is the basic question asked by the novel.

As in the case of Gervasio Pola, with Robles there is a very specific time which constitutes the origin of his power. Almost simultaneously with his acquiring that origin and power, he is radically dissociated from his family and class origin. For most of his life, he believed that that moment was the battle of Celaya, but in fact, as he remembers and the reader discovers only near the end of the novel, the significant encounter of his life was that with Mercedes and all that she brought with her, and his subsequent expulsion from that paradisal relationship.

Federico Robles was born to *purépecha* Indian peasant farmer parents in Michoacán on the estate of the Ovando family, who acquired vast tracts of lands in the Liberal reforms of the nineteenth century. His memories are of his father and his close relationship with the land, and of his older cousin Froilán Reyero, who told the family about the textile strike in Río Blanco and the massacre.[41] He was particularly marked by Froilán's statement 'Si usted lo hubiera visto, ya sabría a estas horas que no está solo. Y también que no estar solo es como morirse de pena' (105). Robles was taken to receive some education and help a priest in Morelia. His mother, Magdalena, was lassoed and raped presumably by Pedro de Ovando and his friends during their 'paseos a caballo' (102).[42] Federico's brother attempted to avenge her, but was press-ganged into the Federal army and the rest of the family made no more protest. Federico claimed to Ixca that he had not understood the incident, and even had he, that would not have been his motive for joining the Revolution, which he had not understood and which came along like a natural phenomenon, 'como llueve o hace hambre' (107). Only later did he find the 'justificaciones', which, according to Ixca, those who did know why they joined the Revolution never found. Of these poor anonymous people who fought the Revolution and received little from it, Robles contemptuously says: 'Ésos siempre sabrán los porqués, pero bendito para lo que les sirve'. When Ixca comments that Robles was one of the 'ésos', the latter replies: 'Como el maíz fue grano antes de ser mazorca. Pero cuando es mazorca, ya no es grano' (107). Robles thus aggressively denies the permanence of his origin: 'hay que olvidar todo aquello. [...] Aquello se murió para siempre' (101).

From Morelia Federico was taken as sacristan to the hacienda of the Zamacona family near Uruapan. He glosses over this period of his life to Ixca with a phrase reminiscent of Lazarillo's departure from the service of the 'fraile de la Merced': 'Por lo que usted guste, me salí de la hacienda' (109).[43] He then joins the Revolution and claims that his experience at the battle of Celaya had been at the origin of the immense power he went on to acquire: 'una brida tensa entre los dientes, en el

[41] The later importance of Froilán Reyero for Federico Robles is foreshadowed by their sharing the initials F. R.
[42] The landowners Atanasio Menchaca in *La muerte de Artemio Cruz* and Miranda in *Gringo viejo* rape the mothers of Artemio Cruz and Tomás Arroyo, but are the fathers of the protagonist.
[43] 'Y por esto, y por otras cosillas que no digo salí dél', *Lazarillo de Tormes* (Madrid: Castalia, 1982), 157.

campo de Celaya, origen del poder' (164). His first lesson in power comes from a general who befriends him because he can sing *Valentina* in Latin, and its message is utter brutality and scorn for the Mexican race: 'Güevos, es lo único que hace falta para dominar a esta raza, y como ni se dan cuenta, cuando menos lo sabes ya estás trepado en sus cogotes. Que los azotes y robes, no les importa, con tal de que tengas buenas viejas, y güevos' (111).[44] This brutality, inseparable from horses and sexual power, comes to a head in a vigorously described scene in the battle:

> el kepí de Federico voló, y en sus cabellos azotados, en la mañana sin viento, por la velocidad y el tumulto, sintió nacer la ambición y la gloria: el machete se irguió con la rapidez del deseo y cayó sobre las nucas y los cráneos, batidos, pegajosos de sudor y sangre, de los hombres de la División del Norte; el pecho inundado de calor, la verga erecta, las piernas tensas sobre el lomo del caballo, los dientes hundidos en la rienda. (114)

After the Revolution, Robles quickly becomes a powerful and unscrupulous man. Power, he explains to Ixca, is inseparable from the verb *chingar*, the violent opening up of an opponent, sexual humiliation of the male, the turning the other into an object as explained by Paz:[45] 'Y así inventamos el poder, Cienfuegos, el verdadero poder mexicano, que no consiste en el despliegue de la fuerza. [...] Nada es más admirado en México que el gran chingón' (121).

This brutality and denial of others is a long way from the values of Robles's home. Only towards the end of the novel do we read of the incident in Uruapan which is presented as decreeing this fatal split in Robles. Mercedes Zamacona was the fifteen-year old daughter of a religious family (a priest, a crippled mother and embittered sister), given to walking through the fertile countryside and cultivating a heady mixture of mysticism and sensuality, somewhat reminiscent of D.H. Lawrence. Christ for her was not in the chapel or the stuffy house, but outside, in a living rhythm of sin and pardon, 'encarnación viva de pecado y perdón' (414), or 'en cualquiera de los hombres oscuros que

---

[44] This is the philosophy Raskolnikov expounds to Sonya in *Crime and Punishment* (Oxford: OUP, 1990), 400.
[45] See *El laberinto*, 67–72.

olían a tierra húmeda y grano de café' (415). Her painfully aroused new breasts and sex, she sees as three twin moons, awaiting, and to be completed by, their other half, or sun (as pardon completed sin), dual in that they are brilliant at night, dark during the day in the sunlight:

> Entonces no eran necesarios el porte y la conciencia de sus pechos nuevos, de la navaja inasible entre las piernas, sino la escueta existencia de los nuevos centros brillantes como tres lunas gemelas que cantaran entre sí, que dialogaran sobre su nacimiento súbito, atónito, y sobre su muerte de vidrios pulverizados: su otra mitad, oscura: lunas redondas, negras frente al sol, plateadas en la noche: así las sentía. (415)[46]

There follows a tremendously violent and sensual scene when Mercedes excitedly watches Federico Robles brutally break a wild horse by lacerating it using a club with nails. A magical power runs between the three centres of the girl's body, a vehicle for all the force of the land, and the 'centaur' formed by the horse and man and their erect flesh:

> su vista [de Mercedes] telegrafiaba, del muchacho con el garrote que se abrazaba al cuello de la bestia, al muñón de carne erecta del animal. Un río de poder corría, magnético, entre las carnes exaltadas del hombre y el animal, trenzados como un centauro roto, y la triple efigie lunar de la muchacha: lunas que pulsaban, levantadas como toda la naturaleza de su tierra, en ese instante de dominación y orgullo. (419)[47]

This scene leads up to the sexual consummation of the relationship between Federico and Mercedes in the afternoons, in the absolute darkness of the sacristy, where she feels that she continues to feed his power: 'ella quería alimentar su fuerza, sólo eso; darle parte de su semilla de poder' (420). The crisis comes when the priest and his sister open the door and let both their scandalised condemnation and the light

---

[46] There would seem to be references to Nahua mythology here. Huitzilopochtli, for example, the sun, falls like an eagle each night to die in the body of the earth goddess, and before being reborn each morning must fight with his sister the moon. See Caso, *La religión de los aztecas* (Mexico City: Imprenta Mundial, 1936), 11-12.

[47] It is tempting to link Federico's violence towards this horse with the vision of the horse from which his mother was lassoed and then raped.

flow in. Federico closes his eyes 'no como si lo cegaran las luces, sino tratando de dividir la luz de las sombras y recobrar éstas' (421). Mercedes, in terror, takes refuge in her class ('ella era decente y él y indio mugroso' (422)) and individuality and ego: 'quiso asirse al yo-soy y dejó de ser lo que era' (421). The unity or rhythm of one and the other, light and dark, nature and man, is broken. As she accepts the strictures of her uncles, the world becomes only half of what it should be, only one half of a dual whole: 'todo [...] se le apretaba entre las piernas como una disecación madura, como las cuerdas rotas por un tijeretazo de palabras, y un medio terror (pues desde entonces se diría que no habría plenitud, que todo se daría a medias [...])' (422).

Mercedes realises she is pregnant, and, like Rosenda, excludes the father from the conception, condensing all the rhythms of the land into 'su propio alumbramiento' (422), ensuring that 'los frutos erguidos y reales de ese poder sólo fueran de ella, que los había germinado en aquel momento' (424). Out of spite, she places a curse on the power of Federico: that he should only find his truth and origin in the dark, but should be a prey to egoism, the self, and should squander his power during the day in a futile and criminal show:

> lo condenó a la oscuridad [...] a vivir a ciegas y a sólo encontrar en lo oscuro su verdad y su satisfacción y su origen y sobre todo [...] a vivir presa del yo-soy, a condenar su poder maltratado [...] a un despeñadero inútil, egoísta [...] lo condenó [...] a recobrar en la oscuridad su poder y a gastarlo en la luz, a no encontrar jamás la fórmula exacta de la razón entre el poder y su fruto. (424)

The origin of his power is plural, the men and land of Mexico, his love and son ('tierra húmeda, frutos de la tierra, ojos y manos y rostros mexicanos que sin verlos fueron testigos de su amor' (427)), but the exercise of his power is individual, ego-bound. Her curse is a split between day and night, between the self and community, but offers one glimpse of hope: the return to her image and that of his son: 'deberás regresar a mi imagen y a la de tu hijo para encontrar la verdad y el origen de tu fuerza y lo demás será la disipación y el orgullo sin frutos y el crimen más horrible' (427). The split in Federico is clearly that between solo and juntos; he is both things, one by night, unconsciously, and the other by day, consciously, but the two never come together in a meaningful rhythm, or complementarity: there is a sort of amnesia which prevents any integration.

His wife and lover, Norma and Hortensia, are associated respectively with the sun and darkness. Norma, who is fair-skinned and has green eyes, 'quiso ser el sol, sentir una semilla de astro que le calcinara el vientre y repitió, en el calor del sol, su nombre, una, dos, varias veces' (124). Hortensia, who is dark-skinned and blind, asks herself: '¿Es la oscuridad lo que le ofrezco? ¿Es la oscuridad el lugar donde puede encontrar su luz Federico Robles?' (355). Norma Larragoiti is part of the power structure of Federico, his chic, confident social dimension and image, distant from any 'original' identity: 'La máscara de Norma, insensiblemente, había sido inventada por aquel rostro inventado y deseado por Federico. Todo el perfil de la mujer, supo Robles, era un producto de su pura voluntad. Ella, sin saberlo, sólo se había amoldado a un deseo imaginario hasta plasmarlo sobre su efigie verdadera, perdida para siempre' (162). Norma forms part of the exclusive sphere of power of Robles, impervious to anything which questions its limits, pluralises its nature:

> Y Robles volvió a sentir (en Norma) su prolongación y avanzada [...]. La plenitud de su poder le subyugaba con una esfera cálida y perfecta que alumbrase todos los rincones previsibles de su vida. [...] Federico canceló automáticamente, todos los momentos anteriores, y todos los que, hoy mismo, querían ligarse a ellos, reconstruir su otra imagen, su vida olvidada y escondida. (164–5)

Hortensia, on the other hand, is very much his equal: her mother had been a maid at the house of Pimpinela de Ovando, while Robles's father had been a *peón* on the estate of Pimpinela's uncle.[48]

The development of Robles's power is not, of course, as clean or straightforward as this ideal image would suggest. The reader learns much of his rise through the testimony of his alter ego Librado Ibarra, who had studied law with him after the Revolution, shared women in the same bed, but had followed a different career as labour lawyer,

---

[48] The various marriages are interesting here. Rodrigo Pola, who had been the fiancé of Norma, marries her eventual enemy Pimpinela de Ovando. Robles marries the daughter of the maid of Pimpinela's family, while Ixca Cienfuegos is forced to live with Norma's maid, Rosa Morales.

representative of the Cárdenas regime in rural areas and political prisoner until he was finally compromised and swindled by Robles and crippled in one of his factories. Robles started making money by means of fraudulent speculations on the property of ruined survivors of the Porfirian oligarchy, before moving north to make himself useful and available to North-American commercial interests, later to flirt with fascists and the military. One episode, however, which Robles remembers only towards the end of the novel, stands as a symbol of the price he payed for his enrichment. In 1938, as a representative of the hard right, he approached a general, probably Juan Abreu Almazán, with the proposal that he assassinate the labour leader Feliciano Sánchez (a friend of Ibarra who had taken in the latter's wife when he was away), in the hope that his followers might be open to the attraction of the right-wing opposition once he was dead. After Sánchez is gunned down 'while attempting to escape', Robles is offered a portfolio in the General's future revolutionary government, which he shrewdly exchanges for urban land which will soon become valuable building plots.

After his miscalculation and failure with Rodrigo Pola, Ixca Cienfuegos turns his attention, and all the power he seems to have to manipulate plot and destiny, to Federico Robles and Norma Larragoiti. His first task is to free Norma from dependency on the power of Robles, which gives rise to some of the most bizarre episodes in the novel. After showing Norma that he knows the secrets of her modest family, and telling her that the difference between Robles and her was 'el poder. Y saber cómo usarlo' (311), he refuses to make love to her before he has made her pregnant with his words: 'Yo no tengo sino palabras, hasta mi cuerpo es de palabras, y esas palabras pueden ser tuyas. [...] Tienes que ser tú, tú entera con todas las consecuencias de tu vida [...] Toma el poder, te pertenece. [...] Y yo no te daré el gusto de que sientas mi carne hasta que te tragues todas mis palabras, te den náusea y te embaracen como a un pulpo, hasta que las hagas tuyas' (312-3).[49] Later, on the beach at Robles's Acapulco house, Ixca repeatedly possesses Norma until she claims to be totally dependent on him and love him more than her own life. Later, however, in a

---

[49] There is a similar scene between Arroyo and Harriet Winslow in the ball-room in *Gringo viejo*.

fantasmagorical scene after their yacht capsizes during a storm, Ixca clearly pushes Norma to try to drown him to gain possession of the only life-belt, which he is clinging to. It is here that he gives her her own independent power, as she chooses to survive at the expense of another: 'Su propia efigie le brillaba ante los ojos, y la sangre le hervía en el pensamiento de su salvación, salvación de su cuerpo, de todo su poder' (331). She quickly turns this new confidence against Pimpinela de Ovando, who had aimed to regain some of the family's lost fortune in exchange for aristocratic connections, but more importantly against Federico Robles himself. At a key moment, and clearly almost physically occupied by Ixca, she refuses to offer any solidarity to Robles, and asserts her own independence and uniqueness: 'yo tengo mis propias fuerzas, no porque esté casada contigo [...] no soy fuerte porque soy tuya; yo sola puedo vivir, y amar y torcer a la gente e imponerme [...] ella sola, singular, Norma Larragoiti' (396). Her option is that of solitude, the solitary exercise of power, though she survives these words only by some brief moments.

In the meantime, Ixca has, with the omnipotence of a Vautrin, manipulated the financial ruin of Robles, advising him to move against some Monterrey bankers and then passing on false information to Pimpinela de Ovando. Robles's son Manuel Zamacona has conveniently appeared on the scene, and his presence and the questions he asks, or those asked by Ixca, but which Robles seems to attribute to Manuel, stir remote memories and longings in Robles. The following statement in particular comes to haunt Robles: 'por cada mexicano que murió en vano, sacrificado, hay un mexicano responsable. [...] para que esa muerte no haya sido en vano, alguien debe asumir la culpa. La culpa por cada indígena azotado, por cada obrero sometido, por cada madre hambrienta. Entonces, sólo entonces, ese hombre singular de México será todos los mexicanos humillados' (378-9).

On the night of the fifteenth of September, that is, the Día del Grito, 1951, there is a remarkable series of deaths which offers a symbolic resolution of the novel. The deaths are clearly linked, by the date, and with other seemingly random deaths earlier in the novel. The link is hinted at by one of the dead, Manuel Zamacona, who opens his copy of Nerval's *Les Chimères* at the lines from 'Artémis', 'Et c'est toujours la seule — ou c'est le seul moment' (390). The line, which also serves as an epigraph to Paz's 'Piedra de sol', refers to the sameness of the various moments of death. The dead are Norma Larragoiti, burnt to death after her husband accidentally sets fire to the house, though Teódula Mocetzuma takes the death to be her desired sacrifice, Jorge Morales, the son of the taxi driver who dies at the beginning of the novel, Gabriel, the migrant worker recently back from the USA, and Manuel Zamacona, shot in a *cantina* because one of the drinkers did not like the way he looked at him. The deaths of Manuel and Gabriel are characterised by utter meaninglessness, as Beto exclaims: 'Morirse así nomás, sin razón, de repente. [...] Es como morirse en balde, señor' (431).

The date of these deaths, and various formal similarites, link them to that of Feliciano Sánchez, shot at Robles's instigation, 15 September 1938. In turn, Feliciano Sánchez is linked in the mind of Robles to his own cousin Froilán Reyero, who was executed together with Gervasio Pola in Belén, 1913, and whose phrase on solitude and communion had stayed with Robles since his youth: 'Los dos rostros [Sánchez and Reyero] se aliaban y confundían en esa zona última de la memoria [...] ambos idénticos en la reproducción mental, no querida, de Robles' (391).

The links are formalised and made significant for Robles in an important scene of anagnorisis, which effectively breaks the curse of duality and amnesia pronounced by Mercedes Zamacona, the mother of his son Manuel. After leaving his burning house in the Lomas de Chapultepec, Robles drives and then walks in an unfamiliar poor neighbourhood, as if controlled by forces or beings outside him: 'Robles caminó sin rumbo, perdido en su afán secreto, conducido por otras manos y otros pies al centro y ombligo de la urbe, al lugar del nuevo encuentro' (429). He enters the wake of the murdered worker Gabriel and hears the prayers of the latter's mother doña Magdalena. It is significant that Gabriel's mother bears the same name, similarly mispronounced as 'Madalena', as Federico Robles's mother (101). This is probably the final name that Robles had earlier been unable to recover: 'Robles quiso volver a recobrar un nombre anterior, anterior y de ese instante mismo [...]' (392). The sameness of the death of his own son Manuel and that of Gabriel makes the coincidence even more pointed. In Gabriel Robles recognises Froilán and Feliciano, inseparable in his mind from his son Manuel Zamacona:

Éste es mi primo Froilán la mañana que lo fusilaron en Belén— dijeron esos ojos cada vez más viejos de Robles sin que su lengua pudiera pronunciar los nombres o su memoria saber cuáles eran; —éste es Feliciano Sánchez, asesinado por la espalda, corriendo en un llano de caliche... Y eran la voz adivinada y los ojos ondulantes de Manuel Zamacona los que repetían estas palabras en el centro carnal de Robles. (431)

More importantly, Robles recognises the death and suffering of others as his own; he is those others and has been nourished by them:

Más allá de sus huesos y de su sangre, en las vidas de otros que en ese minuto de humillación y carne rendida eran su propia vida, en las vidas mudas que lo habían alimentado, sintió la razón verdadera: y esas vidas mudas, cuyos nombres quizá no recordaba, se multiplicaban en una escena de pantomimas fatales, hasta abarcar toda la tierra de México, todas las derrotas y asesinatos y batallas, hasta regresar, hablándole, reconociéndole, al cuerpo de Federico. (432)

The death of his son Manuel, his self-recognition in the worker Gabriel and his acknowledgement of his life debt to a host of anonymous Mexicans, this cluster is inseparable from memory, both personal memory in Robles and the multiple voices from Mexico's past and present in the text of *La región más transparente*. As Robles climbs the stairs to the flat of Hortensia Chacón, each step brings a new memory until finally 'toda la vida es vuelta a sacudir, exigiendo que se le recuerde, que se sepa que fue todo lo anterior, que se niega a ser cancelada' (434). Hortensia herself is the embodiment of the plural, humble Mexico which Robles has recognised in himself. Self and other, solitude and togetherness take on a more fertile relationship in their union, as Federico returns in a sense to the darkness and union that he had originally found with Mercedes only to be denied by her: 'No era como si estuvieran solos, ni como si ya fuesen uno; tampoco como si aún fuesen dos. Eran dos, sí, pero cada uno era otro porque había sido reconocido así, como el otro nuestro, como el otro que me pertenece' (435). Robles marries Hortensia, has a child with her and grows cotton in the North of Mexico.

Robles, thus, seems finally and probably momentarily to have answered the questions raised by Gervasio Pola and evaded by the latter's son, as he relives the situation of his cousin and double Froilán Reyero: 'Detrás de las cortinas más densas de su sueño, Robles se veía con otros nunca más solo, y el rostro que mojaba los bigotes en la jícara de barro le decía que no es la soledad lo terrible, que estar con otros es el único dolor' (435). His position at the beginning of Fuentes's career is emblematic of the latter's recognition and affirmation in the novel of the totality of Mexico, its languages and voices, against the ideological closure of authority and power. Within the vast action of the novel, however, the powerful literary structuring offered by the recovery of memory and reconciliation with origins as described here displays a symbolic closure never fully reproduced in subsequent works.

Las buenas conciencias, 1959: Family Tradition and the Individual Talent

Introduction

A year after completing the exhausting task of writing the ambitious and path-breaking novel *La región más transparente*, Fuentes quickly and easily produced *Las buenas conciencias*, a relatively short *Bildungsroman* written in an unexpectedly realist and traditional fashion. Fuentes described the novel to Rodríguez Monegal thus:

> Mira, es una novela de catarsis simplemente. En un doble sentido; literario, porque quise ver si podía dominar una narración de tipo tradicional, de tipo galdosiano, y quizá no debía de haberla publicado; era para mí una prueba; y también de tipo personal, porque la escribí en un momento de ruptura mía, muy traumática, con mi familia, con mi pasado, con mi educación religiosa, burguesa y demás, que traté de trasladar a la experiencia del personaje.[1]

The double motivation of the novel is thus to 'dominar una narración de tipo tradicional [...] galdosiano' and to document 'una ruptura muy traumática con mi familia'. These two dimensions of Fuentes's work are intimately linked, and here I will describe how the relation with literary traditions and predecessors is played out in the variations on the Freudian 'Family Romance' outlined by Harold Bloom to characterise the struggle between the writer and his strong predecessor.

Las buenas conciencias follows the early life of Jaime Ceballos: his adolescence and sexual awakening, his rebellion against his family, the Catholic Church and society, and his eventual return to the fold of his upper-middle class family in provincial Guanajuato. It documents a search for authenticity of voice and identity in relation to the dominant language and presence of others. The notion of authenticity in this novel, an ideal balance between independence and originality and the sense of belonging to a community is explored within an existentialist /

---

[1] Emir Rodríguez Monegal, 'Carlos Fuentes', an interview, in Giacoman, *Homenaje*, 52.

Christian tradition. Jaime strives for uniqueness, but necessarily imitates: Christ, Raskolnikov, the gestures of his uncle and of the presidential candidate Alemán. The novel was written as the first work of a tetralogy, which was to be called *Los nuevos*. Fuentes claimed that he stewed the last three volumes in a tub and took a bath with them (Rodríguez Monegal, 51). The style was supposed to reflect the atmosphere of the provincial town and act as an ironic base for the writing of the later volumes:

> Yo necesitaba tener esa base temática y estilística para la tetralogía. Quería salir de ese mundo de Guanajuato, que se expresa en estas formas muy siglo diecinueve, muy Pérez Galdós, muy Balzac, para llevar al personaje a la Ciudad de México, llevar concurrentemente un cambio de ritmo, un cambio del estilo de la novela. Es decir, es un estilo que va a ser destruido por las novelas que le siguen.[2]

Indeed, Fuentes confessed that 'se atascó' in this novel, but that the destiny of Jaimes was completed in *La muerte de Artemio Cruz*, where we see him take the role of the heir apparent of the business empire of Cruz, usurping the place of Cruz's son Lorenzo, whose name recalls Ceballos's idealist double in *Las buenas conciencias*, Juan Manuel Lorenzo. Whereas *La región más transparente* was a confident, flamboyant translation of both the realist tradition and the Anglo-American modernism of Dos Passos, Faulkner and D.H. Lawrence into the Spanish American novel, *Las buenas conciencias* is a curiously laboured and painful act of atonement associated with the author's Hispanic and realist forebears: Galdós, Dickens, Stendhal, Balzac, Dostoyevsky, Leonid Andreyev.

Together or alone

The tension between the voice of these precursors and that of the author, the adolescent and his elders, the attempt to establish one's voice as unique and original and the acceptance of the mediated and communal nature of meaning, writing and identity, are again expressed

---

[2] Quoted in Harrs, 365.

in the dichotomy *solo / juntos*, as they were in *La región más transparente*. Jaime demands to be unique, and the novel asks how far his independence is egoism and pride or heroic sacrifice and true individuality. His desire manifests itself on three major fronts: the religious, the family and the linguistic and literary.

He claims an exclusive and privileged communication with Christ: 'El flujo caluroso se establecía, singularmente, entre Jesucristo y Jaime Ceballos [...] quería recuperar la mirada que era sólo para él, capaz de aislarlo y entenderlo a él solo.'[3] He will approach Christ without the mediation of the Church: 'No confesará más. Irá directamente a Cristo.' (95). Both the priest and Christ himself tell Jaime that Christianity can only be communal, never individual: 'Siempre se necesitarán dos hombres para acercarse a Dios. Uno sólo no puede' (147); 'Pero no estás solo, mi hijo. Mi lección sólo se cumple al lado de los demás' (180). The same terms are used in the context of political action. Jaime defends individual, Romantic action ('¿no es una acción personal lo más valioso?'), to which his friend the Indian Lorenzo answers: 'uno solo no puede lograr nada... Todos juntos...' (114-5). The fugitive syndicalist Ezequiel Zuno, the heir to Feliciano Sánchez, makes the same point: 'Pero no eres tú solo. [...] pues ya como que no eres tú, sino los demás' (72). Jaime's exalted sense of his own singularity similarly translates itself into an epiphany or absolute knowledge of the sense of life: 'se imaginaba que la vida se detenía a cada instante, como para celebrarse a sí mismo y otorgar a cada acto un valor final' (183). Linguistically, the equivalent is an all-powerful, original language: 'Debe haber otro idioma, que no sólo refleje, sino que pueda transformar la realidad' (119).

The all-powerful, original voice is owned by others, and Jaime strives to appropriate that voice in a struggle based on a crude, strikingly physical, drama of potency and castration. Christ and the syndicalist own the voice: '¿Buscaba la voz de una estatua de madera barnizada de sangre? ¿Creyó que la única voz humana era aquélla, inolvidable, del minero Ezequiel Zuno?' (79). His uncle Jorge possesses the voice of patriarchal authority: 'Había hablado Balcárcel, y desde ese momento su voz sería la de la autoridad' (32). The raised, erect finger,

---

[3]   *Las buenas conciencias* (Mexico City: Fondo de Cultura Económica, 1970), 52.

'el dedo rígido' (103), 'el índice levantado' (41), which accompanies his pronouncements repeatedly have the castrating effect of paralyzing both Jaime and his aunt: 'No: la lengua se le paralizaba cuando Balcárcel levantaba un dedo rígido y dictaba un precepto hueco. [...] su hombría continuamente expuesta a la duda' (116-7); 'La exclamación de la tía fue paralizada por la mano retórica de Balcárcel' (104). The 'verdadera voz' of the aunt is located in her vagina, 'en el punto solar del vientre, en el declive de la carne más silenciosa', whereas her other lips pronounce a false, social and empty language: '[sus] labios falsos, en un reflejo insospechado de defensa, pronunciaban otras palabras' (108).

The feared castration, linked to the guilt at masturbating,[4] to which both Jaime and his aunt are limited, is obviated in various dramatic ways. One is the fantasy castration of the other in which the central part of his body is emptied out or reified: 'Jaime creyó que la voz gutural salía del estómago, que Ezequiel apretaba un botón de cobre y hablaba' (72). There is a similarly bizarre sequence involving the image of Christ. As Jaime reaches sexual maturity, the church candles one Easter become grotesquely phallic: 'La alegría de la luz consumía al cirio erecto [...] "y en la resurrección de la carne, amén"' (58); 'largos cirios cuelgan su virilidad reposada' (63). As the dripping candles, 'las velas chisporroteantes [...] alargan sus barbas de cera a ambos lados del Cristo', Jaime responds in an ecstasy of mystical and sexual pleasure ('una comezón que nunca había sentido' (66)) in front of the image of Christ, which he narcissistically cannot distinguish from his own body. Out of curiosity he lifts the tunic of the image which had so excited him, the source of the voice directed singularly to him, and finds not a body or genitals, but a simple wooden stick: 'La reproducción natural termina en las rodillas cubiertas. El resto es una cruz de palo que sostiene el torso herido y los brazos abiertos' (67). The returned aggression against the uncle is more physical as he kicks him in the testicles, and culminates in his symbolic castration when Balcárcel 'se paralizó en una posición ridícula' (175).

---

[4] Linked perhaps to writing and literature as a supplementary form of language, as suggested by Jacques Derrida in *De la grammatologie* (Paris: Minuit, 1985), 224.

Church

The notion of a true, transcendent language, and the problematical relationship of the individual consciousness to that language, is explored in terms of Christianity. The family drama is worked out through the theme of Christian education in the middle-class provincial Mexican home. The clear Oedipal struggle makes one also think immediately of the relationship between religion and the killing of the father by the primal horde in the Freud of *Totem and Taboo* and *Moses and Monotheism*. Jaime's relation to the Word of Christ is parallel to that of Fuentes to the great realist novelists, and to that of Jaime to some of their characters such as Pip and Julien Sorel.

Jaime is a great reader of the Gospels, a sign of Protestantism for his uncle, and tries by repetition to make their most dramatic phrases his own: 'Un año era la repetición solitaria de las grandes palabras cristianas' (96). His desire to abolish any distance between himself and the original words of Christ is picked up by the priest Obregón: '¡Crees que puedes igualarte a Jesucristo!', in response to which he has to content himself with imitation: 'Creo que puedo imitarlo' (148). In a sense he wishes to cancel his belatedness to the words of Christ by an act of will or faith. The dilemma of perceiving eternity while trapped in time is central to the thought of a thinker essential to the novel: Kierkegaard. Though Christ walked the earth eighteen hundred years ago, he wrote, yet 'contemporaneousness is the condition of faith'.[5]

Jaime's quest for this 'contemporaneousness' is articulated through the polemic against bourgeois piety by Emmanuel Mounier in *L'Affrontement chrétien*, and through Kierkegaard and Nietzsche, in the name of a more virile and authentic position.[6] Catholicism in Guanajuato means middle-class decency: 'Las palabras "católico" y "gente bien" volvieron a sonar, con sinonimia desde sus labios apretados' (41). Though the polemic is a powerful one, it is placed ironically in the mouth of the hypocrite Jaime Ceballos, ultimately a

---

[5] *A Kierkegaard Anthology*, ed. by Robert Bretall (Princeton: Princeton University Press, 1973), 375.
[6] To the earnest Christian polemic Fuentes adds a satire very much in the spirit of Buñuel, whom he quotes approvingly: 'Para mí [...] el placer erótico está estrechamente ligado a la idea de la religión. Sexo sin religión es como huevo sin sal' ('Luis Buñuel: el cine como libertad', *Casa con dos puertas*, 203).

product of his own class, who is shown to use the 'palabras extremas' to avoid contact with others, the vulgar and humble, especially his own mother, to gain a good conscience for himself and dignify his commonplace adolescent rebellion. The epigraphs of the novel stress the duplicity of bourgeois Christianity. The first is from Kierkegaard: 'Los cristianos hablan con Dios; los burgueses hablan de Dios'. This duplicity is inherent in the *guanajuatense*: 'de propósitos internos claros y manera exterior velada' (15); 'la relación pública por encima de la verdad privada' (16). The second epigraph is from Mounier: 'On s'arrange mieux de sa mauvaise conscience que de sa mauvaise réputation.'

Much of the thought on Christianity in *Las buenas conciencias* is derived from Mounier. The epigraph, for example, comes from a section on repressive and prudish sexual education, which leads to 'couardise spirituelle'[7] and hypocrisy: 'Au surplus le mensonge sexuel des parents est souvent le premier contact de l'enfant avec la dissimulation' (Mounier, 41). The mother's failure to recognise adolescent sexuality and the child's need to relate to outside objects create 'des sentimentalités imprécises et des ferveurs puériles' (Mounier, 42). This is exactly what Asunción does: 'Que nunca crezca, Dios mío' (45). While she begs that he should not frequent prostitutes and wait years before having sex even with his wife, her husband and the priests are obsessed with his masturbation. Mounier sees the 'devirilization' of Christian life as the result of avoiding any real issues within Christian families:

> On y enseigne à [...] masquer sous des affabilités de convention les drames réels que pose toute communauté humaine [...]. Ce besoin, sous prétexte de charité, de ne pas contredire et de n'être pas contredit, de ne pas faire souffrir et de ne pas souffrir, de ne rien brusquer et de ne pas être brusqué, est un poison lent qui dévirilise les cœurs goutte à goutte. (Mounier, 55)

In the Balcárcel household, Asunción's desire for a child, Rodolfo's guilt at abandoning his wife Adelina, Jaime's presence as a pretext for Balcárcel's authoritarianism are all issues which are systematically

---

[7] Emmanuel Mounier, *L'Affrontement chrétien*, Œuvres, vol. 3 (Paris: Seuil, 1962), 39.

avoided according to Mounier's formula: 'Si algo distinguía a esta familia, era la convicción de que la regla máxima de la vida consiste en evaporar los dramas reales. [...] En el fondo, los tres personajes de la casa sabían que es preciso no contradecir a fin de no ser contradicho y de no violentar a fin de no ser violentado' (44–45). It is ironic that Jaime justifies his supposedly rebellious decision to take communion without confession by the family rule: 'Comulgará [...] pero no confesará más. No será juzgado, por no juzgar. No condenará, porque no permitirá que lo condenen' (95).

Jaime glibly uses the idea of the 'devirilising' effect of Christiaity stressed by Nietzsche: 'L'église combat les passions par [...] le castratisme' (cit. by Mounier, 29). He rejects Obregón's criticism of his cowardly behaviour towards his mother and father by asking: '¿Quién era ese hombre disfrazado, que no sabía de las pasiones verdaderas de los hombres, que se había castrado voluntariamente al colocarse esa sotana?' (179). The priest Lanzagorta similarly becomes a 'león desdentado' (180). Jaime himself takes a radical view of Christian commitment as propounded by Saint François de Sales: '¿Cómo decirle que las virtudes han de amarse más de lo que se teme a los vicios?' (116, cit. by Mounier, 45). He makes his own the radical Kiekegaardian view of the demise of Christianity ('Christendom has done away with Christianity, without being quite aware of it'),[8] and parrots it to the priest: 'La Iglesia ya no es Cristo, Padre' (150).

The priest Obregón and his friend Lorenzo seem increasingly to convince Jaime of his own hypocrisy. Following Mounier's denunciation of the lack of adventure and tragic grandeur in the modern Christian, Jaime adopts for himself the affirmation of Mathilde in *Le Rouge et le noir:* 'Quelle est la grande action qui ne soit pas un extrême au moment où on l'entreprend? C'est quand elle est accomplie qu'elle semble possible aux êtres du commun.'[9] He associates this grand Romantic action with Christ: 'Así procedió Cristo. Lo juzgaron un loco extremista, radical como tú dices' (113). And he tries to assume that grandeur when he goes into the desert and lashes himself with thorns in penance for the sins of others. Lorenzo devastatingly introduces the

[8] Kierkegaard, 397.
[9] Stendhal, *Le Rouge et le noir* (Paris: Garnier-Flammarion, 1964), 318; *Las buenas conciencias*, 113; cit. by Mounier, 56.

notion of caricature, suggesting that Jaime cannot reach the individuality and originality he yearns for, but rather becomes the caricature of the gestures and words of others: 'el ejemplo de un solo individuo... a fuerza de repetirse se convierte en caricatura' (113). His heroism is also unmasked by Obregón as pride and self-love: 'Sólo te amas a ti mismo, a los demás les otorgas tu orgullo disfrazado' (177). To use the version of Nietzsche quoted by Mounier: 'Votre amour du prochain, c'est votre mauvais amour de vous-même' (Mounier, 55). Obregón turns against Jaime the phrase of Saint François de Sales that Jaime had used against his uncle. Humility is needed to serve God initially on a human plane and within the mores of the time: 'a Dios se le servía a la manera humana y de acuerdo con el tiempo, en espera de que algún día se le podría servir a la manera divina y de acuerdo con la eternidad' (152; Mounier, 64). Jaime clearly does not gain access to transcendent, original time, 'à la divine et selon l'éternité': his action and language are secondary, derivative.

Jaime himself eventually accepts that his literary, second-hand and 'quoted' Romantic stance was simply a ploy to avoid facing the humble, emotional commitments of reality, the pleas for affection and the unpleasant odours of his dying father: '¿Por qué se justificaba, negando la muerte del padre entre las hojas de un libro, con la certidumbre aprendida de que sufrir y hacer sufrir a los demás es la condición de un espíritu fuerte? Trataba de recordar el pasaje del Evangelio sobre las casas divididas; lo mezclaba con alguna cita de Nietzsche' (165).[10] In what Fuentes describes to Luis Harss as Jaime's only act of honesty in the novel,[11] Jaime finally renounces his bid for solitude and originality, recognising that he needs the support of tradition and society: 'mis tíos, la vida que me prepararon, la vida que heredé de todos mis antepasados' (190).

---

[10] Nietzsche, cit. by Mounier, 56: 'Créer des souffrances à soi-même et aux autres pour les rendre capables de la vie la plus haute.'
[11] Harss, 365.

Family Romances

Ancestors weigh heavily on the shoulders of every member of the Ceballos family. The solid stone house has more reality than any of its fleeting inhabitants: 'los cuadros de los antepasados, la enorme cama y sus mosquiteros, tenían más vida que las dos personas artificialmente quietas y ensimismadas' (144). Dead ancestors are alive within Jaime: 'No eran fantasmas. Los traía metidos adentro, de buena o mala gana' (9). He has little being outside them: 'Nunca se pensó distinto, no sólo de los vivos, sino de los muertos convocados a toda hora en la conversación' (54). Family rules take no account of individuals: 'Reglas, recomendaciones, aprendidas de los padres [...] indiferentes a la personalidad de cada nuevo ser, aplicables a todo lo porvenir' (161).

The generations of Ceballos are mapped out for the reader as carefully as they might be in a novel by Galdós or Zola. Briefly, the founding couple Higinio Ceballos, a draper, and Margarita Machado came from Madrid to Mexico in 1852 and had four children. These were a daughter who married well and forged important political connections, Francisco who died fighting the empire of Maximilian in the 1860s, and two other sons who form an opposition later repeated in the family: Pánfilo, as his name suggests, a dark, heavy individual happy to serve unambitiously behind the counter in the draper's store, and José, blond, outgoing, economically successful. José married a Mexican, Guillermina Montáñez, with whom he had two children: Asunción and Rodolfo. Rodolfo followed the line of Pánfilo, married below him, was forced to repudiate his wife Adelina, but took in his son Jaime Ceballos. Asunción married the successful and ruthless economist Jorge Balcárcel, who is sterile.

In *The Anxiety of Influence* and *A Map of Misreading*, Harold Bloom rather melodramatically applies this sense of being overwhelmed by ancestors to literary influence.[12] The most intimate desires of a poet belong to another poet: 'For the poet is condemned to learn his profoundest yearnings through an awareness of other selves. The poem is within him, yet he experiences the shame and splendour of being

---

[12] I quote from the following editions: *The Anxiety of Influence. A Theory of Poetry* (New York: Oxford Unversity Press, 1975) and *A Map of Misreading* (New York: Oxford University Press, 1980).

found by poems — great poems — outside him. To lose freedom in this center is never to forgive, and to learn the dread of threatened autonomy forever' (*Anxiety*, 26). The precursor, the owner of the original voice vis-à-vis which the writer is always belated, is the poetic father, and the writer has no choice in the matter: 'No poet [...] can choose his precursor, any more than any person can choose his father' (*Map*, 12). But the two volumes do describe the ways in which the writer attempts to reverse the seemingly iron succession, and have the precursor necessarily read through the work of his successor: 'All quest-romances of the post-Enlightenment, meaning all Romanticisms whatsoever, are quests to re-beget one's own self, to become one's own Great Original' (*Anxiety*, 64). He quotes two writers, interestingly two writers already found relevant in the context of Jaime's religious experience, who deny his earlier assertions about the inevitability of sonhood. Kierkegaard wrote: 'He who is willing to work gives birth to his own father', and Nietzsche: 'When one hasn't had a good father, it is necessary to invent one' (*Anxiety*, 26, 56). The writer gives birth to himself by wilfully misreading and misinterpreting the precursor, by the 're-writing of the father' (*Map*, 19). Irrespective of whether one agrees with the highly personalised version of intertextuality propounded by Bloom, his presentation is suggestive for approaching *Las buenas conciencias*, where the quests for an individual voice in the family, religion and literature are inseparable.[13] Bloom sets up various categories of misreading, what Culler calls a 'series of gaudy and exotic tropes', which I will not attempt to apply in any systematic way.[14] The correspondence, however, between the Freudian scenes within which Bloom dramatises the conflict with the precursor and the family drama acted out in the novel is striking.

If the precursor is the father, imagines Bloom, then the Muse is the mother on whom the poet must beget himself:

---

[13] Note the criticism of Jonathan Culler in *The Pursuit of Signs. Semiotics, Literature, Deconstruction* (London: Routledge & Kegan Paul, 1983), 107-9. For a comparison with other models of intertextuality, see the Introduction to Michael Worton and Judith Still (eds), *Intertextuality. Theories and Practices* (Manchester: Manchester University Press, 1990).

[14] Culler, 109.

His word is not his word only, and his Muse has whored with many before him. He has come late in the story, but she has always been central in it [...]. In the wholeness of the poet's imagination, the Muse is mother and harlot at once, for the largest phantasmagoria most of us weave from our necessarily egoistic interests is the family romance. (*Anxiety*, 61, 63)

Bloom uses three essays by Freud which are almost programmatically worked out in *Las buenas conciencias*: 'Family Romances', 'A special type of object choice made by men', and 'On the universal tendency to debasement in the sphere of love'. These pieces largely describe adolescent fantasies which alter parenthood or see the mother as a whore and thus as an accessible sexual object for the son. In 'Family Romances' the child fantasises that he is in fact the son of more exalted parents than his present family; that his mother was unfaithful to his father with varying consequences, for example that the son is the only legitimate child, or with the result of removing the consanguinity of the sister and thus making her a legitimate sexual object. In 'A special type of object choice', Freud looks at the case of men attracted to prostitutes. Various interesting points emerge: that in the unconscious what for the conscious mind is a sharp contrast between mother and prostitute is a unity. As a child, the person who exhibits this preference fantasised, in revenge for some slight, that his mother was unfaithful to his father, that is, that she was a whore, with an idealised and older version of the boy's own personality. In relation to the common fantasy of rescuing the mother from danger, linked to the adult desire to rescue the prostitute, Freud explains that 'the son shows his gratitude by wishing to have by his mother a son who is like himself: in other words, in the rescue-fantasy he is completely identifying himself with his father. All his instincts, those of tenderness, gratitude, lustfulness, defiance and independence, find satisfaction in the single wish to be his own father.'[15]

Such fantasies are a potent tool for undoing family determinism, the dependent status of the son towards ancestors, parents and literary precursors. The family, the father, can be rewritten. Rodrigo Pola in *La región más transparente* chooses Federico Robles as paternal model over his father Gervasio, and there are many similar examples in later

---

[15] In *On Sexuality*, The Pelican Freud Library (Harmondsworth: Penguin, 1977), VII, 240.

works. One of the clearest examples is the novella *Aura*, 1962. There, the protagonist Felipe is literally rewriting the memoirs of a dead general, Llorente, and at the same time is seduced by his widow, or by a magical projection of her younger self. In the process he engenders his own double, Llorente, gives birth to himself as another: 'la concepción estéril de esa noche engendró tu propio doble'.[16] The essays published together with the English translation of the novella, in *Myself with Others*, and elsewhere, 'How I wrote Aura', makes it clear that *Aura* is also the story of the rewriting of Aura from a multiplicity of literary models.[17] Llorente can thus be read as writers like Alfonso Reyes and Fuentes-Felipe becomes retrospectively the author of works like 'La cena', which helped to inspire *Aura*.

Returning to *Las buenas conciencias*, Jaime's real family disintegrates. His mother is expelled from the patriarchal bed and the family home, and his father loses authority to his sister and her husband, and is literally marginalised to a room to which he gains access by an outside flight of stairs. Tony Tanner points out how *Ulysses* grows out of the disintegration of the traditional family.[18] Jaime has a whole alternative family: uncle and father, the aunt Asunción who brought him up and his real, absent mother. The authoritarian uncle and the lenient father embody the split between the castrating and the good father analysed by Freud in 'The Uncanny'.[19] The basic terms of the opposition between Adelina and Asunción, whore and virtuous woman, as in the essays of Freud, are combined in an ambiguous fashion. The mother is a religious person who drinks cognac and frequents prostitutes while the aunt is an eminently respectable *beata* who tries to seduce her nephew, like the aunt in 'Vieja moralidad' from *Cantar de ciegos*.

---

[16] *Aura* (Mexico City: Era, 1976), 51.
[17] The version in Spanish is 'Cómo escribí algunos de mis libros', in *Sábado*, the supplement of *Uno más Uno*, 9 Oct. 1982, 1-3.
[18] 'In this connection it is interesting to note that in *Ulysses* we have both the decomposition of the family — the father a voyeur masturbator, the wife an adulteress, the legitimate child dead — and a study of the composition of the dedicated artist. One is tempted to say that the emergence of the artist-as-hero is coincident with a sense of the family-as-ruin' (*Adultery in the Novel* (Baltimore: The Johns Hopkins University Press, 1979), 99).
[19] Note 1, 'The Uncanny', in *Art and Literature*, The Pelican Freud Library, vol. 14 (Harmondsworth: Penguin, 1985), 353-4.

The mother is in fact split into three figures, which allows great room for manoeuvre for Jaime: biological mother, aunt, and Olga, the prostitute habitually used by his father, and thus clearly linked to the mother. Asunción is sexually frustrated with Jorge Balcárcel, whose 'sterility' and relative impotence ('el sexo viejo del marido' (141)) seem to be related to Freud's comments in 'The tendency to debasement in love' about diphasic sexual object choices and the relative impotence experienced by a man with an object of affection which reminds him of his mother and who thus chooses to find sexual satisfaction with a debased object such as a whore.[20] This situation is presented in an almost caricatural fashion by Balcárcel:

> Puedes pensar que a veces soy frío contigo. Pero ésa es mi manera de respetarte. No traeré la prostitución a mi casa. No soy perfecto: tengo la debilidad natural de los hombres. Pero a ti te respeto; cuando caigo en la tentación me voy lejos, dejo mis tentaciones sucias en León, en Guadalajara o en México. En mi casa soy limpio, y te amo castamente. (143)

Asunción becomes available as a sexual object, but Jaime chooses not to move from auto-eroticism, with the threat of castration, to sex with a woman. If one takes the perspective of the adolescent as writer, Asunción is probably too close to the mother for comfort, too close to the maternal language which would smother the creativity of the artist. This is what Paz alludes to in 'Hacia el poema': 'Encontrar la salida: el poema. [...] Cortar el cordón umbilical, matar bien a la Madre: crimen que el poeta moderno cometió por todos, en nombre de todos.'[21] Bloom is in similar territory when he writes: 'Beyond the pleasures of poetry lies the maternal womb of language out of which poems arise, the literal meaning that poems both evade and desperately seek' (*Map*, 92). Jaime finds a safer maternal option in Olga.

Jaime's real mother, the illegitimate daughter of don Chepepón López, is a highly ambiguous figure. After being forced out of the family house, she is seen with prostitutes, lecturing them on their evil ways. Balcárcel describes her as a 'ramera disfrazada de mística' (143). The ambiguity of her position, claiming to be a 'santa' among whores

---

[20] See *On Sexuality*, 251.
[21] *Poemas*, 228.

('Siempre queriendo presumir de santa. / —No presumo, soy.' (123)) has echoes of the prostitute called Santa in Federico Gamboa's novel of that title: 'No vayas a creerme santa, porque así me llamé'. Like Adelina, Santa is 'desahuciada de las "gentes de buena conciencia"'.[22] Much of Jaime's righteous indignation at his family comes from the fact that they abandoned Adelina, but when he finally comes face to face with her in a bar, he takes refuge in his habitual narcissism, admiring his own face reflected in a beer bottle. We have the classical Freudian case of the mother become whore (as a sexual object or as one to be rescued) but again Jaime is not ready to act.

For much of the novel, Jaime is torn between allegiance and obedience to Balcárcel or his father Rodolfo: '¿A quién debía obedecer más: al señor elegante, autoritario, o al señor gordo, complaciente?' (37). Towards the end of the novel there is an important play on the name of the father, as the latter and his son change places. When Rodolfo falls ill, he collapses on Jaime's bed and indeed dies in it. Spurned by the son, who refuses him any affection, on his death 'ahora su padre no tiene nombre' (166). After the funeral he goes with Juan Manuel Lorenzo to a brothel for the first time and sleeps with a young prostitute, Olga, who is the habitual partner of his father. Rodolfo and Olga 'nunca se dijeron los nombres' (155), and when she asks Jaime his name, after a moment's hesitation, he replies 'Este ... Rodolfo' (174). Jaime is finally his own father, no longer dependent on the other. This is perhaps why Lorenzo now calls him by his Christian name for the first time. Having slept with a woman he has gone beyond masturbation and the fear of castration. Rather neatly, he immediately comes across his uncle Jorge in the brothel, in a particularly undignified position: 'Encima de la mesita de la sala, sin zapatos, sin saco, con grandes manchas de sudor debajo de las axilas y un gorrito de crepé sobre la cabeza rala, el tío Balcárcel bailaba solo, con una botella de ron entre los brazos' (175). Jaime kisses Olga on the lips, and his uncle 'se paralizó en una posición ridícula'. *Paralizarse* was the verb used to describe the castrating effect of Balcárcel's rigid figer on the tongue of Jaime and his aunt. It is now Jaime who acts as the male, while his uncle embraces a surrogate sexual object, a bottle. On the following

---

[22] *Santa, Novelas de Federico Gamboa* (Mexico City: Fondo de Cultura Económica, 1965), 717.

day, whenever his uncle speaks it is from behind the protection of a napkin over his mouth. Jaime is thus the father of both his father figures.

Having gained his independence, Jaime quickly renounces it and joins the conventional order, agreeing to become a lawyer (as his father had wished to become), abandoning his earlier ideals, which he now sees as 'mentiras', and looks forward to a brilliant middle-class future. Looking at Jaime as writer, he has not attained the absolute originality discussed by Bloom, but engages in the ambiguous world of others. As Manuel Echeverría puts it, Jaime 'abandona el mundo de la unicidad absoluta para ingresar en el de la ambigüedad'.[23] In the interview with Rodríguez Monegal, Fuentes says something very similar: Jaime is no longer a 'fariseo que hablaba desde los púlpitos de la pureza [...] para convertirse en lo que es un verdadero escritor, es decir: un publicano; un hombre que participa del pecado, de la culpa' (Monegal, 52).

Intertextuality

If Jaime's life is marked by belatedness and the need to forge an identity by repeating the gestures of others, Fuentes set himself the task of writing originally, but through the voices of Galdós and Dickens. Fuentes quotes the well-known phrase of Alfonso Reyes to the effect that in Mexico 'llegamos siempre con cien años de retraso a los banquetes de la civilización' (Monegal, 29). Latin American writers have to tackle many pressing themes from their own reality which have already been described in other literatures: 'La realidad inmediata de América Latina nos ofrece los temas que ya han tratado en otras literaturas Balzac y Dreiser, pero nuestro problema es cómo retomar esos temas para paralelizarlos, digamos, para darles su relevancia actual, su relevancia nacional' (Monegal, 54). Dependence and intertextuality are examined in sociological terms, in the readings of the characters, and metatextually in Fuentes's self-conscious transposition of elements of works such as *Fortunata y Jacinta* and *Great Expectations*.

---

[23] Manuel Echeverría, 'Prólogo' to *Las buenas conciencias*, in Carlos Fuentes, *Obras completas*, vol. 1 (Madrid: Aguilar, 1972), 607.

The Guanajuato middle classes have been marked by a tendency to import, apply and manipulate the texts and ideology of the Enlightenment and beyond from Europe: '¿Por qué, en la dilatada extensión de la Nueva España, fueron éstos los lectores —y las infanterías— de Voltaire y de Rousseau? ¿Por qué, en nuestra extrema actualidad, se escuchan en los pomposos escalones de su Universidad discusiones sobre Heidegger y Marx?' (14). Fuentes talks to Monegal of the importing of foreign constitutional models, of the 'élite progresista que había leído, desde el tiempo de las guerras de la Independencia, a Montesquieu y a Rousseau, que quería trasladar el mundo civilizado que representaban las constituciones francesa, norteamericana y británica a nuestro suelo' (Monegal, 53). The distance between the ideal official reality and the real countries of injustice and exploitation is as great as that between the great Christian discourse of Jaime Ceballos and his real behaviour and motivation. Fuentes returns to the question in 1990 in the novel *La campaña*, about the Wars of Independence and in the essays of *Valiente mundo nuevo*, where he sets the determinism or 'fatalidad' of the Hispanic tradition against the equal tyranny of the imitation of foreign models used to escape from the first. The way to escape this dual trap is what he calls 'crítica': 'La imitación extralógica, como la llamase Antonio Caso citando a Gabriel de Tarde, nos ha marcado como las más fatales herencias. Sólo hemos superado la imitación o la fatalidad mediante la crítica.'[24] In the case of *Las buenas conciencias* the equivalent of that 'crítica' is the rewriting and opening up of the models through irony, combination, anachronism, parody.

Jaime and Juan Manuel spend much time discussing their literary heroes and models. Jaime identifies with his heroes to the point of taking their names and almost becoming them, as he had wished to do with Christ:

> Su espíritu vuela hasta el humor de Mr Micawber, encarna la figura sombría de Raskolnikov en un desván de Moscú, se postra en el huerto de Getsemaní [...] late su corazón a esos ritmos, porque cree que puede serlo todo (94); La lectura de la epopeya napoleónica le entusiasmaba; se imaginaba en el centro de aquellas grandes batallas, bautizado por aquellos grandes nombres (117).

---

[24] *Valiente mundo nuevo: épica, utopía y mito en la novela hispanoamericana* (Mexico City: Fondo de Cultura Económica, 1990), 11.

Juan Manuel, on the other hand, dialogues with his authors in a more critical fashion, questioning their ideas with his own origin and everyday reality:

> no admitía una afirmación del invisible autor sin ponerlo en duda y buscar su razón. [...] Nietzsche, Stendhal, el Andréiev de Sachka Yégulev, Dostoievsky, Dickens, Balzac, Max Beer, Michelet, eran sus interlocutores cotidianos [...]. No obstante [...] no podía perder la conciencia de su origen y de los problemas diarios de esa raíz. [...] decidía con mayor ardor conjugar las ideas que descubría con la situación que conocía. (115)

José Vasconcelos and Martín Luis Guzmán, our characters muse, speak a language of authenticity and originality, whereas others in Mexico speak the debased, false language of lackeys: 'El tumulto apasionado de la prosa de Vasconcelos, por un lado, y por el otro la claridad serena de Guzmán. ¿Y por qué hablaban estos hombres con un tono de verdad, aunque de manera opuesta, sobre los mismos temas que en otros labios eran mentira, basura, vulgaridad?' (118-9). Vasconcelos and Guzmán wrote as direct contemporaries and participants in the Mexican Revolution. Politicians write a secondary rhetoric derived from the epic action; Juan Manuel, Jaime and Fuentes are belated to the supposedly authentic language of the contemporaries.

The notion of belatedness is echoed and played out in relation to a previous revolution, the Napoleonic epic, and given a universality, a contemporaneity with belatedness, which goes beyond the specifically Mexican or Latin American context. Tolstoy in *War and Peace*, according to the friends, wrote authentic, direct language about the Napoleonic heroes, but the eloquence of Julien Sorel from Stendhal's *Le Rouge et le noir* is devalued in so far as it is distanced from action: 'Julián... tenía una elocuencia maravillosa [...] porque no tenía que actuar como las gentes de la época de Napoleón' (117). Stendhal's character seems to be aware of his own verbosity: 'Julien atteignit à un tel degré de perfection dans ce genre d'éloquence, qui a remplacé la rapidité d'action de l'empire, qu'il finit par s'ennuyer lui-même par le son de ses paroles' (Stendhal, 158). Under Napoleon, life was somehow more real (Stendhal, 316), and Julien's belatedness destroys any chance of happiness: 'ce souvenir fatal nous empêchera à jamais d'être heureux' (Stendhal, 116). The Frenchman's characters are reduced to imitating past gestures, repeating stories, as Mathilde with Julien's head repeats the story of her Renaissance ancestor Marguerite de Valois. Fuentes utilises and neutralises belatedness by a witty anachronism, whereby Julien Sorel writes about the Mexican Revolution:

> trasladaba la acción fulminante de la que hablaba Stendhal a otros hombres y otros campos. La caballería villista en el Bajío, los yaquis que ganaron la victoria de Obregón, la celada a Zapata en Chinameca. Ahora todos esos héroes habían muerto, y en su lugar estaban los Julián Sorel, que hablaban con mucha elocuencia de la Revolución Mexicana. (118)

What is lost in specificity and immediacy is gained in cultural continuity.[25] In later novels Fuentes gradually radicalises this notion. In *La muerte de Artemio Cruz*, and *Gringo viejo* the Mexican Revolution is rewritten or overwritten with literary texts about the American Civil War. Artemio relives scenes from Stephen Crane's *The Red Badge of Courage*, while the Old Gringo quotes and lives out the stories of Ambrose Bierce, *In the Midst of Life*. Layers of historical reference, the U.S. invasion of Mexico in 1848, the American Civil War of the 1860s, the Spanish–American War of 1898, the Mexican Revolution of 1910, become inseparable from a consciousness of the highly mediated textuality of history, any history.

The two main literary precursors, the anteriority of which is to be reversed or modified, are the Galdós of *Fortunata y Jacinta* and the Dickens of *Great Expectations*. By clearly acknowledging his sources, by using a scene from Dickens readily familiar to many readers and by directly referring to a character from the Galdós novel, Fuentes shows not so much dependence as a knowing commentary on his own stylistic intentions. He himself enriches and appropriates the previous text by adding another layer of meaning to it. It is interesting that both foreign novels deal with mysterious, changed or contrived origins: their literal plots become a metaphor of the genesis of the later Mexican text.

The main transposition from *Great Expectations* is the figure of the escaped convict Magwich, who is fed by Pip and recaptured the next day. He becomes the syndicalist Ezequiel Zuno, sought by the police for organising a strike. There is in fact little parody involved here. The

---

[25] See *Valiente mundo nuevo*, 10.

excruciating snobbery of Pip, ashamed of his tutor Joe and his benefactor Magwich, are quite straightforwardly reworked in Jaime's inability to approach his strident and vulgar mother, and his condescension towards Juan Manuel Lorenzo. The mystery of parenthood in the Galdós text is echoed in Jaime's exchanging his real parents symbolically for Asunción and Balcárcel.

The guiding presence of *Fortunata y Jacinta* is indicated in the early pages when the patriarch of the Ceballos clan is revealed to have been an apprentice of the patriarch of the classic nineteenth-century novel of Madrid: 'El jefe del hogar, don Higinio Ceballos, había sido oficial de aquel Baldomero Santa Cruz, notable comerciante en paños del Reino en la calle de la Sal, y de él aprendió la máxima de su comercio: el buen paño en el arca se vende' (15–16).[26] The main element of plot taken from the Spanish novel is the rivalry between Jacinta, the 'mona del cielo', the blond middle-class woman, barren and obsessed with having a child, and Fortunata, the working-class lover of her husband and occasional courtesan. Jacinta is initially cheated when offered the bastard son of Fortunata and her husband Juanito Santa Cruz, but finally takes the child of her husband and Fortunata when the latter dies. Asunción, deprived of a child through the sterility of her husband, plots to expel Adelina and take her son Jaime for herself. Both the English and the Spanish source novels clearly treat the archetypal exchange of parents, the questioning or reversal of parenthood.

Another characteristic element of Galdós is taken up with some humour. Galdós's drama is always on the point of becoming *sainete*, Galdós apparently often on the point of parodying his own techniques. The ups and downs of the Santa Cruz marriage echo and parody the vicissitudes of Restoration Spain, as family dates coincide with political ones, for example: 'Isabel Cordero y D. Juan Prim expiraron con pocas horas de diferencia' (Galdós, 74). His characters take the trait to amusing extremes: 'Sobre aquellos cinco [partos] hay que apuntar doce más en la cuenta, total, diecisiete partos, que recordaba asociándolos a fechas célebres del reinado de Isabel II' (Galdós, 44). Fuentes enthusiastically takes up the technique: 'Cuando el viejo Higinio Ceballos murió, el mismo día en que Maximiliano pisó tierra veracruzana [...]' (17). The self-awareness of the technique is very

---

[26] See Benito Pérez Galdós, *Fortunata y Jacinta* (Madrid: Hernando, 1971), 20.

reminiscent of Galdosian irony: 'Por lo visto, los patriarcas de la familia Ceballos acostumbraban morir en fechas históricas' (24). Various aspects of Fuentes's treatment of religion are also a homage to Galdós: the familiar way in which God talks to Fortunata in *madrileño castizo* or to the protagonist of Nazarín in the final lines of that novel is reproduced in Jaime's familiar chats with Christ (for example, 180).

The risk of being devoured, after the fashion of Goya's Saturn, by the father Galdós is also characteristically obviated by the widening of the intertextual dialogue. Galdós comes to *Las buenas conciencias* through the mediation of another father figure, Luis Buñuel, 'gran destructor de las conciencias tranquilas', as he is described in the dedication of the novel. Something similar happens twenty-three years later, in *Una familia lejana*, also dedicated to Buñuel, where the grand analogies of *A la recherche du temps perdu* are subjected to the delirious fantasy of the Aragonese cineast. Buñuel is, of course, in turn a great interpreter and recreator of Galdós in films such as *Tristana* and *Nazarín*. To use an Unamunian inversion, Buñuel becomes the father of Galdós. The mischievous sacrilege involved in having Jaime lift Christ's tunic points to the presence of Buñuel in the novel, and similar techniques are repeatedly used to break up the overwhelmingly nineteenth-century style of narration. Asunción's repressed sexuality and voice explode into explicit Buñuel fantasy, for example, using an image from *Un Chien andalou*: 'empezaba a decir oraciones mientras sentía que un enorme triángulo negro le cubría la boca, y la lengua de su delirio se alargaba húmeda y enrojecida hacia los labios de un rostro en blanco' (141). Guanajuato may have its origins in the Madrid of Galdós, but the Ceballos house is also the 'gran caserón' in Guanajuato of the grandfather of Francisco in Buñuel's *Él*, which the grandson is fighting to save from usurpers. The attack on middle-class morality in Buñuel is parallel to that of Galdós, but far more strident, and Fuentes is able to move freely between the two styles. Jaime's snobbery may reflect that of the nineteenth-century Pip, but it is also that of Viridiana, finally unable to tolerate the table manners of those whom she set out to redeem.[27]

[27] As Fuentes puts it in 'Luis Buñuel: el cine como libertad', *Casa con dos puertas*, 211: 'El fracaso de la santidad abstracta conduce al fracaso de la fraternidad cuando ésta no rebasa los límites de una compasión sospechosa de repugnancia o, por lo menos, de condescendencia. La fraternidad será

Jaime's reversal of the tyranny of his ancestors, his taking the place and the name of the father, is short-lived and compromised by bad faith. Fuentes's jousting with his precursors is less overtly parricidal. What happens, however, in the spheres both of the family and the intertextual, is a dynamic pluralisation of influence, a loosening of determinism. Hierarchic and chronological sequence becomes dialogue. Through quotation, 'history as a sequence is undone, as is the notion of a single unified, individual voice'.[28] From belatedness, the novel begins to forge a form of ironic contemporaneity.

---

convulsiva o no será. Viridiana no ha querido salvar a los pobres: ha querido salvar su propia imagen impoluta de santidad.'

[28] Worton and Still, 12.

La muerte de Artemio Cruz, 1962: Fathers and Sons, History and Myth

Introduction. Destiny and freedom

La muerte de Artemio Cruz recounts twelve days in the life of a powerful Mexican entrepreneur from the perspective of his death-bed. It covers his involvement in three families which span the history of Mexico from Independence to 1959. Cruz's life seems to embody the promises, the fruits and the betrayal of modern Mexican history. His childhood in Veracruz province is evoked in Arcadian terms until he shoots his uncle. In the Revolution he has an idyllic love affair until his lover is hanged, and he is acclaimed a hero after fleeing from battle and abandoning a wounded companion. He survives the Revolution by deftly shifting allegiances; makes the beginning of his fortune by highjacking land distribution in Puebla; acquires building land in Mexico City in exchange for betraying a priest harboured by his wife to the authorities at the time of the Cristero Wars. By the time of his death, each stage in his life, each choice to survive and prosper, has turned him into a monstrously embittered, arrogant and loveless man, deprived of hope and divorced from any youthful idealism he may once have had. With him, the Revolution has become mired in big business deals with foreign capital, institutional cynicism.

This frighteningly deterministic story of corruption is only one temporal and ideological structure within *La muerte de Artemio Cruz*. The novel also reflects a high degree of idealism and a real sense of optimism felt by Carlos Fuentes at the time when it was written, for example in its treatment of the Spanish Civil War.[1] In fact it weaves together a remarkable number of different structures and discursive threads into a rich and complex pattern. Its meaning cannot be sought in any one thread, but only within the dialectical movement they trace.

---

[1] For an excellent discussion of the importance of the Spanish Civil War in *La muerte de Artemio Cruz*, and the relevance of the Cuban Revolution to the writing of the novel, see Maarten van Delden, *Carlos Fuentes, Mexico, and Modernity* (Nashville, Tenn.: Vanderbildt University Press, 1998), 58-60.

Against the Revolution as epic, he sets history, temporality, betrayal, a movement away from the ideal which seems to have the force of destiny. But to history as linear process, he opposes the circularity of myth, the sort of complex, recurrent patterning of choices at the beginning of each generation which we glimpsed in *La región más transparente*. To such mythical patterns, and to the failure of historical projects, he opposes the straight line of Christian eschatology, a structure of redemption derived from medieval Christianity, a reversal of the fall in time, a recovery of the original historical impulse from the ravages of historical determinism. Utopia haunts the pages of *La muerte de Artemio Cruz*.

Fuentes has returned on various occasions to consider the conjunction of genres in Spanish American literature —myth, utopia, epic, lyric, novel, etc.— which reflect the complexities of the conception and realities of the Continent. In 1971, in *Tiempo mexicano*, he considers the possible fall to neo-colonial Pepsi-coatl from Quetzalcoatl, and the utopian presence in the novel: 'la base de nuestra narrativa moderna, que es transgresión de la norma épica por la herejía utópica: epopeya / espacio violados por novela / utopía que crea su propio tiempo. México no está fatalmente abocado al tiempo de Pepsicóatl'.[2] Later, in an article first published in *Vuelta* in 1983, he takes Bernal Díaz del Castillo's *Historia verdadera de la conquista de la Nueva España* as the origin of Spanish American literature, given its founding conjunction of chronicle and lyricism, reality and desire:

> en el Nuevo Mundo las expectativas exageradas de la Utopía, su victimación por la Épica y el refugio de aquéllas en un barroco doloroso establece de inmediato dos grandes tradiciones: *la crónica* que apoya políticamente la versión épica de los hechos y *la lírica* que crea otro mundo, la historia en la cual todo lo asesinado y sofocado por la historia épica tenga cabida. Bernal es la fuente secreta de la novela hispanoamericana: su libro recuerda, recrea, ama y lamenta, pero se ofrece como 'crónica verdadera'.[3]

---

[2] *Tiempo mexicano* (México: Joaquín Mortiz, 1978), 41, abbreviated as TM.
[3] 'La Ilíada descalza', *Valiente mundo nuevo*, 180.

The different causalities or generic readings outlined above are facilitated by the formal ordering of the novel. The narrative of Artemio Cruz is split into three voices, YO, TÚ, and ÉL, in the present, future and past tenses, in successive sequences on the occasion of each of the twelve historical moments. Temporal succession is shuffled dizzily as the twelve[4] periods are recounted out of chronological order, which allows Fuentes to sow and the reader to develop in his mind a fascinating, multi-directional web of different formal links and echoes between the episodes.

I will principally study two of the causalities or genres, the conjunction of which makes the reading of the novel so memorable. The first is the recurring family structure, observed in three key historical periods, of father, legitimate son and illegitimate son or symbolic heir, which articulates dual or alternative forces in Mexican history and spirit. The second is the structure of redemption of the past within a generally Christian symbolic world, the recovery of promises betrayed in history. I take Dante's *Divina Commedia* as a paradigmatic expression of such redemption to make visible the utopian recovery in the novel, the reversal of destiny into freedom. Finally, I will suggest how in turn the intertextual presence of José Gorostiza questions the completion of the Dantean redemption, hollows out the fullness of its terms.

Two Mexican times, two options

Destiny and freedom are decent metonyms for a whole series of oppositions which the novel uses as its warp and weft. They are also well represented by the vision of the two Mexicos experienced by Rodrigo Pola, Ixca Cienfuegos and Manuel Zamacona in *La región más transparente*, the world of *tú* and the world of *ustedes*. Artemio Cruz inherits an emotionally perceived *tierra* of community forged through struggle, and he bequeathes a *país* of separation, alienation and corruption:

---

[4] Or thirteen, according to José Carlos González Boixo in his useful introduction to his edition of *La muerte de Artemio Cruz* (Madrid: Cátedra, 1998), 30.

> heredarás la tierra
> no verás otra vez esos rostros que conociste en Sonora y en Chihuahua, que un día viste dormidos, aguantándose, y al siguiente encolerizados, arrojados a esa lucha sin razones ni paliativos, a ese abrazo de los hombres a los que otros hombres separaron, a ese decir que aquí estoy y existo contigo y contigo y contigo también, con todas las manos y todos los rostros vedados: amor, extraño amor común [...]
> legarás este país; legarás tu periódico, los codazos y la adulación, la conciencia adormecida por los discursos falsos de hombres mediocres [...] les legarás sus líderes ladrones, sus sindicatos sometidos, sus nuevos latifundios, sus inversiones americanas. (276-7)

Cruz is fatally split. The mirrors in the following passage show him walking simultaneously towards Madero, synonymous with honesty and reform, and towards a meeting with North American partners which will see him radically betraying the nationalist ideals of that Revolution: 'se ajustó la corbata frente a vidrio del vestíbulo y atrás, en el segundo vidrio, el que daba a la calle de Madero, un hombre idéntico a él, pero ten lejano [...] le daba la espalda y caminaba hacia el centro de la calle, mientras él buscaba el ascensor, desorientado por un instante' (22).

Political alienation for Artemio goes hand in hand with the withering of his capacity for love. His splitting in the mirror is echoed in the barrier which pride erects between himself and his wife Catalina, the mirror or pool of Narcissus in which they both risk drowning and perhaps have already drowned. Catalina's much delayed caress to his forehead on his death-bed opens a chink in the barrier from which the text emerges:

> Ella también pensará en su orgullo. Ahí nacerá la chispa. Allí la escucharás, en ese espejo común, en ese estanque que reflejará los rostros de ambos, que los ahogará cuando traten de besarse, el uno al otro, en el reflejo líquido de sus rostros: ¿por qué no miras a un lado?; allí estará Catalina en su carne. (92)

Artemio is not only split in himself, but reflected in various types of doubles which will allow Fuentes to generate the structure of inheritance mentioned above. The wounded soldier whom he allows to die is a twin who embodies the death of his own solidarity: 'si tuviese los ojos verdes, sería su gemelo...' (75). The soldier could in fact literally be Artemio's twin: after giving birth to Artemio, Isabel Cruz 'ya gemía con una nueva contracción' (315). His son Lorenzo in his heroic death in Spain is an inverted reflection of Artemio's betrayed idealism, while Jaime Ceballos, presented at the end of the novel as his symbolic heir, is a fair reflection of Cruz's cynicism.

Cruz is presented as belonging to two sorts of time, fallen, inauthentic time, and transcendental, full time. There is a similar mutual questioning between two sorts of time in Octavio Paz's 'Himno entre ruinas': 'todo es dios [...] La luz crea templos en el mar. / Nueva York, Londres, Moscú. La sombra cubre al llano con su yedra fantasma.'[5] In *La región más transparente*, Federico Robles experienced a time of plenitude with Mercedes which he seems to recover with Hortensia in his return to the land at the end of the novel. In *La muerte de Artemio Cruz*, the question of the recovery of any original time is more complex and problematic, but the utopian thrust is a fundamental underlying force in the novel. An Arcadia in the past is projected onto a utopia in the future. It is often expressed as a *unio contrariorum*. The waves of the sea to which the novel returns so often, as in the paradisal scene of bathing and making love in the Pacific Ocean at Acapulco between Lilia and the aptly named Xavier Adame, exhibit this unalientated fusion of opposites: '—otras las mismas— siempre en movimiento y siempre idénticas, fuera del tiempo, espejo de sí mismas, de las olas del origen, del milenio perdido y del milenio por venir' (157). Yet in the social reality just behind the opulent international seafront, the naked fishermen, their 'chozas con niños barrigones, perros sarnosos, riachuelas de aguas negras, triquina y bacilos' speak of different Mexican time: 'Siempre los dos tiempos, en esta comunidad

---

[5] *Poemas*, 234. Even more dramatic is the dialogue between the two times in 'Piedra de sol': 'busco una fecha viva como un pájaro' (*Poemas*, 263); 'el mundo reverdece si sonríes / comiendo una naranja, / el mundo cambia si dos, vertiginosos y enlazados, / caen sobre la yerba' (272-3) against the sequence which begins 'y el festín, el destierro, el primer crimen, / la quijada del asno, el ruido opaco / y la mirada incrédula del muerto / al caer en el llano ceniciento, / Agamenón y su mugido inmenso / y el repetido grito de Casandra' (273).

Published in the same year as *La muerte de Artemio Cruz*, Carpentier's *El siglo de las luces* alternates in tragic tension between the mythical, feminised time of the sea and the cruelty and fickleness of history on land.

jánica, de rostro doble, tan lejana de lo que fue y tan lejana de lo que quiere ser' (151). In Nahua cosmology the union of origin and future is conjugated in the fifty-two year cycles, at the end of which sacrifices are made to assure the rebirth of the sun, the beginning of another cycle (TM, 27). It has been argued that the New Year party held by Cruz at his Coyoacán mansion, fifty-two years after he started out on his adult life, abandoning his origins in Cocuya, fits into this pattern.[6] The exaltation of the party, however, is not followed by any sort of rebirth, but by a spiteful return to the status quo. In *Tiempo mexicano*, Fuentes sums up the two temporalities evoked here in two figures: Quetzalcoatl and Hernán Cortés. Quetzalcoatl, the Plumed Serpent, God of creation, culture and crops, was exiled to the East and his return eagerly awaited; origin and a beneficent future would become one: 'el regreso de Quetzalcóatl, el retorno al origen sin separación, idéntico al encuentro con un futuro bienhechor' (TM, 22). In his place, however, came the conquistador Hernán Cortés to destroy 'el tiempo y el espacio inventados para recibirlo', to bring genocide and a foreign religion. But the Hispanic tradition in Spanish America, argues Fuentes, is dual, concealing under medieval and imperial organicism the individualism of the Renaissance and the tradition of utopianism. The opposition between the two figures is central to Fuentes's historical shorthand, a metaphor for an opposition already central to *La región más transparente*. In *Terra Nostra* the figure of the Peregrino alternates between being Quetzalcoatl for much of the narration and a cruel Cortés on the *nemontani* or *días enmascarados*. Artemio Cruz can be seen as an avatar of the phonetically similar Hernán Cortés: their Mexican careers begin in Veracruz; the 'violation' of doña Marina, violation and founding encounter, is that of Regina and the conception of Artemio; don Gamaliel in Puebla, whose empire is taken over by Cruz, fulfils the role of the Aztec Emperor Moctezuma, replaced by Cortés. Fuentes adds that both married a woman called Catalina.[7] It is perhaps not too

---

[6] For a discussion of the validity of such interpretations, see González Boixo, 88 et seq.

[7] Fuentes commented on the parallel made originally in the article on which the first half of this chapter is based to María Victoria Reyzábal: 'Pero el propio Boldy propone una asimilación más audaz y, acaso, más inconsciente de mi parte. Boldy llama la atención sobre la similitud fonética Hernán Cortés-

anachronistic, thus, to use the two figures of Quetzalcoatl and Cortés to describe the recurring pairs in the novel of the powerful man of action and the idealist son absent from the novel, and the two times they represent.

The ambiguity and duality of the beginnings of New Spain is echoed in the way key episodes of the novel are given in two distinct versions. The two founding events in Artemio's life, his birth and his encounter with Regina, both merged with the image of the sea and projected onto the future as a paradise to be regained, manifest this dual nature. Artemio's love for Regina is one of total union, oneness with the universe and the seeds of time; making love, they are 'reducidos al encuentro del mundo, a la semilla de la razón, a las dos voces que nombran en silencio, que adentro bautizan todas las cosas' (67). They remember their first meeting as idyllic: '¿Te acuerdas de aquella roca que se metía al mar como un barco de piedra? [...] Se forma una laguna entre las rocas y uno puede mirarse en el agua blanca. Allí me miraba, y un día apareció tu cara junto a la mía' (66). But their union is built on a lie, an 'hermosa mentira' (82), their memory is a redeemed or improved past. In fact Regina was the first anonymous woman Cruz came across on entering a conquered town, she was hoisted onto the saddle of his horse and 'violada en silencio en el dormitorio común de los oficiales, lejos del mar, dando la cara a la sierra espinosa y seca' (83).[8] This act of falsification or transformation repeats Artemio's own

Artemio Cruz. Las carreras de ambos comienzan en Veracruz. Barrenan las naves de su pasado. Violan a Marina-Regina. Someten a Bernal-Moctezuma. Y se casan con Catarinas. Le juro que a mí nunca se me ocurrió esto, pero voy a creer desde ahora en estructuras automáticas y desplazamientos freudianos del trabajo onírico al trabajo material' ('Mantener un lenguaje o sucumbir al silencio', in Julio Ortega, ed., *Retrato de Carlos Fuentes* (Barcelona: Galaxia Gutenberg / Círculo de Lectores, 1995), 87).

[8] Artemio's love for his wife Catalina is similarly dual, but the order of factors is reversed. We learn how she is forced to marry him as part of the agreement whereby Cruz takes over Gamaliel Bernal's lands while protecting the family. He wishes to erase the memory of that mechanism, but realises that appearances are against him, even though he had loved her before the pact: 'Él deseaba borrar el reuerdo del origen y hacerse querer sin memorias del acto que la obligó a tomarlo por esposo. [...] ¿Cómo hacerle creer que la había amado desde el momento en que la vio pasar por una calle de Puebla, antes de saber quién era?' (101).

origins, presented as a paradisal, tropical life by the river near the sea, fishing and swimming in the clear waters and working in harmony with the mulatto Lunero: 'Todo el tono de fruta verde corría por los brazos delgados y el pecho firme, hecho a nadar corriente arriba, con los dientes brillantes en la carcajada del cuerpo refrescado por el río de fondo herbáceo y riberas legamosas' (283). Only at the end of the novel do we learn that Artemio was himself the fruit of a rape, that his mother Isabel, the sister of Lunero, was one of the many casually taken by force by the *hacendado* Atanasio Menchaca.

Artemio is thus an *hijo de la chingada* before confirming the self-perpetuating curse of la Malinche by taking in turn the mask of the *chingón*. As he is planning to change political allegiances yet again and denounce the padre Páez, as Robles had sacrificed Feliciano Sánchez before him, in exchange for the favours of President Calles, the fat policeman is explicit: '¿A poco no somos los meros chingones? ¿Sabes? Escoge siempre a tus amigos entre los grandes chingones, porque con ellos no hay quien te chingue a ti' (129). As an alienated travesty of the cyclical Aztec time, Mexican reality is seen to obey the rule that the outrage practised on one will be avenged in turn by its imposition on another. Artemio's TÚ voice talks of 'el ultraje que lavaste ultrajando a otros hombres' (147). Artemio's grandmother Ludivinia is almost constitutionally aware of the repetitive pattern: '¿Vienes a decirme que ya no hay tierras ni grandeza para nosotros, que otros se han aprovechado de nosotros como nosotros nos aprovechamos de los primeros, de los originales dueños de todo?' (296). The dispossessed will in turn dispossess. This seems to be the meaning of Artemio's enigmatic refrain on his death-bed: 'regresaron, no se dieron por vencidos' (271). The *villistas* whom Artemio's men thought they had defeated return to the village and hang Regina in Cruz's absence. The untranslatable word *chingada*, so memorably analyzed in Octavio Paz's *El laberinto de la soledad*, comes to signify the determinism of cruelty and dehumanisation in the process of Cruz's life and in the Mexican history of which he is emblematic, a sort of Mexican destiny which the writing of the novel contests. The TÚ voice protests at its power: 'déjala en el camino, asesínala con armas que no sean las suyas: matémosla: matemos esa palabra que nos separa, nos petrifica, nos pudre con su doble veneno de ídolo y cruz: que no sea nuestra respuesta ni nuestra fatalidad' (146).

The motif of 'regresaron, no se dieron por vencidos' also refers to the way in which the dead whom Cuz survived and to whom he owes his survival and power, return irrepressibly to his memory. Memory becomes the site where the irreversible process of *la chingada* is contested.[9] The plural voices of the others contest and dissolve the power of the individual, the choices of Cruz's life between community and power are posed again, their promises become a constant virtuality.

The pattern through history

La muerte de Artemio Cruz follows family dramas set in three historical periods, where one group in power replaces its predecessor, each group promising great progress, each one reproducing the negative features of the previous regime. These three periods are the creole-dominated regimes after Independence, Liberalism, and Revolution. The first is best represented by General Antonio López de Santa Anna, president eleven times between 1833 and 1855. Independence from the Spaniards and the Bourbons had promised a proud and wealthy future for the vast country of Mexico. But by the time of his final exile, the operetta-like hero, with a passion for gambling and cock-fighting, who had a funeral for his leg lost in battle, had seen the loss of Texas, the invasion by U.S. troops in 1847 and the loss of half the national territory.[10] The second period, championed by the Liberal Benito Juárez, president from 1858 to 1872, sought to modernise the country, undermining the traditional, conservative forces of the church, the army, the regional *caciques*, and the communal Indian villages. The Lerdo law of 1856 and the radical constitution of 1857 sought to disentail Church property and replace communal landowning with a new class of capitalist small farmers. But the civil war with the conservatives (1858–1861), the French intervention and the Empire of Maximilian (1864–1867) and other factors meant that much of the land was acquired by rich landowners: 'It thus only added to the ecomonic strength and political

---

[9] This is well expressed by González Boixo, 12.
[10] See Enrique Krauze, *Mexico: Biography of Power. A History of Modern Mexico, 1810 – 1996*, translated by Hank Heifetz (New York: Harper Collins, 1997), 135-51.

cohesiveness of an already dominant class of wealthy hacendados.'[11] The next upturn is the Revolution and civil wars between 1910 and 1917 with their own land reform and their own new oligarchy distinguishable from earlier ones mainly by their rhetoric.

Each one of these periods is represented by a patriarch figure who fills the position of his ousted predecessor: Ireneo Menchaca, Gamaliel Bernal and Artemio Cruz. Ireneo Menchaca was given thousands of hectares of land on the tropical coast of Veracruz by Santa Anna, taken by force from the original Indian owners, worked by cheap negro labour from the Caribbean, increased by mortages imposed on the small holders of the region (292). After 1855 they have to return from Mexico City to defend the land against the *juaristas* and offer their estate to the French troops of Napoleon III as a base against the Liberals (288). Ireneo dies in Campeche after joining an aborted return by Santa Anna after the death of Maximilian. Most of the house was burnt in 1868 by the *juaristas* and the son is killed in 1889 by the new landowners now firmly established under Portfirio Díaz.

This class, which replaced the Menchacas, is represented by Gamaliel Bernal, a Puebla businessman who acquired church lands after the disentailment of Lerdo for next to nothing. An indignant Catholic tells the story to Cruz: 'todo lo que tiene se lo robó a los curas, allá cuando Juárez puso a remate los bienes del clero y cualquier comerciante con tantito ahorrado pudo hacerse de un terrenal inmenso...' (43).

Bernal is ousted by the revolutionary officer Artemio Cruz, grandson of Ireneo Menchaca, dispossessed by the Liberals who gave power to Bernal. Cruz comes to an agreement with Bernal who agrees that 'hay que pagar un precio para sobrevivir' (42). Cruz marries his daughter and takes over the debts owed to him with the promise to return a quarter of everything he recovered (48). Cruz takes charge of the land reform in the area after 1919 but keeps the best land for himself, ruins the neighbouring landowners by extortionate loans, selling their land off in lots in exchange for urban real estate in Puebla City while promising it to the local *campesinos* and having himself elected as *diputado* for the area. As Bernal perceives, Cruz is not so much an individual as the incarnation of a new cycle: 'Artemio Cruz.

---

[11] Bethell, ed, *Mexico since Independence* (Cambridge: CUP, 1991), 51.

Así se llamaba, entonces, el nuevo mundo surgido de la guerra civil; así se llamaban quienes llegaban a sustituirlo. Desventurado país [...] que a cada nueva generación tiene que destruir a los antiguos poseedores y sustituirlos por nuevos amos, tan rapaces y ambiciosos como los anteriores' (50).

Towards the end of the novel, there are indications that Cruz has a similar, symbolic, successor in Jaime Ceballos, the hero of *Las buenas conciencias*, whose father-in-law Roberto Régules had been instrumental in dispossessing Cruz's counterpart in *La región más transparente*, Federico Robles.

At the end of each cycle a significant duality is embodied in the two sons of each patriarch, who express the choice between survival, opportunism and idealism, coinciding to some extent with the disjunction Cortés-Quetzalcoatl. Menchaca has two legitimate sons, Atanasio and Pedrito, whereas Gamaliel Bernal and Artemio Cruz had a legitimate son who embodied their better self and a symbolic heir or usurper: Gonzalo Bernal and Artemio Cruz, Lorenzo Cruz and Jaime Ceballos.

When Ireneo Menchaca returned to his hacienda in Veracruz, his son Atanasio, 'el hijo de los ojos verdes, vestido de blanco sobre el caballo blanco [...] cabalgando sobre la tierra feraz con el fuete en el puño, pronto a imponer su voluntad decisiva' (292), defends the lands with the same vigour with which he ravishes the local *campesinas* and indeed lives on there until in 1889. Pedrito meanwhile continued to live frivolously in the salons of Mexico City when there was no real wealth to support him. When Atanasio is murdered after being treacherously called to pick up the bones of his father, recovered from a Campeche cemetery, Pedrito, who was present and carried a shot-gun, abandoned him to his fate, adding an element of virtual fratricide to the opposition between the authenticity of the two sons. Here the vigorous son, true to family and class roots, dies while the coward survives as parasite and alcoholic.

Gamaliel Bernal's legitimate son Gonzalo, though a hedonist, betrayed his father's class by joining the Revolution against it. Artemio had faced the possibility of a firing squad with Gonzalo, but whereas the latter preferred to die idealistically rather than contaminate himself with compromise, Artemio abandons his companion and with Machiavellian skill takes over the position of Gonzalo as heir to the Bernal fortune.

Cruz becomes the new revolutionary oligarch and has his son Lorenzo spend time at the *hacienda* by the Verzcruz coast which he has bought and restored. Against the wishes of his mother Lorenzo chooses to go to Spain to fight idealistically for the lost cause of the Spanish Republic, seen as a mirror of the Mexican Revolution, and dies heroically in 1939 whereas his father had opted to survive at any cost. Jaime Ceballos, the 'twin' of Lorenzo, is his opposite and identical to Artemio in his cynicism and will to succeed.

Textual games

Though I have summarised the generational patterns in a schematic fashion, they in fact emerge only gradually for the reader in a tantalising and pleasurable way in a complex web of intratextual echoes, an elusive order glimpsed in a fragmentary way in the swirling nebula of the mind of the dying Artemio Cruz. The temporal dislocation and the three dialoguing voices release textual elements to be recombined in different threads and rival causalities. On the other hand, the patterns which do appear have a frighteningly archetypal and determining force. The impression of metempsychosis and magical processes link the novel with overtly fantastic works such as the novella *Aura*, published in the same year. Here the witch Consuelo reincarnates her long-dead husband, a Mexican general of Emperor Maximilian, in the person of a young historian, in much the same way as Ludivinia magically foresees the young Artemio as a prolongation of her dead son Atanasio.

Fuentes uses a wide range of techniques to suggest identifications and parallels between characters and situations. They were rivalled only in the early sixties in the novels of Mario Vargas Llosa, such as *La ciudad y los perros*. They include parallel situations, repetition of phrases, authorial comment disguised as the thoughts of a character, magical ceremonies, myth. A typically effective device is the recurring index of the gun with two bullets, which appears in five scenes involving four separate characters. Pedrito fails to use the double-barrelled shotgun he carries on his horse to defend his brother Atanasio, but keeps it oiled and ready; the thirteen-year-old Artemio takes it fourteeen years later to kill the *enganchador* of the local *hacendado* and allow Lunero, the mulatto brother of his mother, to escape, but, firing upwards from the undergrowth, kills Pedrito, the creole brother of his father Atanasio;

Lorenzo in the snowy Spanish Pyrenees uses a similar gun, now rusty and useless, to shoot, again upwards, at the Nazi planes to cover the retreat of the fleeing refugees. The gun also appears in the duel between Cruz and the *villista* officer Zagal in the Mexican Revolution and in the parallel Russian roulette duel with the fat *comandante de policía* at the time of the Cristero troubles, where both rivals spare Artemio's life. The index has some symbolic meaning in itself: it is an obvious phallic symbol, and its two bullets speak of duality. This meaning underlines and expands the meaning of the situation where it occurs, suggesting, for example, that one man out of two usually dies in a duel and that another man dies in exchange, sacrificially, before or after the duel: el padre Páez is handed over to the authorities after the experience with the *gordo* and Gonzalo is executed before the duel with Zagal. It signals the tension between choice and chance: the chance inherent in the Russian roulette and duel against Cruz's choice in the two scenes between political allegiances (Carranza-Villa, Obregón-Calles); the chance by which Artemio unwittingly kills Pedro against his choice to defend Lunero. Being presented originally as an attribute, and metonymically as the whole of one character, when attributed to another, it carries with it much of the meaning developed in the first situation. The identity of the first possessor is superimposed onto the second, making it an effective technique in creating the notion of a collective memory passed from one generation to another.

The partiarchs Ireneo, Gamaliel and Artemio are linked by images of death and dogs. Ireneo dies 'en el verano sin letrinas, hinchado de agua putrefacta' (293), in a similar fashion to his grandson Artemio, whose swollen abdomen is relieved only when he vomits his own excrement. Don Gamaliel on first meeting Cruz is accompanied by a mastiff: 'El mastín saltó con alegría y lamió la mano del amo' (39). At the end of Artemio's life, when he is about to face the parallel interview with Jaime Ceballos, he is accompanied by two mastiffs, who almost drag him out of his seat when a photographer takes a picture.

Cruz's grandmother Ludivinia is seen to foresee and almost magically to control the whole mechanism of inheritance. Born in 1810, the year of the 'grito de Dolores', she is contemporaneous with the birth of Mexican independence. This first 'grito' is one hundred and twenty-nine years before the second cry of Dolores, the Lola whose scream, as Lorenzo is killed in Spain, closes the whole cycle of the hopes of Cruz. Ludivinia had lived for thirty-odd years in the *zona sagrada* of her room in Cocuya, where not even the fire of the *juaristas* and history had dared to penetrate. Like Consuelo in *Aura* in her decrepit old age, she makes grotesque efforts to recover her youth: 'Seguía aquí, tratando de cumplir desde el lecho revuelto los ademanes de la joven hermosa y blanca que abrió las puertas de Cocuya al largo desfile de prelados españoles, comerciantes franceses, ingenieros escoceses [...]' (291). Ludivinia is the memory of Mexico incarnate: 'traía emplastada en el cerebro la memoria de un siglo y en los surcos del rostro capas de aire y tierra y sol desaparecidos' (291); 'creía ser el centro que anudaba la memoria y las presencias circundantes' (298). From this racial memory and long enclosure in her sacred space she is able to dictate the future, reincarnate the dead. She finally wishes to touch the young mulatto on whom she had spied for so many years, and whom she had 'reared in her foresight': 'una forma humana [...] que sólo ahora deseaba tocar y llamar por su nombre, en vez de criarla en el presentimiento' (306). She will live and survive through him with her memory: 'aún existiría un margen de vida fuera de su siglo de recuerdos: una oportunidad de vivir y querer a otro ser de su sangre' (298). It is Ludivinia who utters the curse, the 'maldición natural' which is to become the destiny of the novel, as she screams at her son Pedro and at the *enganchador*: '¡Chingao!' (297, 306). From Ludivina then, Artemio inherits memory, to which is added the accumulated memory of all those who die for him: the hell of memory which constitutes the text of the novel.

Cruz at the crossroads

Two central relationships in the novel are those between Artemio and his double/twin Gonzalo Bernal, and between Artemio and his alternative heirs, Lorenzo and Jaime Ceballos. Cruz and Gonzalo Bernal meet in a *villista* prison, rather like Gervasio Pola and his companions before them, where they await execution together. While Cruz will do virtually anything to survive, Gonzalo is consciously a martyr to a lost cause, an idealist and a purist who believes that 'hay deberes que es necesario cumplir aunque se sepa de antemano que se va al fracaso' (196). They form a clear opposition between thought and action, idealism and opportunism. But Artemio is not impervious to the presence of Gonzalo, who expresses thoughts parallel to his own, memories which Artemio is desperately trying to avoid, thus becoming a formidable enemy: 'ese nuevo enemigo armado de ideas y ternuras, que sólo estaba repitiendo el mismo pensamiento oculto del capitán, del prisionero, de él' (197). The opposition between openness and closedness is momentarily resolved in the 'abrazo violento' between the two men as Artemio struggles to silence Gonzalo, to silence his own memory. This aggressive embrace characterises doubles in Fuentes elsewhere too, as in the final fight between Franz and Javier in the pyramid in Cholula in *Cambio de piel*.

The moment represents the end of a cycle. '¿Para qué ilusionar a esos pobrecitos con un nuevo sol? (198), comments Zagal, their captor. If there is a rebirth, and the sun does rise just after Gonzalo's death, then there is a tension between Nahua and Christian conceptions: Gonzalo dies in solidarity with the Indian Tobías to propiciate a new cycle; Artemio survives but, Christ-like, assumes the cross of the life and sins of all Mexicans. Memory is central to the process of inheritance. Gonzalo is an invitation to remember: 'Dicen que es bueno recordar' (191), he says, while Artemio refuses to remember, tries to 'disfrazar esa ansia de recuerdo' (189). 'No hay mucha vida por detrás' (191), he lies. But after the 'violento abrazo' with his 'new enemy', Artemio suddenly becomes conscious of his role as memory and decides to live and survive so that his dead lover Regina will live on in him:

> Él sólo sentía ese dolor perdido de Regina, esa memoria dulce y amarga que tanto había escondido y que ahora brotaba a flote, pidiéndole que siguiera viviendo, como si una mujer muerta necesitara del recuerdo de un hombre vivo para seguir siendo algo más que un cuerpo devorado por los gusanos en un hoyo sin nombre, en un pueblo sin nombre. (198)

Artemio assumes not only the life and death of Regina, but also the unfulfilled possibilities of Gonzalo's life together with his material heritage. It is the fact that Artemio incorporates his double and opposite that allows him to split in two in turn when his own destiny is exhausted, and delegate the eternally unfulfilled promises of Gonzalo onto another, his son Lorenzo. In one moment of lucidity, Artemio is completely aware of the logic of inheritance:

> La ironía de ser él quien regresaba a Puebla, y no el fusilado Bernal, le divertía. Era, en cierto modo, una mascarada, una sustitución, una broma que podía jugarse con la mayor seriedad; pero también era un certificado de

vida, de la capcidad para sobrevivir y fortalecer el propio destino con los ajenos. [...] sintió que entraba duplicado, con la vida de Gonzalo Bernal añadida a la suya, con el destino del muerto sumado al suyo: como si Bernal, al morir, hubiese delegado las posibilidades de su vida incumplida en la de él. Quizás las muertes ajenas son las que alargan nuestra vida, pensó. (43)

Gamaliel Bernal accepts Artemio as his heir, bowing to historical necessity and fatality, like Moctezuma perhaps faced with Cortés, but also because he recognises in him a survivor like himself.

The final couple of twins are Lorenzo and Jaime Ceballos, Quetzalcoatl and Cortés. Lorenzo's identification with the former is perhaps suggested when 'el brazo levantado del muchacho indicará hacia el horizonte, por donde salió el sol' (225). The two never meet, and are only contrasted in their relationship with the father figure. Cruz forces Lorenzo to do what he did not do, to recover his life: 'lo obligarás a hacer lo que tú no hiciste, a rescatar tu vida perdida' (246). In the Spanish Civil War Lorenzo lives out the ideals betrayed by his father in the Mexican Revolution. The episode is related in a third person section and the reader initially reads the *Él* which refers to Lorenzo as referring to Cruz, thus blurring their identities. Indeed Cruz accepts that he invented the details of the episode: 'ah, soñé, imaginé, supe esos nombres, recordé esas canciones, ay gracias, pero saber, ¿cómo puedo saber? [...] invento paisajes, invento ciudades [...] ay, gracias, que me enseñaste lo que pudo ser mi vida' (243-4). The section is a reworking, an inversion of many elements from Cruz's career: the *azotea* is the same one from which Artemio watched the execution of Gonzalo; both hear a baby cry; the man at the balcony who 'esperaba el regreso de alguien o [...] aguardaba la salida del sol' (234) echoes the reference to the 'new sun' at the time of Gonzalo's execution, and foreshadows Cruz's position at the New Year's Eve party as spectator, seeming to await the return of his own son. The rifle with two bullets is there, and Lorenzo's relation with Dolores is clearly an inverted reflection of Cruz's love for Regina, even in their projected reunion by the sea.

Lorenzo, of course, dies and it is Jaime who takes his place at the party. In a complex three-page sequence (266-9), Artemio's memories of his last days with Lorenzo by the sea in Veracruz are brilliantly superimposed on or alternated with a dialogue between Artemio and

Jaime. The disjointed phrases from the two discourses seem to answer each other, Jaime falling ambiguously and ironically into the questions and interpellations addressed mentally by Artemio to his dead son. Jaime's ideals, for example, becoming part of Cruz's business empire ('Pero ya ve, yo tengo otros ideales...') are juxtaposed with the universality of Lorenzo's ideals, embodied in the ocean: 'al mar libre, al mar abierto, hacia donde corrió Lorenzo'. The vision of a promised land intuited by Cruz and his son ('distinguirán en la otra ribera un espectro de tierra, un espectro, sí...') is painfully contrasted with the superficiality of the present ceremony for Ceballos: '¿Qué le parece esta fiesta? ... vacilón, qué rico vacilón, cha cha cha'. Perhaps the most significant juxtaposition is that between the leitmotif with which Artemio always refers to his hopes in his son ('lo esperaba con alegría esa mañana') and the reality of the return of a very different figure: '¡Bah! llegó usted tarde.'

The final identification between father and heir, Cruz and Ceballos, takes place at the New Year's Eve party in the Coyoacán mansion which is a reproduction of the room of Ludivinia, the original *zona sagrada* of the novel. It is signalled by the repetition of a crucial phrase denoting the rebelliousness of Cruz's life. Jaime has broken the sacred rule that nobody should talk to Cruz during his parties and, when challenged, answers defiantly, 'Esas reglas fueron hechas sin consultarme, don Artemio.' This rebellion corresponds to Artemio's first lesson in life, not to be 'esclavo de los mandamientos escritos sin consultarte' (125), and to his dictum to the pretender at the party: 'el verdadero poder nace siempre de la rebeldía'. Artemio seems to recognise himself in the young intruder: 'dio la cara a Jaime y el joven lo miró sin pestañear ... picardía en la mirada ... juego de los labios y las quijadas ... del viejo ... del joven ... se reconoció, ah ... se desconcertó, ah'; 'se vieron a los ojos, se sonrieron'. The pattern continues, the opportunist is poised to take over while Lorenzo rots on a foreign mountain side. The curse of *la chingada* has not been broken.

The Mexican Divine Comedy

By approaching *La muerte de Artemio Cruz* through the lens of Dante's *Divine Comedy* it is possible to make visible a structure of redemption and a basically Catholic-inspired notion of good and evil which questions and symbolically reverses the determinism of the curse, the course of which was followed above. Fuentes has cited Dante as the most important influence on his work after Cervantes[12] and described the TÚ voice to Emmanuel Carballo as an 'especie de Virgilio que lo guía [a Artemio] por los doce círculos de su infierno'.[13] My argument is to suggest that the three alternating voices of the novel, YO, TÚ, ÉL, correspond to the three *cantiche* of the *Commedia* and that the redemption of Dante by Beatrice and Christ corresponds to the redemption of Artemio by Regina and Lorenzo.[14] Many of the elements of the novel I adduce may, of course, correspond simply to the wider text of Catholicism.

Our starting point, then, is a schematic correspondence: ÉL, narration in the past, as *Inferno*; YO, narration in the present tense, as *Purgatorio*; TÚ, narration in the future, as *Paradiso*. Published after Fuentes's novel, but offering fascinating information, Frances Yates's *The Art of Memory* suggests that the *Commedia* is a mnemotechnic device to remember the sins and their punishments and that its *cantiche* correspond to the three parts of prudence as defined by Cicero: *memoria*, remembering vices and their punishments in Hell, *intelligentia*, the use of the present for penitence and the acquisition of virtue, and *providentia*, the looking forward to Heaven.[15] The medieval forms of *prudentia* were the three powers of the soul defined by Saint Augustin as memory, understanding and will, the image of the Trinity in man.[16] According to this scheme, Él becomes memory; YO intelligence; TÚ providence or will.

In many works of Fuentes, the desire to deny the fixity of the past, to undo its determinism, and the inevitability of its alienating structures, is a powerful agent. The idea is formulated in the first novel: 'noches rezando para que no suceda lo que ya sucedió' (*La región*, 378). In *La*

[12] See Wendy Faris, *Carlos Fuentes* (New York: Frederick Ungar, 1983), 9.
[13] See René Jara, 'El mito y la nueva novela hispanoamericana: a propósito de *La muerte de Artemio Cruz*', in *Homenaje*, 174.
[14] Georgina García Gutiérrez, in *Los disfraces: la obra mestiza de Carlos Fuentes* (Mexico City: Colegio de México, 1981), 19, suggests that the triad into which Artemio is split corresponds to the Catholic trinity.
[15] See Frances Yates, *The Art of Memory* (Harmondsworth: Penguin, 1978), 104.
[16] See Yates, 62.

muerte de Artemio Cruz, the TÚ voice is seen to reverse what was recounted in the ÉL sections, for example,: 'tú escogerás abrazar a ese soldado herido que entra al bosquecillo providencial' (246). The clearest cases are the version of the encounter between Artemio and Regina as idyllic when it was in fact an abduction and rape, and the presentation of the heroic death of Lorenzo as a correction and reversal of the cowardice of his father in historical time. In *Terra Nostra* the modifications of the past through the Theatre of Memory happen on a much larger, combinatory scale, as when the *comuneros* are seen to be victorious at Villalar.

The difficulties and mystery of the TÚ voice go well beyond the techniques of Butor's *La Modification* or the dilemmas of destiny and freedom in *L'Être et le néant*, which have been rightly invoked in this context.[17] To recount the past in the future, as TÚ does ('Ayer volarás' (13)) is to speak at the same time of liberty and predestination. Without the syntactic and semantic stridency of Fuentes's text, many of Dante's interlocutors situate themselves in a similar position, since they know as much of the future as of the past. Cacciaguida, for example:

> Cosí vedi le cose contingenti
> anzi che sieno in sè, mirando il punto
> a cui tutti i tempi son presenti. (*Para.* xvii. 16–18)[18]

And in the famous prediction of his exile, he recounts, in 1300, the year in which according to the text the action of the *Commedia* takes place, things which will happen to Dante in the future, although they had in fact happened to him before he wrote the poem: 'Tu proverai sí come sa di sale / lo pane altrui' (*Para.*, xvii. 58-9). For Dante this predestination does not affect freedom, it is not a destiny fixed in advance, in the same way as the movement of a ship is not determined in its reflection in the eyes which observe it.[19] Such rational

[17] See R. Reeve, 'Carlos Fuentes y el desarrollo del narrador en segunda persona: un ensayo exploratorio', and C. Allen, 'La correlación entre la filosofía de Jean-Paul Sartre y *La muerte de Artemio Cruz* de Carlos Fuentes', in *Homenaje*, 75–87.
[18] The quotations from Dante are taken from *La Divina Commedia*, Milano: Lucchi, 1967.
[19] See the commentary of Sinclair in Dante, *The Divine Comedy*, vol. 3,

contradictions can only be resolved in a vision which is somehow divine, or in the divine mind itself, where temporality does not exist. In the ÉL voice, determinism, the modern form of predestination, is ironlike, but a divine vision is glimpsed in the TÚ. It is only from this perspective that some rationally incomprehensible phrases can be approached. For example, in 'la memoria es el deseo satisfecho / hoy que tu vida y tu destino son la misma cosa' (209), the three dimensions of time are almost mystically reconciled: memory or past, desire or future, satisfaction or present. Such contradictions suggest a redemptive role for memory. The TÚ voice, which Fuentes associates with Dante's first guide Virgil, is equivalent in this context to those interlocutors of Dante who know the future in the past, show him the 'diritta via' and offer him a second chance: they recount to him his future tribulations (in fact past ones) no longer as predestination but as the possibility of salvation.

Another fundamental aspect of the *Commedia* for the novel is the Catholic concept of good and evil. The anti-Manichean concept expounded in Virgil's 'discourse on love' derives from Augustine, but finds its classical formulation in Dante. Evil does not exist per se, and all the mortal sins have their origin in the love for some good, which is falsely perceived or pursued in an insufficient or excessive fashion.[20] Virgil expresses this as follows:

> Quinci comprender puoi ch'esser conviene
> amor sementa in voi d'ogni virtute
> e d'ogni operazion che merta pene. (*Purg.*, xvii. 103-5)

Artemio's TÚ is similarly incapable of conceiving of evil in an isolated form:

> El mal. Tú nunca podrás designarlo. Acaso porque, más desamparados [que los protestantes norteamericanos], no queremos que se pierda esa zona intermedia, ambigua, entre la luz y la sombra: esa zona donde podemos

---

Paradiso, trans. by John Sinclair (New York: OUP, 1979), 252.
[20] See Sayers's Introduction to *The Comedy of Dante Alighieri the Florentine. Cantica II, Purgatory*, trans. by Dorothy L. Sayers (Harmondsworth: Penguin, 1965), 66.

encontrar el perdón. Donde tú lo podrás encontrar. ¿Quién no será capaz, en un solo momento de su vida — como tú — de encarnar al mismo tiempo el bien y el mal, de dejarse conducir al mismo tiempo por dos hilos misteriosos, de color distinto, que parten del mismo ovillo para que después el hilo blanco ascienda y el negro descienda y, a pesar de todo, los dos vuelvan a encontrarse entre tus mismos dedos? (33)

Love does not lead directly to salvation, the pardon apparently promised by the TÚ voice. On showing this, Fuentes exhibits the same mixture of tenderness and cruelty as Dante in his encounter with Paolo and Francesca, the most pitiable pair in the poem. Artemio's love for Regina, while it is presented as an essential union and a rediscovery of the world, brings about his first, fundamental fall: his cowardice and betrayal in battle as he tries to save his life for his love. He abandons an injured soldier, who is his twin and an essential part of himself, only to return to the village to find his lover hanged. The unon between two lovers is frustrated if it is divorced from the union between man and society, the individual and a political cause. In the *Commedia*, however, it is precisely the ambiguity of love which allows salvation, and the function of Purgatory is to purge the faults of perverted, excessive, or insufficient love until it is renewed. Both *Artemio Cruz* and the *Commedia* have as their starting point the love for a woman (Regina and Beatrice), a love which provides their most intimate symbolism. The discourse of the dying Cruz is a purging of the faults of his love for woman and country.

The correspondences between the symbolic schemes of both works may be seen in the arch they spread between two woods: in *Artemio Cruz* between the 'bosque bajo pero tupido' (74) of the protagonist's cowardice during the Mexican Revolution and the 'campo de álamos desnudos' (234) of his son's heroism during the Spanish Civil War; in the *Commedia*, between the 'selva selvaggia ed aspra e forte' (*Inf.* i. 5) where Dante is lost and the 'divina foresta spessa e viva' (*Purg.* xxviii. 2) of the Earthly Paradise. In both cases the two woods are the same wood transformed by a process of redemption.[21] This redemption may be seen as having been brought about by a woman: by Beatrice, firstly on earth and later in a semi-divine form; by Regina first and later by

[21] See Sayers, 293.

her double Dolores. It is also brought about by a man: by Christ, Son of God and Adam, and by Lorenzo, the son of Artemio.

The episode of Artemio's cowardice and abandonment of the soldier echoes in some detail the plot of a novel by Stephen Crane on the American Civil War: *The Red Badge of Courage*. There is a nice link here between inter- and intratextuality: an episode from the American Civil War is reflected, in another text, in a similar episode from the Mexican Revolution, which in turn is reflected, with an inverted meaning, in a scene from the Spanish Civil War, where Lorenzo repeats many of the actions of his father. But Lorenzo heroically dies to save his companions and Dolores survives where Regina had died.

At the beginning of his poem, Dante is lost in a wood: 'mi ritrovai per una selva oscura, / che la diritta via era smarrita'. He is morally lost in his public life on having lost sight of the example of Beatrice. The meanings carried by Beatrice are many: she is the real and ideal woman of Dante's early poetry, she is Florence, the Empire, and the Church.[22] Seeing Dante from Paradise heading for damnation despite his virtues, she determines to show him the fate of the 'perduta gente' and descends to Hell to ask Virgil to show him the *Inferno*. On leaving Hell, he climbs with Virgil the levels of Mount Purgatory to the boundary of the Earthly Paradise, where he joins Beatrice, who takes him through the celestial spheres until he is granted the ineffable vision of divinity. Regina may be seen to represent the Revolution in the same way as Beatrice the ideal of empire. Artemio's love for her displays the same mixture of tendernsss and violence as characterises the Revolution. For Octavio Paz, revolution is an attempt to restore a mythical golden age,[23] and this is perhaps why, superimposed on the brutal rape of Regina in a village taken by the revolutionary forces, we have the idyllic meeting by the river bank which is clearly the same river where Artemio lived out his paradisal early life with Lunero in Cocuya. Regina's symbolic death when Artemio betrays his 'gemelo' signals the progressive degeneration of any political idealism in Cruz.

The scene in the wood is thus the fall of Artemio, who, like Dante, realises he is lost: 'El hilo estaba perdido. El hilo que le permitió

---

[22] For a fuller treatment of the figure of Beatrice, see Charles Williams, *The Figure of Beatrice. A Study in Dante* (London: Faber and Faber, 1950).
[23] See *El laberinto de la soledad*, 129.

recorrer, sin perderse, el laberinto de la guerra' (78). From this wood, guided by the TÚ, he descends to the inferno of his life. In fact the wood hovers between paradise, 'bosquecillo providencial' (75) and hell: 'más arriba no había luz: el cielo descendió un peldaño y era un cielo de pólvora' (74). Regina, hanged from a tree by the *federales*, is a tree herself, her eyes black cherries: 'cerezas oscuras del árbol de carne y entrañas calientes' (81). In his later life, for example in Coyoacán, Artemio strives to recreate his first garden, 'el jardín sombreado de cerezos' (258). But on a realistic plane, as Catalina insists, he will never recover his original garden: 'Quizás tuviste tu jardín. Yo también tuve el mío, mi pequeño paraíso. Ahora ambos lo hemos perdido' (113). The second fundamental wood and specifically a tree in Dante comes towards the end of *Purgatorio*. Virgil has taken Dante to the rivers which mark the boundary of the Earthly Paradise, from where he watches a liturgical ceremony in which the pole of the Chariot of the Church is detached and leaned against a dried up tree, which immediately flowers. Allegorically the pole is the Cross, made with wood from the Tree of Life, by which Adam sinned. The restoration of the Cross to its origin symbolises the redemption of Adam from his Fall by Crucifixion, and hence the flowering of the tree, of Adam's stock.[24] Beatrice is waiting for Dante at the other side of the river. After confession, Dante faints and is helped across the river by a woman, Matilda. As a prelude to his ascent to Paradise, Dante has to cross two rivers and he crosses the second one hand in hand with Beatrice. These rivers are the Lethe and the Eunoë; the first makes him forget everything, the second, the river of 'blessed remembrance', returns to him the memory of his sins, but now freed from guilt, transformed into the promise of Grace.

Without trying to labour the point, it is significant that the counterpoint between remembering and forgetting is one of the main characteristics of the novel. Artemio, for example, would wish to forget the least honourable of the motives behind his marriage, financial interest: 'Él deseaba borrar el recuerdo del origen y hacerse querer sin memorias del acto que la obligó a tomarlo por esposo' (101). But before he can forget, he has to face up to the hell of his memory. Regina

[24] See Sayers, 326-7.

compassionately offers to efface the brutal side to her meeting with Artemio, but in a sense it can only be effaced once he has, vicariously, crossed the river in Spain. The meeting will be remembered in its purified state only in its reenactment by Lorenzo and Dolores as a second Regina.[25] Writing about the painter Féliz Cuevas, Fuentes seems to be speaking about his own novel: 'El arte de Félix Cuevas es, a la vez, una memoria indecible y una promesa que habla con los acentos de la resurrección. Una resurrección es una transfiguración: es la imagen del origen sensiblemente re-aparecida.'[26]

Faced with the defeat of the Spanish Republican army in 1939, Lorenzo and his companion Miguel resolve to cross the Pyrenees towards France. They meet three women who accompany them, Dolores, Nuri, and María, reminiscent perhaps of Dante's three female guides Beatrice, Lucia and the Virgin Mary. On approaching the bridge over which they must cross a swollen river, they traverse a 'campo de álamos desnudos'. The density of the symbolic language attached to the river immediately suggests its importance: 'El puente se alargaba, parecía atravesar un océano y no este río encabritado (236).[27] The similarity of images used seems to link this river to the 'tajo de España [que] se abre de mar a mar' (237). In the *Commedia*, the Lethe is compared to the Hellespont, which does link two continents. The Spanish river links two seas, the Mediterranean and the Gulf of Mexico, and the destinies of two men, Lorenzo and his father. Lorenzo had already crossed a river with his father in Cocuya, where 'distinguirán en la otra ribera un espectro de tierra' (167), the same river where, in the idealised version, Artemio meets Regina.

Lorenzo hesitates before crossing, fearing the bridge is mined, but Dolores, taking his hand, gives him courage: 'Él dudó un momento.

[25] Borges, in 'La otra muerte', *El Aleph*, offers a parallel case of memory and the past transformed by divine grace. Pedro Damián is granted the chance to die as a hero in a battle in which forty years earlier he had survived because of his cowardice: 'Así, en 1946, por obra de una larga pasión, Pedro Damián murió en la derrota de Masoller, que ocurrió entre el invierno y la primavera de 1904' (575).
[26] *Casa con dos puertas*, 239.
[27] On the symbolism of the river and the tree, see Liliana Befumo Boschi and Elisa Calabrese, *Nostalgia del futuro en la obra de Carlos Fuentes* (Buenos Aires: Fernando García Cambeiro, 1974), 63–4 and 183.

Ella no. Los diez dedos unidos les dieron calor' (235). Beyond the bridge rises the beautiful and clearly transcendental vision of an elm tree:

> Del otro lado del río, surgió lo que no habían visto. Un gran olmo sin hojas, grande, hermoso, blanco. No lo cubría la nieve, sino un hielo brillante. Brillaba como una joya, de tan blanco, en la noche. [...] así de ligero, luminoso y blanco le parecía ese olmo que los esperaba. [...] Corrieron y abrazaron el tronco desnudo, blanco y cubierto de hielo, lo mecieron mientras esas perlas de frío caían sobre sus cabezas, se tocaron las manos abrazándolo y se separaron violentamente de su árbol para abrazarse Dolores y él [...]. 'Qué tibia, Lola, qué tibia eres y cómo te amo ya.' (236)

Especially if one takes into account the death of Lorenzo, this marvellous elm tree seems to fulfil the same role in *La muerte de Artemio Cruz* as the tree in the Earthly Paradise rejuvenated by the sacrifice of the Son. The love of Lorenzo and Dolores is sealed by their embracing the tree and then each other, and, through them, Artemio can be seen to be reunited with Regina, as Dante is with Beatrice at the equivalent moment. On the following day, Lorenzo dies, machine-gunned from a plane as he tries to defend his companions. The passion of Lorenzo is the acting out of the purification of Artemio through the hell and purgatory of his memory, the reflowering of the seeds of love and revolution in the former revolutionary. Lorenzo by reliving and correcting the story of his father is Christ redeeming Adam.[28]

Death without end

José Gorostiza's *Muerte sin fin* serves as a sort of intertextual ghost to the confident faith of the *Commedia*. With its central theme of the trinity it provides one of the epigraphs of the novel: '... de mí y de Él y de nosotros tres ¡siempre tres!'. His presence reemerges in a chapter where the tension between freedom and destiny, unity and dispersion,

---

[28] On Artemio as Christ, see, among others, Befumo Boschi, 27, 80–81, 85. There are many other Christ-like figures in the novels, who die to 'redeem' another such as Felisberto in 'Chac Mool', Manuel Zamacona in *La región más transparente*, Franz in *Cambio de piel*.

utopian project and tyrannical reality is more keenly felt than ever. The last fragment belonging exclusively to the TÚ voice seems simultaneously to describe the vision of the young Artemio as he leaves his origins in Cocuya and that of the dying old man. Its backdrop is the night and the stars, and, if one accepts the guiding presence of Dante, an evocation of the stars which close the three *cantiche* of the *Commedia* becomes inevitable. In the *Inferno* they represent beauty and hope after the horrors of hell: 'e quindi uscimmo a riveder le stelle'. In the *Purgatorio*, they are the promise of Paradise after purification in the waters of the Eunoë: 'Io rintornai dalla santissim'onda, / rifatto [...] / puro e disposto a salire alle stelle'. In the *Paradiso*, a timeless motor, divine love, lends an equal movement to the world from human will to the stars: 'l'amor che move il sole e l'altre stelle'.

Towards the end of Gorostiza's poem, the full unity or harmony, however fleeting, between man and his Creator, the water and the glass, is reduced to a pathetically unfounded hope. God is a dead star whose light still travels through the universe and in the mind of men, but no longer possesses an origin:

> de ti, que sigues presente
> como una estrella mentida
> por su sola luz, por una
> luz sin estrella, vacía,
> que llega al mundo escondiendo
> su catástrofe infinita.[29]

The star at which the young Artemio is gazing seems to be the same one: 'Muerto en su origen lo que estará vivo en tus sentidos... Perdido, calcinado, el manantial de luz que seguirá viajando, ya sin origen, hacia los ojos de un muchacho en una noche de otro tiempo...' (312). When the light of the star of his youth, with its promises and betrayals, reaches the dying man, it will be a light without origin. The 'amor che move il sole e l'altre stelle', the divine or mythical plane where chaos takes a form and the opposites can be reconciled is absent. The structure of redemption traced by the death of Lorenzo is undermined,

---

[29] José Gorostiza, *Muerte sin fin*, in Héctor Valdés, ed., *Los Contemporáneos: una antología general*, (Mexico City: SEP/UNAM, 1982), 129.

and, given the emptying out of divine time, the sufficiency of a time marked by isolation is questioned: 'tiempo que sólo existirá en la reconstrucción de la memoria aislada, en el vuelo del deseo aislado' (312).

In his final vision in the *Paradiso*, Dante is granted the insight for which Artemio is searching, the ineffable:

> Nel suo profundo vidi che s'interna,
> legato con amor in un volume
> ciò che per l'universo si squaderna;
> sustanzia ed accidenti e lor costume,
> quasi conflati insieme per tal modo,
> che ciò ch'io dico é un semplice lume.
> La forma universal di questo nodo
> credo ch'io vidi. (*Para.*, xxxiii, 85-92)

Cruz's TÚ voice intuits the Dantean 'forma universal', which he calls 'orden universal' and Gorostiza 'pura forma'. In Gorostiza's poem, the opposites which attract each other, form and content, God and man, are reconciled, but only at the very same instant of absolute and final death:

> En la red de cristal que la estrangula
> el agua toma forma,
> [...] un instante, no más,
> no más que el mínimo
> perpetuo instante del quebranto,
> cuando la forma en sí, la pura forma,
> se abandona al designio de su muerte
> y se deja arrastrar, nubes arriba,
> por ese atormentado remolino
> en que los seres todos se repliegan
> hacia el sopor primero,
> a construir el escenario de la nada.
> Las estrellas entonces se ennegrecen.
> Ha vuelto el dardo insomne
> A la noche perfecta de su aljaba. (Gorostiza, 121)

For Cruz, freedom and destiny, the individual and the other, reality and desire will similarly be reconciled, what was 'squadernato' will be reunited in 'un volume', but the secret, given the absence of any paradise where such volumes could be shelved, will remain irrevocably without a reader: 'Vas a ser el punto de encuentro y la razón del orden universal [...]. Para que tú encuentres el secreto y mueras sin poder participarlo, porque sólo lo poseerás cuando tus ojos se cierren para siempre' (313).

The three works considered here rest on a trinitarian form which is intimately a unity. This mystery in Dante is of an orthodox Christian nature. In *Artemio Cruz*, the longed-for unity would be the inconceivable union of the three voices, with their three temporal dimensions. In Gorostiza's poem, the trinity is stalked by unity, but that unity is nothingness. It is the mysterious third element in God, I and...; glass, water, and... At a certain point in the poem it is an abstract, sterile intelligence which refuses to take body in language:

> sin admitir en su unidad perfecta
> el escarnio brutal de esa discordia
> que nutren vida y muerte inconciliables. (Gorostiza, 112)

As an accomplice of death, that intelligence mocks the possibility of any union:

> Con Él, conmigo, con nosotros tres;
> como el agua y el vaso, sólo una
> que reconcentra su silencio blanco
> en la orilla letal de la palabra. (Gorostiza, 113)

There is a parallel passage in *Artemio Cruz*: 'El niño, la tierra, el universo: en los tres, algún día, no habrá ni luz, ni calor, ni vida... Habrá sólo la unidad total, olvidada, sin nombre y sin hombre que la nombre' (313).

Much of *La muerte de Artemio Cruz* revolves around the nostalgia for paradise, the Paradise visited by Dante, that which takes shape by a tree in the Pyrenees. Again, the terrifying vision of Gorostiza comes to undo the hope generated by the Dantean structure. The final origins will not be the paradisal life with Lunero in Cocuya, but silence:

> Cuando todo [...]
> regresa a sus orígenes
> y al origen fatal de sus orígenes
> hasta que su mismo eco se instala
> en el primer silencio tenebroso. (Gorostiza, 124)

For Fuentes too, entropy is waiting at the end: 'El sol se está quemando vivo, el fierro se está derrumbando en polvo, la energía sin rumbo se está disipando en el espacio, las masas se están gastando en la radiación, la tierra se está enfriando de muerte...' (312-3).

In *La muerte de Artemio Cruz*, Dante and Gorostiza do not cancel each other out, they coexist and dialogue. The desire for order and love, for a revolution which would embody the ideals of Lorenzo, coexists and dialogues with the consciousness of death, the fragility of human projects, the curse of Ludivinia, *la chingada*. This dialogue is the tragic consciousess of evil within good, tyranny and corruption within the revolution.

II: SERIOUS GAMES

Cambio de piel, 1967; *Zona sagrada*, 1967

Cambio de piel and *Zona sagrada* encapsulate the exciting dismantling of aesthetic hierarchies and the moral and political ferment of the late sixties. *Cambio de piel* is a major novel which combines radical literary experiment with intense ethical speculation and while the latter dimension is largely absent from the much shorter, playful but pretty demanding *Zona sagrada*, the two novels have much in common. *Zona sagrada* was written after the main bulk of *Cambio de piel* had been completed, but before its conclusion.

Both novels largely move away from the preoccupation with Mexico, its history and national identity, which marked the early novels. The powerfully structured plots of *La región más transparente* and *La muerte de Artemio Cruz* have also disappeared. *Zona sagrada* is set in Mexico City and Italy. The present of *Cambio de piel* is a car trip from Mexico City to Cholula, but evokes not only Mexico but Germany, Greece, Argentina, the USA and elsewhere. These are highly literary novels, self-aware, flamboyantly experimental and wide open to all the intellectual concerns of the moment. They are marked by paradox and contradiction, and play with the conventions of representation and referentiality in a way that decentres and perplexes the reader.

Cambio de piel takes on some extremely weighty themes, the recurrence of violence through history from the genocide of the native Mexicans, through the Holocaust, to the imperialist excesses and authoritarianism of the Cold War period. The radical play with literary convention aims to undermine the certainties and unquestioned naturalness of the position of the powerful subject, narrator and reader, which allows what is different to be reified, turned into spectacle, demonized or exterminated. Though both are powerful novels, it is the discourse of power which they have in their aim.

Both, but more explicitly *Cambio de piel*, appeal to a wide range of disciplines and engage in a lively dialogue with many thinkers and other texts. Foucault's writing, for example, on authority and on madness are important for Fuentes's treatment of madness, the asylum at Cholula and generally the notion of the Other. Many thinkers on the notion of tragedy are evoked, especially Friedrich Nietzsche. Tragedy is seen as a practice or attitude which allows a meaningful relationship with evil and otherness in oneself and in others, set against facile optimism and Enlightenment certainties.

The debates on language, or more generally artistic representation, depth and humanism, are also carried over into *Zona sagrada*, where Susan Sontag against interpretation, Robbe-Grillet for surfaces and against psychological depth, and Charles Baudelaire on the dandy become interlocutors and collaborators. The two-dimensional cinema screen is important here: the novels are both about cinema, German expressionism, Fellini and the Mexican films of María Félix, etc., and experiment with techniques derived from cinematic practice. Allied to the presence of cinema is that of the structuralism and structural anthropology of the time, especially that of Claude Lévi-Strauss and his ideas on myth. Myths no longer depend on a hierarchy of originality, but are the sum of all their versions. Well-known myths such as that of Ulysses or Jason and Medea are evoked and used to suggest a powerful structural underpinning only to be dissolved and ironised by alternative versions, inconclusiveness, carnivalesque mockery.

The writing here is often highly stylised and marked by a corrosive coexistence of registers, of densely packed high cultural reference and the popular: Beatles songs and Nietzsche, Baudelaire and Elvis Presley, Renaissance frescoes and pinups of sexy Italian divas. Underneath the noise, however, and the dizzying transfigurations, many basic themes are carried over from the early novels. The rather solemn, provincial Oedipal struggles of *Las buenas conciencias* are translated into the altogether racier, sexier and more privileged scene of the Mexico City film actress and her court. Whereas Jaime Ceballos finally manages to visit the local brothel and see his uncle in a silly position, Guillermito turns into a dog and imagines watching while his mother copulates with his double Giancarlo. The doubling between the doer Artemio Cruz and the idealist Gonzalo Bernal is reworked in that between the architect Franz and the unproductive writer Javier in *Cambio de piel*. The youthful writing of Rodrigo Pola spied on and resented by the mother Rosenda is reflected in Javier and the disapproving vigilance of first his mother and later his wife Elizabeth.

Cambio de piel, 1967: Literature and Evil

Cambio de piel is perhaps Fuentes's most difficult and disturbing novel. Its challenge is summed up for me by the question '¿Nietzsche y Breton, jefes de pelotón en Auschwitz?', followed by the injunction 'En todo caso, tú cita a tus clásicos y sé feliz'.[1] In a novel which certainly does quote its classics, which is overwhelmingly intertextual, it is impossible to discuss the nature of evil without questioning the status of literary discourse as represented there. Literature and evil can both be extreme forms of encounter with the Other. One of the few certainties the reader has on closing *Cambio de piel* is the relentless recurrence of evil and violence throughout history. When the four characters, Javier, Elizabeth, Franz and Isabel, enter the ancient religious centre of Cholula on Palm Sunday 1965, they repeat the entry of Cortés over four centuries before in the early stages of the genocide of the indigenous Mexicans. They are in turn shadowed by their doubles, the hippie Monjes in their Lincoln convertible, who finally kill one of the party in the pyramid. The pyramid is echoed in construction and function by the concentration camp at Terezin built twenty-odd years before by Franz. The ultimate evil, the Holocaust, which is enacted there is echoed by evocations of pogroms throughout the history of the West. What the Spaniards did to the *cholultecas*, and Gentiles to the Jews, man is seen to do to woman, dressing her in the guise of otherness as with the witches Jeanne Fréry and Mrs Samuel, and the character Elizabeth, often called Medea by her husband Javier. What the Nazis do to the Jewish prisoners in making them sing their own requiem, turning them into spectacle, the Paris bourgeoisie did to the insane in Charenton, and the characters to those in the lunatic asylum in Cholula. What is different in the novel, the Other, is repeatedly seen to be enclosed or exterminated.

---

[1] *Cambio de piel* (Barcelona: Seix Barral, 1974), 83.

Some Thoughts from the Essays

Fuentes's essays of the period, *La nueva novela hispanoamericana* (1969) and *Casa con dos puertas* (1970), contain a series of considerations which help with a reading of *Cambio de piel*.[2] Particularly relevant is his treatment of what I have called the 'Other' and various forms of discourse. This relationship involves discussion of the concept of tragedy, of recuperation, isolation, and the play between structure and its dissolution. Tradition and intertextuality provide the framework within which the text pluralises and challenges structure. As in previous novels, but in a more complex fashion, the relation to pre-existing textual structures and their repetition is in turn linked to relationships with parents.

The most primitive reaction to the Other is the temptation to exterminate it. Writing on *Moby Dick*, Fuentes sees Ahab's determination to kill the whale as springing from pride and solipsism: 'El activismo individualista debe llegar a su extremo afirmativo: la muerte de la ballena blanca, del 'otro'. ¿Qué mejor prueba de *yo* que la supresión de *no-yo*?'(CDP 43). From Ahab, the essayist extrapolates to the Cold War politics of the USA and specifically to McCarthyism:

> La verdad de los demás [for many North Americans] es sospechosa y debe ser destruida. Sí: en nuestros días el capitán Ahab sigue viviendo y se llama McArthur y Dulles, McArthur y Johnson; la ballena blanca está en Cuba, en China, en Vietnam, en Santo Domingo, en una película, en un libro ...
>
> (CDP, 49)

As efficient as extermination is the process of taming or recuperation whereby rebellion is turned into a consumer article or exhibit:

> La fuerza de esas sociedades ha consistido en que incluso la palabra enemiga era transformada en bien de consumo. La rebeldía degeneraba en moda, al rebelde se le adulaba, compraba, consagraba; y el icoloclasta terminaba en icono, encarcelado, como un simio detrás de la reja del zoológico, tocando

---

[2] *La nueva novela hispanoamericana* (Mexico City: Joaquín Mortiz, 1972) and *Casa con dos puertas* (Mexico City: Joaquín Mortiz, 1970), abbreviated herein as NNH and CDP.

la guitarra eléctrica y agitando la melena frente a los consumidores-domadores satisfechos. (NNH, 89-90)

Turning to the classical Latin American novel, the *novela criolla* or *novela de la tierra* of the 1920s and 1930s, he argues that the ills of the continent, such as those encapsulated in Sarmiento's notion of *barbarie*, were treated in such a mythifying manner as to isolate them from the rest of reality, alien to the writer, outside the realms of his responsibility: 'La mitad negra de la historia latinoamericana emergía en la viejas novelas de Gallegos, Rivera e Icaza como la encarnación de un mal aislado, impenetrable, tremendista, finalmente irrisorio por ajeno y por definido' (NNH, 66).

The term *isolation* used here in 'la encarnación de un mal aislado' is an important one for Fuentes's vision of the period. Fuentes likes to quote from Styron's novel *Lie Down in Darkness* the lines 'Didn't that show you that the wages of sin is not death, but isolation?'[3] The world is described as 'nuestro mundo de esferas aisladas' (NNH, 9). In a letter to Octavio Paz, Fuentes complains of the same isolationism in Mexican criticism: 'el aislamiento es el virus maligno de la crítica en México'.[4]

The character who represents the temptation of Nazism in the novel, Herr Urs, significantly claims: 'Mi libertad es mi aislamiento. [...] Desde mi aislamiento, ejerzo el poder de una lejana contaminación. [...] Soy una tentación porque nadie me reconoce. Muero en el momento en que alguien cree descubrirme' (480). The Narrator of the novel has been confined in a lunatic asylum / lazaretto: 'Lazarillo: a lo largo y ancho de este lazareto en que el aislamiento de la lepra crea la ilusión de la vida gracias al amor de la crueldad' (496). The main masculine characters Javier and Franz are forged by a complex dialectic between isolation and complicity, escape and participation, separation and identification, in a way similar to the disjunction between *solo* and *juntos* in *La región más transparente* and other novels. In the German Franz, the 'sueño heroico' (421) and the 'exaltación solitaria' (403) of the individual lead to 'complicidad ciega' (421) in evil and collective crime. For the Mexican writer Javier the relationship between the two

---

[3] *Cambio de piel*, 184; William Styron, *Lie Down in Darkness* (London: Black Swan, 1984), 269.

[4] 'Seis cartas de Carlos Fuentes a Octavio Paz', *Revista iberoamericana*, 37:74, 1971, 21.

terms is far more self-consciously internalised and complex. He is more of an idealist when he speaks of transforming 'las relaciones del mundo para que todos [...] seamos personas solas y solidarias' (426). More lucidly despairing is Freddy Lambert's phrase: 'entre escapar y participar, sólo nos queda escoger nuestra enfermedad, nuestro cáncer personal, nuestra parodia de las grandes síntesis' (122). Only to the Beatles is it given to reconcile 'la lejanía cesárea y la participación satánica' (268). To separation and isolation Fuentes in his essays opposes poetry, myth and tragedy. The reference to the tragic, especially, in the two volumes of essays, is constant. *La nueva novela hispanoamericana* carries an epigraph from Jean-Marie Domenach's *Le Retour du tragique*, and quotes from it in the text, drawing on its treament of the tragic thought of Hegel, Hölderlin, Goldmann, and others. Traces of Steiner's *The Death of Tragedy* are apparent in the novel, especially in the quotations found there of *King Lear*, Büchner and Kleist. Nietzsche, whose *The Birth of Tragedy* is central to the novel, even has his photograph reproduced in its pages. The writer whom Fuentes chooses to discuss under the rubric of tragedy in *Casa con dos puertas*, William Faulkner, is from the USA, where tragic thought, according to Fuentes, is least at home. It is significant that Faulkner is from the South, a region which, like Latin America, has known failure and defeat.

Against the certainties of power, 'la tragedia es ambigua' (CDP, 57), a characteristc which it shares with poetry: 'Sólo la poesía, en este sentido lato, sabe interrogar, porque sólo la poesía puede proponer, simultáneamente, argumentos conflictivos entre sí' (CDP, 60). Both ambiguity and the simultaneous use of conflicting arguments are essential characteristics of *Cambio de piel*. Tragedy shows up the limits of optimistic rationalism, saving one from alienation in its promises and from falling into nihilism when they are disappointed: 'Gracias a escritores como Dostoievski, Kafka y Faulkner, que restauran la advertencia trágica, podemos acompañar a la razón dentro de sus límites sin enajenarnos en sus ilusiones' (CDP, 78). In this sense, tragedy as a limit to rationalism plays a role close to that of madness, not surprisingly, perhaps, given the role of Dyonisian madness in tragedy according to Nietzsche. Erasmus's *In Praise of Folly* serves as a similar model in the later collection of essays *Cervantes o la crítica de la lectura*.

The tragic is also a consciousness of one's own guilt and responsibility; fatality is not simply an outside force, but another within: 'Creyéndose libre, el hombre descubre que no puede separarse de sí mismo: el desafío final de la libertad consiste en saber que *el otro que me domina soy yo mismo*' (CDP, 72). Tragic consciousness thus works against the complacent separation of the one from the other, against *aislamiento*. The consciousness of one's separation from oneself and from the realisation of one's desires renews human effort: 'la visión trágica [...] es, a un tiempo, el hecho de la separación y su conciencia, hecho y conciencia que renuevan la voluntad revolucionaria' (NNH, 90). Thus, while being aware of the repeated failure of human projects in history, the tragic word continues to affirm hope and freedom: 'Y porque su visión [the novel of the sixties] es la de la tragedia (ya no la del drama o el melodrama): el hombre, como sus palabras, es el vehículo de una esperanza que, a sabiendas de su inevitable fracaso, se mantiene en el acto de manifestarse' (CDP, 82). Fuentes comes very close here to the vision of the tragic as expressed in the novels of Alejo Carpentier from *El reino de este mundo* (1949) to *El siglo de las luces* (1963).[5]

Against the partial languages of ideology and authority, literary language offers a totality and a belief in the total powers of expression and desire which were to explode in the *événements* of May 1968, one year after the publication of Fuentes's novel which, the novelist argues, only takes on its full meaning in the light of the events of the period.[6] The novel of the 1960s, including the Latin American novel, becomes

[5] In *El reino de este mundo* Ti Noel watched the mythical project of the black monarchy in Haiti turn into tyranny in the historical reality of Henri Christophe, as the Narrator of *Los pasos perdidos* listened to Schiller's *Ode to Joy* being sung in Auschwitz, and Victor Hugues in *El siglo de las luces* saw the French Revolution culminate in the prison camps of French Guyana. Ti Noel 'comprendía, ahora, que el hombre nunca sabe para quién padece y espera. Padece y espera y trabaja para gentes que nunca conocerá, y que a su vez padecerán y esperarán y trabajarán para otros que tampoco serán felices' (*El reino de este mundo* (Barcelona: Seix Barral, 1967), 147-8).

[6] In private conversation, 1986. Fuentes's interest in the phenomenon is reflected in his *París, la revolución de mayo* (Mexico City: Era, 1968). Note also the link made by Elena Poniatowska between the novel and the protests and subsequent massacre at Tlatelolco in *¡Ay vida, no me mereces!* (Mexico City: Joaquín Mortiz, 1986), 28.

internationalist in its language and world of reference. Fuentes associates this tendency with the decentring project of structural anthropology and linguistics:[7]

> Al abrirse a la universalidad de las estructuras lingüísticas, el novelista de los sesentas se abrió también a los supuestos de esa universalidad: la multiplicidad y validez contingua de los lenguajes en sentido histórico-cultural, la disolución de las distinciones culturales entre pueblos 'civilizados' y 'primitivos', la extensión ecuménica del espacio del pensamiento'. (CDP, 85)

The breaking down of centralised hierarchies in this movement clearly also works against the separation of discourses decried by Fuentes, and his subversive juxtaposition of widely different discourses in the novel reflects the new consciousness.

Literary structures, themes and texts are 'lugares comunes', common places against the 'esferas aisladas'; clichés provide a common ground, a communal habitation: 'Después de todo, el lugar común es eso, un sitio de encuentro, una posibildad inicial de diálogo y, como tal, posee ciertas virtudes que nuestro mundo de esferas aisladas no debe sacrificar' (NNH, 9). This 'sitio (lugar de resistencias)' (NNH, 66) is repeatedly invoked in *Cambio de piel* in the question of origins (and destination):

> Hay que estar en un lugar, cualquier lugar, aunque lo inventemos, para poder empezar de vuelta, para renacer.
> —Un sitio, dragona, un lugar donde resisitir. ¡Jalisco, que no se raja! ¡Veracruz, que sólo es bello! [...]

---

[7] This internationalism and insistence on the primacy of language provoked intemperate responses from critics such as the Cuban Roberto Fernández Retamar. See his *Calibán*, in José Enrique Rodó, *Ariel* and R. Fernández Retamar, *Calibán* (Mexico City: SEP / UNAM, 1982), 125. A similarly hostile response, from a specifically Mexican point of view, is intelligently and energetically developed by Jorge Ruiz Basto in *De la modernidad y otras creencias (en torno a 'Cambio de piel' de Carlos Fuentes)* (Mexico City: UNAM, 1992). For a detailed commentary on this study, see my review in *Literatura Mexicana*, 4:1 (1993), 236–9. For an account of Fuentes's relations with Cuba, see Maarten Van Delden, 41–50.

—Grecia, ¿qué tal?, la armonía, el clasicismo, el espíritu, nuestra maldita cuna. (96)

The mention of Greece is very important. In Javier and Elizabeth's (possible) trip to Greece, Javier searches for the 'noble simplicity and serene greatness'[8] which so many Germans sought there after it had been perceived by Winckelmann in the eighteenth century in the Laocoön group sculpture. Nietzsche discovered a far harsher and more exhilarating culture there, but looked upon Greece as a home in a centreless world: 'One is no longer at home anywhere, so in the end one longs to be back where one can somehow *be* at home because it is the only place where one would *wish* to be at home: and that is the world of Greece!'[9] Javier's trip to Veracruz is a local version of the epic journey back to the homeland in Greece, 'punto de partida y retorno' (264) according to his poem *El vellocino de oro*. What he expects to find there is the serene detachment from reality and the emotional balance expressed by Rainer Maria Rilke in the second of his *Duino's Elegies*: '¿No te sorprendió la circunspección del gesto humano es las estelas áticas?' (109). But his wife Elizabeth comes to embody a terrible religious certainty and a voracious sexual exigency. His fear is projected onto the fat German tourist Rudy, who amuses himself flicking pebbles at his wife and who that very afternoon is drowned by her in the sea. The sea, about which Javier often dreams (48), is the threat from the maternal, the unconscious that Javier yearns for and dreads. The serene Greece of Winckelmann, Goethe, Lessing and Rilke turns into the Dionysian panic described by Nietzsche in *The Birth of Tragedy*.

Origins and originality are equally problematical in the novel. Elizabeth may or may not be a New York Jewess; Elizabeth and Javier may have invented their stay in Greece and the origins of their love there from a collection of old papers in a chest. If Javier sought for origins in Greece, in his literature he sought for originality, Faustian knowledge: 'lo que el mundo aún no descubre y quizá jamás descubra

---

[8] Quoted by E.M. Butler in *The Tyranny of Greece over Germany* (Cambridge: Cambridge University Press, 1935), 46. See also M. Van Delden, 'The Banquets of Civilization: the Idea of Ancient Greece in Rodó, Reyes and Fuentes', in *Annals of Scholarship*, 7:3, 1990, 303-21.

[9] Quoted by Silk and Stern, *Nietzsche on Tragedy* (Cambridge: CUP, 1983), 4.

en sí mismo' (297). He writes a story where the protagonist manages to reincarnate his youth in order to love again with retrospective desire. He seems to refer to Fuentes's novella *Aura* where Felipe Montero loves the young Aura only to discover that he is acting for another: the long-dead General Llorente. Elizabeth reveals to Javier that she had got the story-line for him by going to bed with the writer Vasco Montero (surely a relation of Felipe Montero). Where he thought he was alone and original, he finds the other, Bloom's 'strong ancestor'. Literature, like life, demands the presence of others, being a collective creation. Literature is man's house, *zona sagrada*, and hence the inescapable intertextuality of the novel, its dialogue with classical texts. In *Casa con dos puertas* Fuentes makes this explicit: 'Lo cierto es que una obra siempre está escrita (o inscrita) en el lenguaje, como el destino de Valentín en la piel de zapa: el lenguaje es, por definición, creación colectiva' (CDP, 76). The fact that his own text has been written before is then perhaps the meaning of the enigmatic phrase on the first page of the novel: 'Terminado, el libro empieza.'

Repetition is thus inherent in literature as it is in living. For Mircea Eliade ritual is the repetition of the original founding acts. For Borges, famously, 'Quizá la historia universal es la historia de unas cuantas metáforas.'[10] In *Cambio de piel* we read: 'Cada hombre que nace es la creación original. Debe repetir para sí y para el mundo todos los actos antiguos, como si nada hubiese sucedido antes de él' (489-90). (Javier's ritual in the motel with Elizabeth and then with Isabel is the same and yet different.) The parental model here as elsewhere is central, as Javier says of his parents: 'Le juro que sólo he recordado a Raúl y a Ofelia para saber si ya vivieron en mi nombre. Si puedo dejar de repetir lo que ellos ya hicieron' (447).[11] And later the text asks: '¿Enloqueció Becky para que la locura de Elizabeth mereciera el nombre de razón? ¿Desapareció Raúl para que la fuga de Javier mereciera el nombre de encuentro?' (474).

This repetition of models, parental and textual, produces a sense of unfreedom or destiny. In Cortázar's 62. *Modelo para armar* (1968), in

[10] 'La esfera de Pascal', in *Otras inquisiciones, Obras completas,* 636.
[11] Note Freud's quotation in a similar context of the phrase from Goethe's *Faust*: 'What thou has inherited from thy fathers, acquire it to make it thine' (*Totem and Taboo*, in *The Origins of Religion*, The Pelican Freud Library (Harmondsworth: Penguin, 1985), XIII, 221).

many ways the twin novel of *Cambio de piel*, the *figuras* which dictate aspects of the lives of the characters are similarly literary texts and myths.[12] Various characters in Fuentes's novel are made to repeat previous texts: Javier and Elizabeth those they write and collect in the chest: 'cada vez que escribíamos una escena posible [...] nos condenamos a repetirla después, tarde o temprano' (96-97). More literally, the Jewish singers are made to repeat the text of Verdi's *Requiem* by the Nazis, and the Monjes are forced to repeat the script of the trial of Franz and Javier.

When asked whether the all-pervasive intertextuality was not a sign of determinism for the characters, Fuentes agreed and added that one 'se da cuenta de que uno no es libre, para luego afirmar su libertad'.[13] One is again reminded of Cortázar: 'A la luz de figuras arquetípicas toda prohibición es un claro consejo: abre la puerta, ábrela ahora mismo.'[14] The answer to this dilemma is hinted at by the Jewish singers and the Monjes: to rebel within the text, modify it, contaminate it, make it mean something other than it originally did. The Monjes, who occasionally deviate from the script they have to read, are in turn repeating the literary model of Peter Weiss's *Marat / Sade*, the full title of which explains its content: *The Persecution and Assassination of Marat as Performed by the Inmates of the Asylum of Charenton under the Direction of the Marquis de Sade*. At one point, the madmen actors break out of the straitjacket of the script to chant: 'Freedom Freedom Freedom'.[15] Echoing this outburst, the Jewish musicians break the rhythm of Verdi and his text when they come to the words 'Libera me', which they repeat to the banging of drums and the dismay of the organisers of their concert (409). These images are a clear indication of Fuentes's relationship to the texts he uses in his novel. The pattern is parallel to that which he distinguishes in tragedy: the recognition of fatality and its conversion into freedom.

[12] See Boldy, *The Novels of Julio Cortázar*, 115-37.
[13] In conversation, 1986.
[14] 'Para una espeleología a domicilio', in *Último round* (Mexico City: Siglo XXI, 1969), bottom deck, 50. Fuentes has told me that it was Cortázar's idea, after reading the original manuscript, that he should write and add the final parody trial section.
[15] Peter Weiss, *Marat / Sade* (London: Marion Boyars, 1978), 21.

Myth or Epic as Structure, Infanticide, Doubles

In the essays Fuentes describes his relation with the intertextual model in structuralist terms borrowed from Paul Ricœur: structure and change, system and event. No meaning is possible without the pre-existing structures of language and literature, the *lugares comunes*; no life or meaning is possible without the constant change, use and modification of those structures: a dialectical rebellion against their inevitability. In the novels of Fuentes, myth is often used as a metonym for authoritarian structures. The control, closure, certainty and inevitability of myth is in various novels represented by the story of Ulysses, his inexorable return home to his origins in Ithaca and his faithful wife Penelope. In *Zona sagrada*, which makes much use of this epic journey, the repetition of the story is a clear accomplice of the status quo: 'El mito [...] debe tener un final, feliz o desgraciado, pero previsto. [...] El varón clásico, la mujer fiel, el hijo pródigo. Y fueron muy felices.'[16] As an image of his undoing of the univocality of the epic structure, *Zona sagrada* offers an alternative ending to the story: Ulysses is murdered by his son Telegonus whom he fathered with Circe. Telegonus marries Penelope, while Telemachus marries Circe. Penelope and the sorceress Circe becomes ciphers for permanence and change.[17] The soldier father of Giancarlo is reported dead and considered a hero, whereas his son believes that he has simply stayed with a whore in Tripoli, that is, with Circe. In *Gringo viejo*, Harriet Winslow's father, similarly considered a hero of the 1898 Spanish American War, stays with a mulatta in Cuba. His empty grave in Arlington is fraudulently filled by the body of another man.

The dialectical use and subversion of the myth is seen as an assertion of openness against closure, polysemia and ambiguity which will not easily be recuperated by conventional, ideological meaning:

---

[16] *Zona sagrada* (México: Siglo XXI, 1976), 5.
[17] Ortega y Gasset in *La deshumanización del arte* (Madrid: Revista de Occidente / Alianza, 1983), 28, uses a remarkably similar image to describe the struggle of the modern artist against representational realism: 'La "realidad" acecha constantemente al artista para impedir su evasión. ¡Cuánta astucia supone la fuga genial! Ha de ser un Ulises al revés, que se liberta de su Penélope cuotidiana y entre escollos navega hacia el brujerío de Circe.'

La novela de los sesentas, al definirse como forma verbal abierta e inasimilable a los 'mass media', inmediatamente adquiere un rango revolucionario (CDP, 82);
El lenguaje, en suma, de la ambigüedad: de la pluralidad de significados, de la constelación de alusiones, de la apertura. (NNH, 32)

Immobility becomes fluidity: 'El mito es renovable' (NNH, 22). The text becomes the 'sitio' where renewal, 'change of skin', emerges from what was potentially a fatality.

In *Cambio de piel*, myth has the same meaning: 'Es un mito, date cuenta. No hay suspenso. Ya conoces el desenlace de antemano. Ulises regresará a Ítaca. Penélope será fiel a su telar. Medea matará a sus propios hijos. ¿Qué esperabas?' (237). Javier travels back from Argentina to Mexico-Ithaca, but rather than Ulysses, Jason is the main figure associated with Javier. The journey provides a general framework for the novel as the four characters set off from Mexico City for a beach holiday in Veracruz in a Volkswagen Beetle. Veracruz, the home state of the Fuentes family, is in a sense the origin of modern Mexico, the landing place of Hernán Cortés. But the journey is interrupted when the car breaks down and ends in the death of some of the characters in the pyramid at Cholula, near Puebla. *Cambio de piel* is thus, as Fuentes has called other Spanish American novels, a 'peregrinación inconclusa' (NNH, 67). Javier's own work, *El vellocino de oro* (The Golden Fleece) is similarly unfinished; the ultimate Faustian secret is left unrevealed. The destination is not reached, the return to the origin is suspended, mocked.

Elizabeth is particularly affected by the temptation to return. In Xochicalco, she is attracted by the embrace of the circular stone serpent, and the equivalences developed in the text are revealing: house, return, religion, nature, power, Faustian knowledge:

Conozco tu tentación. Lo sentiste como un círculo de violencia que lo aprisiona todo. [...] Estuviste a punto de decir que así, así, así lo querías, deseabas ser tragada, perder la identidad o perder la voluntad, ser la esclava abúlica de un poder semejante. Casi dijiste que esto buscabas, que aquí te quedarías, en esta casa sagrada, esta casa de oración, esta Beth Hattefilah, otra vez. [...] ibas a creer que en esta pérdida encontrarías la semilla secreta del país. [...] O.K. Has leído bien tu D.H. Lawrence [...] volvió a tentarte ese caudal de palabras aprendidas. [...] Ibas a gritarle a la tierra que te dejara regresar, que no te volviera a arrojar al exilio. Ibas a orar por ese sitio donde te tentaba vivir con los ojos cerrados. Otra vez tu Juiverie, [...] tu maldito Ghetto. [...] Óyeme, dragona: se acabó Fausto. (42-43)

Religious certainties in the novel are more associated with women than with men, whose identity and freedom are threatened by them. Elizabeth acquires another, similar certainty on a mountain top in Greece and pursues Javier with her beliefs and desires in the same way as her mother had done to her father Gerson, while a similar figure to the latter, Javier's travelling salesman father Raúl, is expelled from his house to wander as a latter-day, unheroic and disoriented Ulysses.

In fact Elizabeth attempts to do to Javier what his own mother had earlier done to him. The 'seguridad', the 'mentira suficiente que nos consuela y paraliza' (294) acquired by Elizabeth in Greece, is associated with a church interior seen as an asphyxiating womb: 'ese viente dorado, [...] ese claustro irrespirable' (295). Ofelia had refused to sell the family house, believing it to be a force of order and certainty against chaos and the 'algo brutal que acechaba fuera de la casa': 'un deseo de vencer la anarquía desde el centro de una fuerza doméstica en la que él pudiera crecer protegido' (234). Writing is a rebellion against such certainties, as it is against nature. Both women spy on Javier and open the letters about his publications: his mother when his first book is accepted and Elizabeth when a manuscript is rejected (198, 226, 488-9). Both occasions are traumatic and Ofelia is as mortally offended by her son's writing as Rodrigo Pola's mother had been in *La región más transparente*: 'Me has humillado, me has mentido, eres indecente' (307).

The return to the origins, to the permanent house, is mocked in the treatment of the parental bed, the seat of legitimacy, which takes on a dizzying plurality of roles. It is in Ofelia's bed, now in Prague, that the corpse of the dwarf Herr Urs, associated with Nazism and the making of obscene dolls, is found. We come across the bed again in the final parody section in Mexico City when an orgy is held in the brothel which Javier's house had later become.[18] When he sells the house,

---

[18] There is a parallel scene in Proust's *À l'ombre des jeunes filles en fleurs*, where Marcel gives a 'grand canapé' which had belonged to his aunt Léonie to a brothel. On rediscovering it there, he muses that 'j'aurais fait violer une morte que je n'aurais pas souffert davantage' (*À la recherche du temps perdu*

Javier does not reclaim the bed and what it represents: 'Nomás no regresó' (462). Any sense of sacrality or permanent identity is thoroughly undone:

> Veo en esa cama revuelta, con remates de urnas y vides, en medio de los almohadones inmensos, a la Pálida que dice ser Elizabeth que es llamada Ligeia que es famosa como Elena que es frecuentada como la prostituta del templo fenicio que es adorada como María salvada que es madre del Salvador. (458)

But this fertile desecration and transformation allows the scene to become the occasion of a birth, a new beginning, as a porcelain doll representing Christ is born to La Pálida. This dialectical consecration and profanation of the origins is expressed well in a slightly different context by the Monjes: 'este baile es pura improvisación y al mismo tiempo es un rito, ahí está lo durazno' (432). The 'improvised ritual' of the text creates the fertile new space for the 'change of skin'.

The tragedy of Jason and Medea structures the novel in considerable detail. It introduces the theme of filicide or infanticide, which provides an important link between the doubles Javier and Franz, who develop key oppsitions such as those between action and contemplation, certainty and doubt, animal and man. Euripides's *Medea* is quoted verbatim in the text and the general plot line echoed throughout.[19] Elizabeth, often referred to as Medea by her husband Javier, is only one of a long line of witches in Fuentes, and it may be relevant, given the theme of the recovery of the past or the failure to do do, that Medea was able to restore youth.[20] Medea, like Elizabeth, was taken from her

(Paris: Gallimard, 1999), 459).

[19] For example, 'I'd rather stand three times in the front line than bear / one child' (*Medea and Other Plays* (Harmondsworth: Penguin, 1979), 25); 'Pues yo preferiría salir a luchar en una guerra que dar a luz una sola vez...' (*Cambio de piel*, 374, 277). Also: 'I married you [...], no woman, but a tiger' (*Medea*, 58); 'Me casé con una tigesa, no con una mujer; [...] Javier, ahora no; no repitas palabras que no son tuyas' (*Cambio de piel*, 370).

[20] The return from the dead in another form is also the theme of Poe's 'Ligeia', another name given by Javier to Elizabeth. Elizabeth is reborn in a way in her namesake, the young Mexican Isabel, as Ligeia is in Lady Rowena. A phrase which Poe uses an an epigraph to his story and repeats throughout his text is also used in *Cambio de piel*: 'Man doth not yield himself to the angels, nor

homeland by Jason-Javier, after defeating the monsters with her aid. As they escaped she killed her brother to slow down their pursuers. Elizabeth's brother Jake is killed while she and Javier are together with him in the park. At the beginning of the Euripides play, Jason has just decided to abandon Medea in favour of Glauce, daughter of king Creon. Medea takes her revenge in two ways: she sends a magic dress to Glauce which bursts into flames and kills her rival and then murders the children from her union with Jason. Both episodes are re-enacted in the novel: Elizabeth the foreigner is abandoned towards the end of the novel for her young alter ego and namesake, the Mexican Isabel, to whom she gives a shawl which Javier subsequently uses to strangle her. The filicide comes with the abortion that Elizabeth mentions briefly (323, 375), and for which each spouse blames the other: Javier claiming that she did not wish to lose her youthful looks and she claiming that he did not want interference with his literary production, which was not eventually forthcoming. Such bickering and mutual recrimination are also present in the Euripides text, and therein, of course, lies the tragic ambiguity. (Freddy Lambert reads a parallel story of triple filicide from the newspaper, where he also finds parallels for other episodes (33).)

This abortion is perhaps Javier's real sin, the one which most approximates him to the ex-Nazi Franz, who allows the son of his abandoned Jewish lover Hanna to be sent to Auschwitz and watches children taken off the trains for his own camp. This theme refers us back to the final birth of the doll-saviour, which seems to be all the children who have been killed in the text, as it is given to Elena (a Greek woman from the couple's trip to Greece, a helper in the brothel, a dwarf and as 'elenano' (Elena, *enano*) linked to the doll-mender dwarf Herr Urs, as Helen of Troy, archetypal woman): 'Escóndelo de la policía, chaparrita. No dejes que te lo degüellen. No dejes que te lo tiren al basurero. No dejes que te lo metan al horno. Ten tu niño perdido' (459). The mention of the *horno* refers us to Nazi Germany, to Franz, while the 'niño perdido' refers us to the Calzada del Niño Perdido (74, 232, 441), where Javier's childhood home was (and thus

    unto death utterly, save only through the weakness of his feeble will' (Edgar Allan Poe, *Selected Writings* (Harmondsworth: Penguin, 1975), 110; *Cambio de piel*, 148, 330, 457).

the brothel), and where Javier is described as having been lost. Elena is thus again linked with the figure of the mother. Javier, by refusing to publish, finally does not sell his soul for literature, but nevertheless his child dies exactly like the child of Faust, in both Goethe's and Thomas Mann's versions. Franz, on the other hand, clearly does receive the visit of a Mephistopheles character, Herr Urs, which seems to reinforce the parallels between them. The fact remains that Javier the writer is linked with filicide, literature with the death of the child. Elizabeth's mother makes a weighted comment which may provisionally serve us to approach the question: 'Sí, Becky, el Dios de Israel existe fuera de nosotros. No es un fantasma más, inventado por estos hombres que aman mujeres irreales y matan niños inocentes' (461). Literature, as we have seen, is a rebellion against religious certainty and nature, both associated with women. Javier, with Elizabeth and elsewhere, prefers the 'representación de la naturaleza' to 'la naturaleza misma' (292) that Elizabeth desires to embody, the 'mujer irreal' which he invents to the ultimate and complete knowledge of the real woman, which would threaten absorption and madness.[21] As in Nietzsche's *The Birth of Tragedy*, the Dionysian contemplation of the destruction and formlessness of nature must be compensated by the invention and individuation of the Apollonian spirit if one is to avoid madness and death. Literature lies, and negates or postpones truth: 'La mentira literaria traiciona a la verdad para aplazar ese día del juicio en el que el principio y fin serán uno solo' (464).

If the mythical association between Elizabeth and Medea might pin her down to a stable identity, Javier refuses any such univocality, preferring plurality and invention. Rather against Elizabeth's will, he enjoys acting as if she is someone else, as when they go to a party and he pretends that he is meeting her for the first time. He confuses her with other representations in Modigliani's woman at the Tate Gallery; he pluralises her by inventing or watching her doubles, such as the dark Jewess Miriam on whom he spies. The purpose with Miriam is to complete Elizabeth's unfinished duality: 'completar la dualidad trunca, yo la judía rubia, la judía sajona, Miriam la muchacha de enfrente, una hebrea de orgasmos negros, casada, entretenida, viuda, soltera' (174).

---

[21] Fuentes may have had in mind D.H. Lawrence's discussion of Poe's 'Ligeia' and 'vampirism' in *Studies in Classical American Literature*.

This duality parallels that between the blond Nazi Franz and the dark Mexican writer Javier, as it does the two halves of Isabel, both 'demonio' and 'ángel' (118, 167), and the invention in *Zona sagrada* of the 'Bestia' to Claudia's 'Bella'. Such contradictions are also associated by Fuentes as a sign of tragedy against facile optimism: 'La tragedia es la memoria vivificada del ángel y de la bestia que coexisten en cada individuo.'[22] The other double that he invents for her is Isabel, the Lady Rowena in Poe's story in whom the dead Ligeia comes back to life. On other occasions, the couple play out different literary roles, including *Phèdre* (124–5, 126, 131) and *King Lear* (125, 370), curiously mimicking or participating in the creation of the novel.

The characters and the text create their own doubles so they can relate to them, to that side of themselves or that dimension of reality which is repressed or excluded from discourse and consciousness by official, conventional or ideological language. The Narrator at one point claims that characters need doubles as witnesses after the death of our former witness, God:

> la virtud sin testigo, y el mal sin testigo, son impensables y cuando Dios dejó de ser el testigo del hombre, hubo que inventar otro testigo: el alter ego, Mr Hyde; el doble, William Wilson. A ver si Blake no era muy ponchado: Thou art a Man, God is no more; Thine own humanity learn to adore, y a ver si Kleist no agarró volando la onda: Ahora detente a mi lado, Dios, pues soy doble; soy un espíritu y recorro la noche. Y lo malo es que también esto se volvió vieux jeu, en cuanto cerraron el círculo esos cuates de variedad, Pirandello y Brecht. Cáete cadáver: cada personaje es otro, él y su máscara, él y su contrasentido, él y su propio testigo, contrincante y victimario dentro de él. (352)

He goes on to quote Swinburne on the strife between opposites in Nature necessary for creation to continue. The shape of the argument seems to derive from Steiner's *The Death of Tragedy*, as does the quotation from Kleist. Steiner argues that tragedy declines in the seventeenth century as the organic world view disappears.[23] The passage

[22] *Cervantes o la crítica de la lectura* (Mexico City: Joaquín Mortiz, 1978), 17.
[23] George Steiner, *The Death of Tragedy* (London: Faber and Faber, 1982), 292. In the light of the presence of myth in *Cambio de piel*, note Steiner's argument that 'when it is torn loose from the moorings of myth, art tends toward

from Swinburne is again invoked on the birth of the Christ-doll from Elizabeth-la Pálida. Similar arguments are of course constant in William Blake, whose presence seems to suffuse the novel, for example, 'Without Contraries is no Progression. Attraction and Repulsion, Reason and Energy, Love and Hate, are necessary to Human existence.'[24]

Given the constant creation of doubles, their link to tragedy and the completeness of man, Freddy Lambert is an interesting figure. He is the double of all the characters and indeed the double of the text, and the embodiment of the narrative process like Ixca Cienfuegos before him.[25]

The most disturbing doubling in the novel, between Franz and Javier, the writer and the ex-Nazi architect, is inseparable from the relation between culture and its Other, culture and evil. What is more the accomplice of evil: optimistic rationalism or the writing of the demonic, the Romantic Agony, irrationalist vitalism? The tragic line between high culture and anti-humanism in the West is made very explicitly. After several pages about fourteenth-century massacres of Jews in Europe, Fuentes talks of the

> Renacimiento hecho y robado por Vico y Calvino y Descartes que terminó, hundido en su razón y su historia y su bien y su mal y su predestinación y su hombre natural y su activismo fáustico y su orgullo gnóstico y su voluntad trágica en los hornos de Auschwitz y el llano arrasado de Hiroshima.
>
> (271–2)[26]

Writers are seen as controllers of the reverse of culture, its Other in nature and madness: 'El escritor, el artista, el sacerdote, el político, anarchy' (321).

[24] Blake, *The Marriage of Heaven and Hell*, in *Complete Writings* (Oxford: OUP, 1984), 149.
[25] See Fuentes's comments to Emir Rodríguez Monegal, in *Homenaje*, 42.
[26] In a less iracund dialect, as he might have said, Borges similarly juxtaposes humanism and anti-humanism in the figure of the condemned Nazi zur Linde in '*Deutsches Requiem*': 'También frecuenté la poesía; a esos nombres [Brahms y Schopenhauer] quiero juntar otro vasto nombre germánico, William Shakespeare. [...] Sepa quien se detiene maravillado, trémulo de ternura y de gratitud, ante cualquier lugar de la obra de esos felices, que yo también me detuve ahí, yo el abominable' (577).

todos los que ofrecen otra imagen del mundo, la imagen artificial y falsaria, la interpretación, el salmo incantatorio, saben que manipulan a los locos' (350-1). But, alienated in the illusion of their superiority, they are in turn controlled and manipulated by madness: 'no saben que la razón se ha vuelto loca'. And another list of indictments of the West follows: 'Mira a dónde fuimos a parar. Candy y Lolita, la tortura y el horno crematorio, los procesos de Moscú y el asesinato de Trotsky, Bahía de Cochinos y los perros policía contra los negros de Montgomery' (351).

Authority: Spectacle and Enclosure

Dealings with the Other, with what is different, are dramatically represented in the novel in terms of enclosure and spectacle. Different structures are linked by formal similarities, for example the temple at Xochicalco, the concentration camp at Terezin, and the school where Javier is punished one evening (42-43, 79-81). There is also a clear analogy between the characters looking at the madmen in the Cholula asylum, the madmen displayed at Charenton, and the Jewish musicians displayed performing their own requiem. The place from which the characters view the insane could not be more dramatically eloquent, and in fact the situation described is exactly as it is in the real Cholula. They stand on the *mirador* of a Catholic church built by the Spaniards on top of the original pyramid as their answer to the indigenous religion. The Spaniards seem to have driven what they thought they were controlling underground, where it becomes more powerful, and where the old gods mock the official religion: 'Estos monstruos se ríen de los santos de allá arriba [...]. Hacen muecas feroces y se ríen de la muñequita ampona' (420). The situation is the same with the madmen who seem to be under control, but in fact control their blindly self-confident guardians: 'el loco se burla de su mentor y lo convierte, a su vez, en el loco del loco' (351).[27]

---

[27] The phrase comes from Diderot's *Le Neveu de Rameau* (Paris: Garnier-Flammarion, 1967), 116: 'Celui qui serait sage n'aurait point de fou. Celui donc qui a un fou n'est pas sage; s'il n'est pas sage, il est fou; et, peut-être, fût-il roi, le fou de son fou.' The importance of this phrase and the attitude it

Javier explains the meaning of the spectacle of the madmen: 'En Charenton los locos eran ofrecidos como espectáculo a los burgueses de París. [...] Y los burgueses regresaban a sus casas con la conciencia tranquila. Ellas [sic] no eran así' (350). The paradigm of the asylum and especially Charenton comes from various sources. One is Julio Cortázar, whose asylum in *Rayuela* has a green-eyed inmate like that of Fuentes, but more specific models are Foucault's *Histoire de la folie à l'âge classique* (translated as *Madness and Civilization*), and Peter Weiss's *Marat / Sade*. Foucault's study documents the 'broken dialogue'[28] between madness and reason in the modern world. In other ages, he argues, the terms were not nearly so polarised, and 'the Greek Logos had no contrary'.[29] Up to and during the Renaissance, the madman was an important source of knowledge to reason; madness a communication with the 'great tragic powers of the world', an awareness of the limits of humanity in animality and death, a salutary and accepted complement to reason. Only in the Enlightenment did bourgeois rationalism enclose madness as a threat to its order and nascent authority. Significantly, madness came to occupy the same symbolic role and literally the same buildings as had leprosy years before. Hence the mention of contagion by the mad Narrator of the

> represents within eighteenth-century rationalism is discussed by Foucault in *Madness and Civilization* (London: Tavistock, 1982), 199-201. The curious inversion, so close in spirit to Fuentes's novel, is repeated in *Jacques le fataliste* (Paris: Garner-Flammarion, 1970), 199, where the servant, Jacques, 'mène son maître'. Other phrases from *Le Neveu de Rameau* are drolly echoed in *Cambio de piel*, for example, 'On est dédommagé de la perte de son innocence par celle de ses préjugés' (113); 'lo bueno de perderla [la inocencia] es que al mismo tiempo se pierden los prejuicios. N'est-ce pas?' (*Cambio de piel*, 363). Also: 'S'il importe d'être sublime en quelque genre, c'est surtout en mal. On crache sur un petit filou; mais on ne peut refuser une sorte de considération à un grand criminel' (131-2); 'lo malo no es ser ladrón, sino un raterillo pinche; lo malo no es ser asesino, sino un asesino incompetente y descuidado' (*Cambio de piel*, 241).
>
> [28] *Madness and Civilization. A History of Insanity in the Age of Reason* (London: Tavistock, 1982), x.
> [29] *Madness and Civilization*, xi. Compare with Cortázar's notion of a non-dualistic sanity / madness: 'por la locura se podía acaso llegar a una razón que no fuera esa razón cuya falencia es la locura', *Rayuela* (Buenos Aires: Sudamericana, 1969), 93-94.

novel, Freddy Lambert,[30] who refers to the asylum as a lazaretto and to himself as Lazarus. Madness was not differentiated from that other threat to the bourgeois work ethic, idleness, and the poor were given a similar treatment to the mad. Though secrecy was the rule for such inmates in the eighteenth century, an exception was made with madness, as Foucault describes happening, for example, at Charenton:

> La folie devient pur spectacle, dans un monde sur lequel Sade étend sa souveraineté et qui est offert, comme distraction, à la bonne conscience d'une raison sûre d'elle-même. Jusqu'au début du XIXe siècle [...] les fous restent des monstres — c'est à dire des êtres ou des choses qui valent d'être montrés.[31]

Authority, then, is seen to repress what is different, either defusing its force or succumbing to the temptation to exterminate it. When the Other is repressed it is not always simply neutralised, but takes on an evil force it did not have originally. Freddy Lambert-Fuentes has a curious, rather Cortazarian passage on monsters, which illustrates this point. The monster-killing hero is a 'cómplice de lo unívoco' (179), a destroyer of healthy plurality. The monster is given a greater power on death, returning in a more sinister form, but disguised as order: it is allowed to 'reaparecer con su sangre envenenada pero con la simulación del orden, sin la espontaneidad real de su lugar en el mundo, disfrazadas de concierto para sembrar el desconcierto' (180). The relation with madness is made clear by the repetition of the word *disfrazar* in the following passage: 'la razón se ha vuelto loca y la disfrazan de erotismo, de gloria militar, de necesidad de Estado, de salvación eterna' (351). The link between the sublimation of the Other and the cold and rational madness of Nazism becomes clearer.[32]

The analogy between the position of the guardians of the asylum and the writer is emphasised by these examples. Moral questions are raised, such as the argument that Gentile writers have no right to describe the Holocaust, to exploit it for literary purposes. The writer must ask

---

[30] His name refers us to two geniuses who ended up deranged: Friedrich Nietzsche and the hero of Balzac's novel *Louis Lambert*.
[31] Michel Foucault, *Histoire de la folie* (Paris: Gallimard, 1979), 162.
[32] See also Julio Cortázar, 'Irracionalismo y eficacia', *Obra crítica*, vol. 2, ed. by Jaime Alazraki (Madrid: Alfaguara, 1994), 189–202.

whether all he is doing is to neutralise and recuperate the Other for his bourgeois readers. Javier is very clear about this. After discussing Charenton, he adds:

> ¿Quién puede escribir y temer que no hace no mismo? Qué indecencia, presentar el horror sólo para que un banquero diga, gracias Dios mío, porque no soy como los monstruos que acabo de ver... El pobre autor puede creer de buena fe que es capaz de escandalizar a los burgueses. Vaya risa. Después de *La edad de oro*, los burgueses se inventaron su mecanismo interno de defensa. ¿Ustedes creen que Tennessee Williams los escandaliza? No. Sólo los conforta, como los locos de Charenton. (350)

As a writer, Javier's own reaction is to cease to write, in order to avoid justifying one system or another (224, 315). Fuentes patently does not take this path, even though he does try hard enough to disturb the reader with the buggery of Isabel and some trying scenes between Javier and Elizabeth. The strategy of the text is rather to attempt to avoid recuperation by refusing separation, hierarchy and sublimation.

A couple of droll episodes illustrate Javier's own attempt to break down the separation between himself as spectator and the Other. For the educated bourgeois Javier, what is most other is his own country, Mexico, and especially its *pueblo*. He returns to Mexico because if he 'no se enfrentaba a todas las terribles negaciones de México [...] su obra carecería de valor' (149-50). On seeing the child rolling in the dust with the dog, Elizabeth screams '¡No quiero este terror! ¡No aguanto más el terror de esta gente!' (274). It is as if such aspects of Mexico are a privileged but unbearable Dionysian vision of the origins, of chaos.[33] Only Apollonian lies can make such a reality bearable. One night, on the way back from a party, and quoting *Phèdre* interminably, Javier insists on entering a *cantina* with Elizabeth. The *mariachis* are the Mexican Other, still, according to Javier as they sing a *corrido*, screaming the awesome scream of the origins: 'Los gritos del parto. Como si la madre y el hijo siguieran gritando de dolor toda la vida. [...]

---

[33] Compare with Ixca Cienfuegos's vision of Mexico in *La región más transparente*, 377: 'El pueblo de México, que es el único contemporáneo del mundo, el único pueblo que aún vive con los dientes pegados a la ubre original. Este conjunto de malos olores y chancros y pulque vicioso y carne de garfios que se apeñusca en el lodo indiferenciado del origen.'

Como si el parto no terminara nunca. Están aullando ciegos [...] atados por su cordón azul a la madre que aúlla con ellos, envueltos siempre en su placenta '(128). And yet even they are recuperated through the picturesque, through ignorance and class difference. They become a distant spectacle like animals in a zoo or the madmen in Charenton:

> Somos unos marcianos. No hablamos como ellos. No pensamos como ellos. Nunca nos hemos detenido a mirarlos. Les damos órdenes. Si venimos a verlos es como ir al zoológico. A ver a los changuitos. Unos monos vestidos de carnaval que aúllan como coyotes. Somos enemigos. Ellos saben que están detrás de la reja. (129)

Javier heroically attempts to break down the barrier, to join the actors on the stage,[34] provoking the *mariachis* by throwing peanuts at them. One of them eventually beats Javier up and, as he lies in the blood and dirt, he feels that, finally, 'estaba del otro lado de los barrotes. Como ellos' (131). The original animality with which he believes he had made contact is, however, shown to be of a conventional literary nature, a mixture of Douanier Rousseau and Blake: the *mariachi* walks 'como una bestia que aparta con la cabeza los helechos y lianas de la selva: como el tigre del Aduanero: burning bright in the forests of the night' (130). Elizabeth later deflates this literary vision talking to Freddy: '¿Musculoso y grácil como una pantera? Qué va. Yo lo vi, gordo, fofo, un mariachón bien nilo, pero con muchos sopletes y sus bigotes a la mechingué' (279). However hard Javier tries to go beyond sublimation and distancing, literature has its way. There is a curious metatextual element in this episode. The *corrido* of Benjamín Argumedo that the *mariachi* sings resounds through the text,[35] and his introduction is used by the Narrator in the first page of the novel: 'Para empezar a cantar, pido permiso primero' (131). The implied question again must be

---

[34] The protagonist of Cortázar's 'Instrucciones para John Howell' (*Todos los fuegos el fuego*) finds himself literally in this position and, like the characters of *Cambio de piel*, has to work within a preordained script in order to subvert it and work against the inevitability of its outcome.

[35] See Margo Glantz, '*Cambio de piel*: Fuentes y las fiestas imposibles', in *Repeticiones: ensayos sobre literatura mexicana* (Xalapa: Universidad Veracruzana, 1979), 35–46.

whether the novel will be viewed by the reader like the *mariachi*-monkey behind its bars.[36]

Textual Strategy

So far, in specific examples and in metaphorical metatextual commentary, the Other seems almost automatically to be sublimated by literature. Textual means are developed, however, to overcome sublimation and separation. The main aim is to subvert the certainties and stabilities which allow one to assert the naturalness of one's position, identity and the stability of ego-centred discourse against what he decrees Other. The novelist's objective thus becomes the reader and the stable, safe and confident position from which he can view the text. In a way similar to Cortázar in *Rayuela*, Fuentes is looking to create a space for a 'lector cómplice'.

A well established way of disconcerting and decentring the reader is to include a representation of his activity in the text, and the theme of the spectacle in the novel clearly invites a consciousness of one's own reading activity. The legitimacy of that activity is questioned in a significant inversion. Elizabeth's father, Gerson, becomes a policeman, an official figure of authority, and part of his job is to observe sexual offences in the public toilets in the railway station. He also forces Elizabeth to watch (329). The family theme of becoming invisible, as Jews in a foreign land, is ironically echoed. At the end of the novel, however, the official, critical status of that watching is inverted when it is revealed that Gerson was prosecuted for criminal voyeurism: 'La policía lo había sorprendido espiando en los excusados públicos.' The Narrator adds, almost directly addressing the reader: 'Era un voyeur, como tú y yo' (490). The reifying gaze of the reader is then clearly implicated in all the watching that goes on in the novel.

Another effective way of making the reader question his own activity is to destabilise the reading contract between author and reader, to scramble the instructions encoded in the generic presentation of the material. In a way similar to that described by Fuentes in his

---

[36] This episode is echoed in the episode in Greece where the German flicks pebbles at his wife, later to be drowned by her.

presentation of *Cien años de soledad*, here too there is a great ambiguity and questioning of the status of representation.[37] The novel is neither pure fantasy, nor *nouveau roman*-style formal experiment, nor yet classical realism, but belongs ambiguously to all these categories. At the same time as we are powerfully drawn into the intense relationship between Javier and Elizabeth and invited to believe in it, we are told that they invented their lives from the papers, books and films contained in a chest. The Narrator figure who would normally present a form of stable reference for the reader is similarly treated. At once he is a real character who follows the protagonists into Cholula with the Monjes and is implicated in the murder of Franz, and is also seen as a madman who either invents the story or has it recounted to him by the women. Even if one tried to naturalise the information in the latter manner, that is, concluding that he accumulates information from the dialogues between himself and Elizabeth ('dragona') and Isabel ('novillera'), there are still some difficulties. When, for example, his voice is first introduced, it does not invoke a definite referentiality or narration of a conversation that really happened: 'Me ibas a contar algún día, Elizabeth, que [...]' (27). However, in his incarnation as a taxi-driver, we do see him make love to Elizabeth while Javier is drunk, most of the conversations are impossible to locate temporally or spatially. In this context he is the double of the characters, for the conversations between the four, in different pairs, throughout the night, are impossible to justify realistically. They stand ambiguously between a thinly disguised narrative convention and highly detailed, often moving personal confrontations.

The pact between reader and narrator is similarly subverted in the final parody trial of the characters, mainly Franz and Javier, where Freddy Lambert seems to act as judge. He decides at one point against Javier but then gives in to pressure from the Monjes. Though he does not agree with their verdict against Franz he does not interfere:

> No supe o no pude decir más para detenerlos dragona. No quise pedir más, es la puritita verdad. Me venció el entusiasmo de una participación y la conciencia de que voy que chuto para la cuartentena. Yo iba a ser joven con

---

[37] See 'Gabriel García Márquez and the Invention of America' in *Myself with Others. Selected Essays* (London: André Deutsch, 1988), 180–95.

ellos, dragona (492); sin que yo me atreviera a dar mis verdaderas razones para impedir el crimen y sin que obtuviera la camaradería, la participación o el amor a cambio de los cuales me callé. (496)

Not only is the judge-narrator corrupt, which might simply make him the classic 'unreliable narrator', but by participating in the crime by default almost, for fear of contradicting the majority, he reproduces the basic crime of Franz, the person they condemn for not opposing the Nazi movement. What seemed to be a position outside the shifting perspectives of the action, perhaps similar to the judgemental position the reader believes he can adopt, is firmly revealed to obey the same laws and ambiguities.

The reversal of our perception of Freddy from sanity to madness is an important paradigm in the destabilisation of the position of supposed sanity from which one could declare the other insane. Though such ambiguities or reversals of vision are common in Blake's *Marriage of Heaven and Hell*, for example, or in much of Unamuno,[38] a more direct model of the inversion is to be found in *The Cabinet of Dr Caligari*, to which the text often refers, and a still from which is reproduced in the novel. There, the spectator is led to believe in the story told by one character and watches the mad crimes of a fairground charlatan Dr Caligari and the somnambulist Cesare whom he controls in order to perpetrate his crimes. Finally, however, the narrator is revealed to be mad, and the story to be his paranoid fantasies about the benign director of the asylum where he is confined. The spectator, however, is never fully convinced of the truth of the matter. The questioning of the sanity of authority in Germany between the wars in this film is of course relevant to the novel, as it is in others to which allusions are made, for example, *Dr Mabuse*, *The Student of Prague*, *The Golem*.[39] The main Caligari-like figure is Herr Urs, who modifies dolls by adding masculine features to female dolls and vice-versa, in a way remarkably

---

[38] For example, 'Y después de todo, ¿qué es la locura y cómo distinguirla de la razón no poniéndose fuera de una y de otra, lo cual nos es imposible?' (*Del sentimiento trágico de la vida* (Madrid: Austral, 1967), 192).

[39] On *Dr Caligari*, see S.S. Prawer, *Caligari's Children: the film as tale of terror* (New York: Oxford UP, 1980), 164–200; more generally, see Siegfried Kracauer, *From Caligari to Hitler: a psychological history of the German film* (New York: Dennis Dobson, 1947).

similar to the character M. Ochs (an avatar of Jules Verne's Professor Ox) in Cortázar's *62. Modelo para armar*, published about the same time. As corruptor and manipulator of German youth he acts the role of Caligari, and Franz that of Cesare. But when he appears as a doll himself on the knee of the Narrator, it is the latter who becomes Caligari, while Urs plays Cesare. Finally, Freddy Lambert takes the role of Francis, the narrator, especially in the final revelation that he is mad.

Peter Weiss's *Marat / Sade*, with its madmen actors directed by Sade, is another, related model. A Brechtian distancing technique is used which makes the spectator aware, and wary, of his position. The characters are madmen playing roles in a play (like Javier in his literary role-playing and the Monjes in the trial), and perfectly conscious of their roles. The spectator / reader is not allowed to naturalise his reactions to the actions and issues. The fictionality of the characters in *Cambio de piel* is again stressed by the reference to Pirandello and his *Sei personaggi in cerca d'autore*, as the six Monjes come to look for the Narrator Freddy Lambert (429).

Cervantes's *Don Quijote* provides another important paradigm, both in the context of madness and of intertextuality, as the knight goes out into the world to question it with his texts. For Fuentes, Don Quixote's madness ironically questions the sanity of the nascent bourgeois order in the same way as Erasmus in *Praise of Folly*.[40] At the beginning of the second part of the novel, Fuentes includes a nicely problematical quotation from Foucault's *Les Mots et les choses*: 'Et puisque cette magie a été prévue et décrite dans les livres, la différence illusoire qu'elle introduit ne sera jamais qu'une similitude enchantée.'[41] The context of the phrase is the four similitudes discussed by Foucault as basic to Western culture until the sixteenth century, which would include the analogy between signs and things, words and reality. Don Quixote puts this system to a tough test by trying to read the world according to the chivalric novels which he has read. Reality does not conform to Don Quixote's books, but he concludes that this is only because sorcerers have maliciously transformed reality. Since this

[40] See *Cervantes o la crítica de la lectura* (Mexico City: Joaquín Mortiz, 1976), 66-8.
[41] *Cambio de piel*, 25; *Les Mots et les choses* (Paris: Gallimard, 1984), 61.

activity has previously been described in books, the signs after all are true. The phrase is ambiguously placed in the novel, but many issues are clearly alluded to: the relation between text and intertext; the transformation of reality in novels; the power of language actually to change reality, with clear political resonances; the ambiguous status of representational realism in the novel.

One of the main elements in recuperation or reification which we have seen in the novel is separation or isolation. One of the most striking responses of the text is to dissolve literary hierarchies with stylistic techniques, including the abundant use of slang, vulgarisms and barbarisms used in contexts where they would normally be excluded, for example, in theological or philosophical discussions. The death of a student is described in a bizarre combination of classical myth and the comic strip: 'Al estudiante se lo fildeó la pelona y el azul, el cuico, el genízaro, como siempre, se voló la barda y chau. Puro mito, dragona' (238). Generic borders and hierarchies are breached, as they were in Cortázar and Puig at much the same time, in a various ways including the use of much essayistic content and even photographs. Startling juxtapositions and contaminations are made across seemingly uncrossable barriers: when, for example, in the parody trial a Nazi becomes Christ who, in turn, comes close to the hero of Lautréamont's *Les Chants de Maldoror* in his dealings with children (473).

Perhaps the most effective anti-recuperation device is to give contradictory answers to every question. He quotes Artaud: 'creemos en el poder absoluto de la contradicción' (61). Blaise Pascal, 'el Pascales, ese draculón trotaconventos' (299), becomes the hero of paradox. According to Goldmann, for Pascal God is always absent and present, he answers every serious question with a 'yes' and a 'no', demands a radical clarity from the irremediable ambiguity of the world.[42] Following the Nazi-Christian parallel in the novel, Christianity is at one point seen to be responsible for the hatred of the body and thus for the splitting of man, the loss of half his being. The 'posibilidades' of man, talked of by Cortázar, are invoked only to claim that they have been hidden by Christianity:

---

[42] See Lucien Goldmann, *Le Dieu caché* (Paris: Gallimard, 1979), 21, 46, 65.

Porque ustedes las han escondido. Han creado un hombre mutilado, sin la mitad de su ser. Ay Máistro Veloz [that is, Swift], tú que odiabas al animal hombre [...]. Sólo hombre completo cuando acepta y exhibe y explota su rostro nocturno. [...] Su corazón de tinieblas [...]. Su mitad oculta por los siglos de la barbarie judía y cristiana que amputa a los hombres. (440)

The accused, that is, Franz as Nazi, is then seen to have recovered this lost half for man by living out those terrible possibilities: 'alguien tiene que estar Loco y Enfermo en un Mundo que se creía incurablemente Sano y Racional. [...] ¡El acusado ha estado Loco y Enfermo en nombre de Todos, por la Salud de Todos!' (441). The Nazi thus becomes the hero, the tragic scapegoat (437, 439). Yet suddenly it is Christ who takes on this role with reference to the topos of the Madness of the Cross: 'hoy ustedes se sienten justificados y cuerdos en contraste con la Locura Salvadora del acusado' (441).[43] The argument thus comes full circle. Within the delirious logic there is a return to the spectacle theme and a reminder that the non-German West looks on Nazism as something alien to itself rather than as a possibility to be avoided.

To the argument that literature recuperates and defuses any threat to the bourgeois order, the opposite is posed: the spectacle of evil corrupts and literary irrationalism leads, as argued by Lukács, to fascism. Franz, for example, referring to the painings of Herr Urs, says: 'Nos perdimos ante ese espectáculo' (159). Famous surrealist and Nietzscheian provocations are easily cited in this context: '"Avez-vous déjà giflé un mort?" "Avez-vous déjà tué un juif?"' (453); '"el acto surrealista más simple consiste en bajar a la calle y disparar indiscriminadamente sobre la multitud"' (83), etc. Hence the presence too in the novel of the more extreme forms of Romanticism: Kleist, Büchner, Sade, Swinburne. Herr Urs, the tempter and corrupter of Franz, has much in common with the Devil of Thomas Mann's *Doctor Faustus*. Various of his phrases are echoed in the text, for example, 'The artist is the brother of the criminal and the madman';[44] 'yo acabo de estremecerme al pensar

---

[43] On the concept of the Madness of the Cross, see Unamuno, *Del sentimiento trágico de la vida*, 89, and Foucault, *Madness and Civilization*, 78-80.
[44] Thomas Mann, *Doctor Faustus* (Harmondsworth: Penguin, 1985), 229. Note also, from the same page of Mann's novel: 'Item, a man must have been always ill and mad in order that others no longer need be so'; and from *Cambio de piel* (441), '¡El acusado ha estado Loco y Enfermo en nombre de

que ellos [...] los criminales y ellos [...] los poetas, pudieron salir de la misma madre: ¿Sade se llama Auschwitz, Lautréamont se llama Treblinka, Nietzsche se llama Terezin?' (448). Mann himself explains the links between the daemonic in literature and fascism elsewhere when he talks of the 'flight from the difficulties of the cultural crisis into the pact with the devil, the craving of a proud mind, threatened by sterility, for an unblocking of inhibitions at any cost, and the parallel between pernicious euphoria ending in collapse with the nationalistic frenzy of Fascism'.[45] Similarly, Lukács saw *Death in Venice* as one of the 'great forerunners of that trend towards signalling the danger of a barbarous underworld existing within modern German civilisation as its necessary complement'.[46]

Javier and Franz: Conclusion

While, then, we have seen how the novel avoids recuperation by various means, we come across the opposite question: that daemonic literature partakes of the same phenomenon as fascism, and we again come up against the insistent parallel between Franz the Nazi and Javier the writer. The question is extremely difficult, but a few points can be made here. Both have heroic dreams which fly in the face of reality and aim to change it. The freedom of the construction of the concentration camp is described in terms very reminiscent of the freedom of literature and its assault on reality, and indeed on the shuffling of characters in the novel:

> todo Terezin, el campo, el ghetto, debía ser una respuesta de la imaginación libre a la realidad esclava (402); la transformación de rostros y manos y glúteos barajados en este laboratorio donde el universo es vuelto a ordenar libremente, sin límite. (403)

Todos, por la Salud de Todos!'
[45] Cit. in Lillian Feder, *Madness in Literature* (Princeton: Princeton University Press, 1980), 231.
[46] Cit. in Feder, 232-33.

Both men, it can be argued, are responsible for the death of a child. The way the two exchange and alternate the two women at the hotel in Cholula is recounted in such a non-realist, or unlikely, manner that it almost seems that the women alternate between two aspects of one man. The differences, however, are also stressed. Faced with the bull guarding the stream, they react in very different ways. Franz follows the model of the classical hero, Jason fighting against the monsters, facing the bull physically and using his coat as a matador's cape. Javier deflates any heroism, refuses the rhetoric of myth by honking the horn of the car, and frightening the animals away. He takes up a similar position *vis-à-vis* myth, in fact, as do certain areas of the text.

The relation between the two doubles repeats aspects of doublings in earlier novels: that, for example, between the doer, Artemio Cruz, who is inevitably corrupted or falls, and Gonzalo Bernal, the person who refuses to act so as not to compromise himself. Similarly, Franz, the architect who preferred to build, even though his building was to be used as a concentration camp, is opposed to Javier the writer who, *grosso modo*, refused to create out of consciousness that his product would be appropriated and used by society for its own ends: '¿Qué no nos será arrebatado, destruido, prostituido por la sociedad? Mejor el silencio' (225).

The opposition between the thinker and the doer is also explored by Peter Weiss in the confrontation between the political activist Marat, the purist with so much blood on his hands, and the Marquis de Sade, the theorist of violence and destruction, of the futile attempt to go beyond nature and destroy it. Peter Weiss questions the direct link made by Mann between the literary demonic and real violence. In the play, Sade suggests that his writings are a sort of exorcism of evil, a facing up to it: 'In a criminal society / I dug the criminal out of myself / so I could understand him and so understand / the times we live in.'[47] And this is the position in the novel voiced by Jacob against Herr Urs:

> Jeanne, ningún poeta es profeta de la tortura, ningún filósofo anunció la justicia y necesidad de la muerte, hablaron del mal, Jeanne, para que lo

---

[47] *Marat / Sade*, 55. For similar appreciations of the thought of Sade, see Maurice Blanchot, *Lautréamont et Sade* (Paris: Minuit, 1984), 48–49, and Foucault, *Les Mots et les choses*, 339.

viéramos de frente y lo incorporáramos a la vida: para que nosotros corrompiéramos el mal, Jeanne, para que el mal no nos venciera aislado.

(481)

Indirectly with reference to Javier, then, we return to the question of *aislamiento* with which we opened the discussion. Whereas authority and power separate and isolate the other, literature faces up to it, brings it out into the open to reduce its negative charge and power of seduction. This is clearly seen in the personal lives of Elizabeth and Javier as against that of Franz: 'Javier y Elizabeth han mantenido su infierno. Él no. Franz cree haberlo evadido' (492). Whereas Franz thinks he can leave his past behind him, Javier and Elizabeth accept their guilt: 'la lucha es entre culpables, ¿ves?, y por eso es trágica' (381).

Javier is not, of course, fully representative of the novel and its functioning. What is more significant than his own characteristics is the fact that the two characters are brought together, that the novel makes the link between them in an ambiguous and difficult fashion, avoiding the isolation practised by authority. Indeed, it can be argued that the complementary nature of the characters reproduces the dialogic functioning of the text. Franz is associated with construction, the epic and heroic, and Javier with the questioning of that structure, with plurality, parody, modernity, doubt. Similar roles are taken by Mito and Giarcarlo in *Zona sagrada*.

It is Jacob who suggests to Jeanne a way of life which is the behavioural equivalent of the practice of the novel, and seems to be related to that led by Javier and Elizabeth. The attitude is one of a tragic recognition of failure and a constantly renewed hope, an embracing and living out of contradictions to ensure renewal:

> tú y yo lucharemos contra nosotros mismos, tú y yo fracasaremos, desearemos, volveremos a fracasar, volveremos a desear, tú y yo iremos hasta el final de todas las viejas contradicciones para vivirlas, despojarnos de esa vieja piel y mudarla por la de las nuevas contradicciones. (482)

Collective violence, he argues, can be avoided or exorcised by working that violence out against oneself as an individual, that is, accepting and incorporating the duality of life, not allowing any force of otherness to be at the disposal of a collective movement which could harness and manipulate it for evil:

> venceremos su violencia colectiva con la violencia individual hacia nuestras mentes, nuestros cuerpos, nuestra arte, nuestros sexos, los derrotaremos derrotándonos antes, para que ellos no puedan encontrar más víctimas, convivir, regalarse, gastarse, Jeanne, hacer historia con nuestras vidas para que ellos no hagan historia con nuestras muertes. (483)

This preventive violence is that done by the text to itself, the techniques to avoid recuperation or manipulation, the ready espousal of contradiction.

The one and the other, Franz and Javier, finally confront one another in the pyramid. As the opposites, the passive and the active, come together to fight, their hatred is turned into desire in a rather Lawrentian scene reminiscent of the embraces between Artemio and Gonzalo in *La muerte de Artemio Cruz*, and between Mito and Giancarlo in *Zona sagrada*. In the Ancient Mexican world of the pyramid, the opposites are necessary complements, and the scene is presided over by the 'dioses negros y amarillos de la vida y de la muerte' (421), the yellow and black colours which have recurred throughout the novel, for example in the shawl with which Isabel is strangled. But here it is Franz who dies, sacrificed perhaps so that the other can live, like Lorenzo and Gonzalo in *La muerte de Artemio Cruz*.

The mysterious *bulto* which haunts the last pages of the novel would seem to be related to the embrace between the two men and the death of Franz, with whose corpse it shares the boot of the Lincoln convertible of the Monjes. The *bulto* is double, reproducing the unity or inseparability created in the embrace between the two men, the 'racimo de pijas' (421), and thus prefiguring the hermaphrodite created in the final pages of *Terra Nostra*. It contains a child and a yellow dog: the child that Elizabeth saw rolling with a yellow dog in the dust by the road, and which she picks up as she does the *bulto*, which she saves by leaving it at the lunatic asylum. The child is also the children who have died in her life: her brother Jake and the foetus aborted in Mexico City (274). As such, the *bulto* is also related to the porcelain doll born to la Pálida-Elizabeth in the brothel. Another passage makes it clear that the dog is all that we have described as the 'Other', all that was repressed by Christianity: the body, the instinctive and the irrational. We hear of the hatred of the 'animal hombre' and almost immediately afterwards of the contents of the *bulto*: 'Serán dos cuerpos, uno el animal del otro, abrazados, quietamente devoradores' (440). Ultimately, the *bulto* is the novel itself: the image of the original dual and complementary nature of existence, of the inseparability of man and his 'cara nocturna', dissociated at such a price by authority and modernity.

Zona sagrada, 1967: Carnival Time

Zona sagrada is a dizzying theatre of representation. A realist narration of life in Mexico in the fifties and sixties[1] in which the relationship between Guillermo and his actress mother Claudia Nervo, readily identifiable as María Félix, is combined, overlaid, and in the third part replaced, by a far less traditional discourse. This other writing embodies the new sensibility and attitudes towards meaning and representation emerging in the sixties, and closely associated with cinema and structural anthropology.[2] From at least the time of *Las buenas conciencias* the struggle for language in Fuentes's work (issues of originality, authenticity and influence) has been played out within the family in the Oedipal manoeuvrings of the Freudian 'Family Romance'. Whereas Jaime Ceballos in the earlier novel sought an absolute, pristine language, 'otro idioma que no sólo refleje sino que pueda transformar la realidad',[3] Guillermo, inseparably actor and writer, demented victim and tyrannical director of *Zona sagrada*, has a different view of the novel: 'Y un libro no nos remite a un significado: un libro es. Un libro no se hace para que nos reconozcamos en él' (156).[4] The anthropology of Lévi-Strauss, the articles of Susan Sontag on cinema, camp and interpretation, and parallel essays by Alain Robbe-Grillet are essential in grasping the new direction in Fuentes's work.

Non-literary forms of representation jostle rather frantically throughout the text commenting on themselves, each other, and the

---

[1] Andrés Avellaneda, 'Mito y negación de la historia en *Zona sagrada* de Carlos Fuentes', *Cuadernos americanos*, 175:2 (1971), 239–48, 243, establishes the chronology of the novel.
[2] In *La nueva novela hispanoamericana*, 20, he writes that 'la novela se acerca cada vez más a la poesía y a la antropología'.
[3] *Las buenas conciencias*, 119. Jonathan Tittler, in his article 'Cambio de zona/Piel sagrada: Transfiguration in Carlos Fuentes', in *World Literature Today*, 57:4, 1983, 585–90, also notes this phrase.
[4] Note Susan Sontag's phrase from 'On Style' in her *Against Interpretation* (London: André Deutsch, 1987), 21: 'Art is not only about something; it is something. A work of art is a thing *in* the world, not just a text or commentary *on* the world.'

story, which is in turn a kaleidoscopic metaphor for its own status within signification. Paintings, myriad versions of the devouring Claudia Nervo, photographs of Mito's cultural heroes and major contributors to the novel's intertextuality such as Charles Baudelaire,[5] pin-ups and religious images, the paintings of Signorelli as 'gestador solitario' (164, one of the many in the novel), the delirious montages of Giancarlo facing the fading Renaissance frescoes, clamour from every wall. Myth, ritual and game, equated and opposed[6] — Claudia has 'un pie en el rito y el otro en el juego' (46) — are omnipresent: from the football matches in Mexico and Positano to Mito's funeral rites for the young birds in Chapala, the use of dolls, effigies and sweaters in complex magical chains, and the version and counterversion in conversation and cinematic performance of classical myths, especially that of the Odyssey. The return of Ulysses to Ithaca in Homer's version becomes a cipher of traditional narrative order and closure. Cinema is similarly present in different ways: Claudia is a movie star and we see her son Mito obsessively watch sequences from her movies and comment on them, caught in a labyrinthine game of mirrors between his own narcissism and the many projections of his mother: in her films, in her protegée Bela, in images of the French actress Sarah Bernhardt, and

---

[5] Some of the quotations are attributed, such as 'Ausente, podría repetir para ella las palabras de Baudelaire, la tontería, la bêtise [sic], es siempre la conservación de la belleza' (92). The phrase comes from 'Choix de maximes consolantes sur l'amour', *Œuvres complètes* (Paris: Robert Laffont, 1980), 315. Future references to Baudelaire will be to this edition. Andrés Avellaneda, 247–8, mentions the role of the Baudelairian dandy and identifies a number of quotations.

[6] There is a similar play in Cortázar between game and ritual. The child's game of hopscotch referred to in the title of *Rayuela* replaced the original title *Mandala*, with its connotations of sacrality. Note Oliveira's insistence on 'evitar como la peste toda sacralización de los juegos' (*Rayuela*, 44). For Johan Huizinga, games and ritual are virtually indistinguishable in form, as are the 'campo de juego' and the 'lugar sagrado'. See *Homo ludens* (Madrid: Alianza-Emecé, 1972), 22. For Lévi-Strauss, on the other hand, game has a disjunctive effect in that it starts with the symmetry of competitors and ends with winners and losers, whereas ritual conjoins in that it postulates assymmetry between the sacred and the profane, faithful and officiating, etc., and by structural means proceeds to a merging. See *The Savage Mind* (London: Weidenfeld & Nicolson, 1989), 32.

in the many fierce roles associated with her, such as Salomé. These mirrorings Mito perhaps uses to avoid a dangerous approximation to a real woman who may lie behind the reflections. Towards the end of the novel the mythical and the cinematic come together when a demented von Stroheim[7] directs Claudia and Giancarlo in a grotesque performance of the murder of Ulysses at the hands of his son Telegonus, a performance which is at the same time part of the plot of the novel.

Zona sagrada was partly written and set in Italy, and Federico Fellini is a fertile presence in the novel. The epigraph from *Giulietta degli Spiriti*, 'Ma chi non ha bisogno della Mamma' (11), a dismissive reply by a detective to a trite Freudian statement by a psychologist in the film, is little more than a homage and an obviously over-determined and trivialising reference to the theme of incest. The ritualistic and crowd scenes in the novel seem to derive their surreal energy and oneiric absurdity from Fellini. The scene in Giancarlo's castle Madonna dei Monti, with its chilling *chiaroscuro* of light and sentiment and its description of the rotting frescoes, could well be inspired by the drunken rituals in the party in the 'vecchia villa' in *La dolce vita*, where Marcello strikes a match to illuminate a gallery of female portraits and Maddalena imitates these likenesses. Important, too, is the example of the disconcerting play in Fellini's films, especially *Otto e mezzo*, between the supposed portrayal of real life and the performance and reworking of that life in cinema, seen both from outside on the set and in the semi-finished form of clips and trials. This technique, facilitated by the fact that Claudia is an actress, is effectively translated into the novel. Non-realistic scenes, such as the ritual murder, the transformation of Mito into a dog, presumably by Claudia-Circe, or his pursuit as an animal or blind man through the labyrinth-womb of the Paris metro, which in a more conventional novel would be naturalised and subordinated to psychological realism by being explained as nightmare, hallucination and metaphor, are here given the same status as other narrative elements. In a nice comment on Fellini's inversion of the priorities of role and actor, Fuentes has 'un bandolero italiano, vestido como Marcello Mastroianni' (169).

[7] See Frank Dauster's 'The Wounded Vision: *Aura, Zona sagrada*, and *Cumpleaños*', in Robert Brody and Charles Rossman, eds., *Carlos Fuentes: A Critical View* (Austin: University of Texas Press, 1982), 106-20, 114.

Another reference to Fellini seems to show Fuentes's recognition of the role of film in breaking down the barrier between popular and high art: 'schifoso Fellini que convierte a Botticelli en Madrake el Mago' (28). In *Zona sagrada*, Fuentes has not written something which, in the style of Puig's *Boquitas pintadas* or *El beso de la mujer araña*, can be read as either high or low art. What he often does is to use cultured references in the style of pop art icon or catchword, with the effect of divesting them of any depth of resonance as *mise en abyme* or key to intertextual readings. Claudia's court of starlets, or Erynnes, for example, are given mythologically significant names in a pointedly unsignifying fashion, for example, Ifigenia, Hermione. References to their fashion accessories are given the same status by contiguity with quotations from Nerval's 'Artémis' and Baudelaire's 'Hymne à la beauté': 'las largas medias iluminadas por rombos color naranja: ¿eres la primera o la última? [...] tus brazos desnudos, Ute, bronceados, ¿vienes del cielo profundo o desciendes del abismo, belleza?' (119). Such signifiers come close to being pure surface. Some critics have questioned Fuentes's attempt to translate cinematographic technique into the novel, pointing out the clear difference between the linguistic sign and the filmic image, which signifies little outside itself.[8] This is clearly the case, as Fuentes is aware, and the momentary silencing of connotation achieved is in itself a signifying gesture, pregnant with intent. Contiguity of high and low sometimes gives way to replacement in the same space: Mito's photograph of Baudelaire by Nadar is replaced in its frame by one of Elvis Presley, while his recording of *Rigoletto* is forcefully replaced on the turntable by the bolero 'Luna que se quiebra', in the same way that the mythically connoted love between Claudia and her symbolic son Giancarlo is replaced by the altogether coarser coupling of Mito's maid Gudelia and Jesús.

Conceptual oppositions such as that between low and high art are often given a spatial and visual expression in the novel, in a way which Mito for one associates with the cinema: 'Claudia pasa por la pantalla y no hay, para mí, diferencia entre el espacio y el pensamiento' (157). In Madonna dei Monti, for example, the Renaissance frescoes of decaying angels are already dual, suggesting beginning and end: 'una forma final [...] de feto y cadáver, de útero y tumba' (98). These frescoes face the

---

[8]   See Befumo Boschi and Calabrese, 122-3.

montage of Giancarlo which combines rotting pigs' heads with condoms and the images of 'las vampiresas mudas' such as Francesca Bertini (99). This combination of bits and pieces from a pre-existing signifying code into a new configuration is an instance of the *bricolage* given great prominence at the time in Lévi-Strauss's *La Pensée sauvage*.[9] The 'frescos gemelos' (101) suggest both the twinning of Giancarlo and Guillermo and are an eloquent embodiment of the struggle in the novel between 'el arte que heredaste y el arte que creaste' (103), traditional art with a great sense of temporal depth and an art of instant combination which abolishes temporality, the space of the sacred and that of the profane. In *Cumpleaños*, the palace of Capodimonti and that of Diocletian in Split embody in more specifically architectural terms a similar dichotomy between opposing notions of meaning: theocentric, classical univocality against palimpsest, layering and combination: 'El Palacio de Diocleciano en Spalato es la moderna ciudad dalmática de Split: los corredores, allí, son las calles; las plazas públicas, los patios; las basílicas imperiales, los templos comunes; las cocinas del monarca, las fondas del pueblo.'[10] Capodimonti, on the other hand, is an 'inmenso cubo de piedra cuyas cámaras circulares desembocan, indefectiblemente, en un patio solitario, rodeado de ocho murallas sin ventanas. Pero desde allí, situado en el centro del patio desnudo, sí se observa la eternidad mutante de los cielos' (C, 25). The house in which most of *Cumpleaños* takes place tantalisingly combines elements of both spaces, as it does dogma and heresy, the individual author and the Borgesian rewriter. *Zona sagrada* is also split between two rival zones, ambiguously sacred and profane: Claudia's house and that of her son Mito. Just as Claudia herself is associated with Immaculate Conception and self-fecundation, the light in her zone is timeless, pure origin, a denial of development: 'esa luz [...] no llega a esta estancia con el signo evolutivo que queremos concederle a todas las cosas vivas. [...] Esta luz se refracta desde un cuarzo incandescente, original y sin tactos o visiones anteriores a él' (117). In comparison with the dissolving mineral light of Claudia's house, that of Mito is vegetable and animal, it has grown, has a history, has developed from previous models: ' [...] mi naturaleza. Ha crecido como una selva; [...] lo que he logrado a

---

[9]   See *The Savage Mind*, 16-22.
[10] *Cumpleaños* (México; Joaquín Mortiz, 1969), 24.

partir de ti, de una vieja fotografía del apartamento de Sarah Bernhardt, de un viejo volumen de la Salomé ilustrada por Beadsley; mi continuidad está aquí' (30). I suspect that the complexity of such spatial games, at which we have arrived from the example of Fellini's cinema, is a complexity specific to literature, and to the novel as devourer of foreign discourses.[11]

It seems to be the intent of *Zona sagrada* to dissolve the oppositions in space, signification and temporality sketched out above, many of which respond to the axis surface/depth. In a novel, like *Zona sagrada*, of shifting locations and identities, no item comes fixedly to embody these oppositions, which constantly shift, relocate, dissolve. Elements such as the songs of the Beatles and the Sirens change meaning almost within one sentence. In the first few pages, for example, the Sirens are presented as 'una sola imagen', as 'risk' — 'te arriesgas', as 'esos seres que quisieran romper el orden natural' of epic resolution, and associated with Giancarlo against Mito, who is 'distraído por la belleza, el juego, la vida'. 'Estás perdido en la imagen única de las islas; yo, distraído con todos los accidentes de la playa' (6). Almost immediately, however, they come to represent exhaustion and renunciation: 'el canto de las sirenas que sólo es escuchado por quienes ya no viajan, ya no se esfuerzan.' With the Beatles, there is a similar slip in appreciation: 'el nuevo tacto', 'el sonido nuevo' quickly becomes 'la melancolía de un reposo bienganado, la bella fatiga', only to end up signifying 'ese apetito satisfecho de [...] regüeldo y esperma' (118). As we shall see later, the superimposition of all the versions of a myth, in which any one reading is partial and meaningless, is taken from the structural anthropology of Lévi-Strauss. To the 'official', Homeric version of Ulysses's encounter with the Sirens Fuentes adds the version of Kafka in 'The Silence of the Sirens' and that of Julio Torri in 'A Circe' in which the Sirens did not sing: 'Las sirenas, esa vez, sólo esa vez, no cantaron' (6).[12] Later Giancarlo says that Ulysses 'escucha el canto de las sirenas y sucumbe [...] se quedó en las islas' (183).

[11] This function, attributed to the novel by Bakhtin, is attributed to film by Susan Sontag: 'Cinema is a kind of pan-art. It can use, incorporate, engulf vitually any other art: the novel, poetry, theater [...]', 'A Note on Novels and Films', in *Against Interpretation*, 245.

[12] In the short piece 'A Circe', Torri has Ulysses say: 'Como iba resuelto a perderme, las sirenas no cantaron para mí', in Octavio Paz et al., eds, *Poesía*

Susan Sontag, with the keenest of antennae for the new sensibility of the sixties, brought out the revindication of surface as a vital trend in film, the *nouveau roman*, and 'camp'. In the context especially of the cinema, the dyad face-mask, face-soul is reversed or dissolved: 'Our manner of appearing is our manner of being. The mask is the face' (18). In 'Godard's *Vivre sa vie*', she quotes the phrase from his *Le Petit Soldat*, which Fuentes use as epigraph to his chapter 'Cinta de plata' (152): 'To photograph a face is to photograph the soul behind it. Photography is truth. And the cinema is the truth twenty-four times a second' (201). She takes the lesson of *Vivre sa vie* to be 'that freedom has no psychological interior' (205). Whereas Mito mostly subscribes to this view of film and prefers his mother Claudia on celluloid almost to the real thing, rather as in Cortázar's 'Queremos tanto a Glenda', he sometimes takes the opposite position: 'Puedo mostrar tu alma última, la que no te han robado las cámaras' (167). In this he comes closer to his double Giancarlo, who listens in the Sirens to 'la parte escondida [de la naturaleza]' (5). Interpretation for Sontag was 'reactionary, stifling, poisoning our sensibilities'; it makes art tame and manageable, and is seen as a 'revenge of the intellect upon the world'. The difficulty of *Zona sagrada* is designed to make interpretation of the novel virtually impossible. Sontag heads her seminal essay with a quotation from *The Picture of Dorian Gray*,[13] which Fuentes quotes twice in *Zona sagrada* (90, 157): '[It is only shallow people who do not judge by appearances.] The mystery of the world is the visible, not the invisible.'

Oscar Wilde seems to be a important model for Guillermo's aestheticism: Beardsley's illustration of his *Salomé* is yet another version of his mother, while Giarncarlo seems to seduce Guillermo in Switzerland by changing his reading habits in much the same way as Lord Henry does with Dorian by sending him what is probably a volume by Huysmans, *À rebours* or *Là-bas* (the second of which Fuentes quotes in an epigraph). Giancarlo in a bookshop takes Mito's hand from the copy of *Great Expectations*, one of the models of *Las buenas conciencias*, which he was about to buy, and leads his hand to the decadent satanism of the 'lycanthrope' Pétrus Borel and to François Villon, whose 'Ballade des dames du temps jadis' tells of one of

---

en movimiento: México 1915-1966 (México: Siglo XXI, 1975), 406.
[13] *The Picture of Dorian Gray* (Harmondsworth: Penguin, 1971), 29.

yesteryear's beautiful queens, 'neiges d'antan', Marguerite de Bourgogne, who murdered her lover of one night Buriden and threw him into the Seine. Guillermo insists on casting Claudia and her co-star the 'galán' in this role of Buridán (25). Dickens, and emblematically *The Cricket on the Hearth*,[14] seems to represent in *Zona sagrada* literature as a mask of the darker truths. Sontag sees Wilde 'between the old-style dandy and an anticipation of the democratic esprit of camp', which she memorably defines in a reformulation of Walter Benjamin's essay title: 'Dandyism in the Age of Mass Culture' (289). Camp, like other phenomena studied by Sontag, denies depth: 'the lens of camp, which blocks out content' (281) and is absolutely incompatible with the humanism of the 'tragic spirit'. Fuentes's text in itself is far too self-conscious and aggressive to be camp, except perhaps in its simultaneous espousal of the mass culture and the erudite, which 'transcends the nausea of the replica' (289). The taste of Guillermo for Art Nouveau Decoration, on the other hand, is certainly camp. Indeed the decoration of his 'encantada gruta' (30-31) seems to have sprung to some extent from Sontag's check-list of camp objects and taste: Tiffany lamps, Guimard, Aubrey Beardsley, Ronald Firbank, 'lighting fixtures in the form of flowering plants, the living room which is really a grotto' (279). Other elements in his room come from that of the proto-dandy Des Esseintes. The latter's celebrated description in *À rebours* of the Salomé by Gustave Moreau in his room and Mallarmé's *Hérodiade*,[15] is superimposed intertextually on Mito's fixation on Beardsley's Salomé,[16] replicating, again, Lévi-Strauss's recording of myth as the sum of all its versions.

Fuentes through Mito, in one of the uncharacteristic programmatic statements in the novel, which help the reader, but go against its own

[14] Mito talks of his favourite writers: 'sobre todo Dickens y la imagen que me capturó, la del Grillo en el hogar y su prodigioso mundo de una fábula inventada por el padre para que el hijo [sic] nunca conozca la verdadera realidad: una realidad que ese niño, ciego, no tiene por qué conocer' (72).
[15] *À rebours* (Paris: Editions Fasquelle, 1968), 83-86 and 240-1.
[16] Beardsley made the illustrations for Wilde's *Salomé*, written for Sarah Bernhardt. See Mario Praz, *The Romantic Agony* (Oxford: OUP, 1985), 312-7. Praz is an excellent source of material on the archetypes Fuentes is using and on the Decadent movement in general. See especially the chapters 'La Belle Dame sans merci' and 'Byzantium'.

spirit somehow, is clear that his loving description of the sinuous surfaces of his room is an aggressive gesture against traditional spiritual depth: 'describir y redescribir como la única burla que nos queda: los inventarios, los catálogos son la ironía final con la que se puede contestar a todas las historias gastadas, a todos los personajes vencidos, a todos los significados vacíos. Los objetos, que son el reino de las apariencias, se vengan del mundo impalpable, espiritual, que antes nos sojuzgó' (67-68).

Mitos's other model dandy is Baudelaire, a line from whose 'Sed non satiata' he uses as an epigraph, and whom he quotes throughout. From Baudelaire's dandy he takes the ideal of appearance and impassivity: 'Viviré y dormiré, Baudelaire, frente a un espejo' (93).[17] Clothes and make-up are stressed, in the Baudelaire he quotes, over nudity: 'La mujer y su ropa, una totalidad indivisible' (133);[18] the 'œil maquillé' is the 'fenêtre ouverte sur l'infini'[19] ('las ventanas que dan sobre el infinito' (107)). It is important to note, however, that in Baudelaire this love of artifice and surface is accompanied by an obsession with and a horror of the bestial, the natural, woman as nature: 'La femme est naturelle, c'est-à-dire abominable.'[20] Love is seen as penetration, opening, wounding: 'Fue Baudelaire quien comparó el acto de amor con una tortura o con una intervención quirúrgica' (26).[21] It is in this spirit that for once Mito desires to break out of the surface, the safe aestheticising gaze with which he defends himself from both his mother and her projection Bela, from mirrors, behind a car windscreen, in front of a movie projector, in his reflection in the Gucci shop window in Rome, and the promise which comes with unfulfilment. In an extraordinarily violent passage, his vision suddenly lurches beyond the 'piel mentirosa':

perfume, brillo en movimiento, piel como papel de seda, mujeres pálidas ahogadas en el satín: tubo de excrecencias, mucosas blandas, pulmones teñidos de tabaco [...] quisiera amarlas desolladas, como realmente son, sin

[17] 'Mon cœur mis à nu', 406.
[18] 'La femme', in *Le Peintre de la vie moderne*, 809.
[19] 'Eloge du maquillage' in *Le Peintre,* 811.
[20] 'Mon cœur mis à nu', 406.
[21] See 'Fusées', XI, 395.

la piel mentirosa, sin el perfume volátil, pura organización de las corrupciones, depósitos de semen inútil. Caguen, putas. (70)[22]

It may be useful to link this passage to another in which another sort of 'piel mentirosa', literature, cannot for once defend Mito from the animality which he loathes, but constantly toys with in dogs, baby birds, ants, spiders. From his bed he suddenly senses the hostile presence of the animal: 'Que otras presencias husmean y palpitan en la oscuridad [...] sólo un aura. Pero es olor de sangre seca y metálica. De cicatrices que no se cierran. De pelambre húmeda y erizada. De anos rojos' (136). He attempts to exorcise that presence by conjuring up fiction, his collection of decadent and camp books, the fictions perhaps of *The Cricket on the Hearth*: 'imagino los libros de la misma cabecera, los libros inevitables, *Les Caves du Vatican, À Rebours, The Picture of Dorian Gray, The Quest for Corvo* [A.J.A. Symons], *Cardinal Pirelli* [Ronald Firbank], como si su propia existencia ficticia pudiese disipar la de la otra ficción, inmediata: mediatizarla. Es inútil' (136). As he puts his hand out, he touches 'la carne húmeda, los belfos espumosos' (137). In a similar vein, though Claudia embodies image and style for Mito, he is also aware that she herself has a seemingly animal dimension beyond the shiny surface. Whereas her lovers have invented her fictional nature, 'inventar en defensa propia tu fábula', she devours and castrates because she will not accept any fiction: 'mi madre devora porque no admite la ilusión y castra porque su vida es más violenta que tus lentos sueños' (26).

As Sontag suggests, perhaps the most radical champion of the surface against depth, humanism and the 'tyrannie des significations'[23] in the arts of the sixties was Alain Robbe-Grillet, in films like *La Dernière Année à Marienbad* with Resnais, his now virtually unreadable novels, and, importantly, his essays, which Fuentes seems to echo in *Zona sagrada*. For Robbe-Grillet film should serve as an example for literature. There, things are not just a meaningful prop in a world of humans, but physically present and visible in their own right for the first time: 's'il arrive encore aux choses de servir un instant de support

[22] Reminiscent of the final lines of Paz's 'Las palabras': 'Chillen, putas', (*Poemas,* 69).
[23] 'Une voie pour le roman futur' in *Pour un Nouveau Roman* (Paris: Gallimard, 1963), 24, abbreviated as RG.

aux passions humaines, ce ne sera que temporairement, et elles n'accepteront la tyrannie des significations qu'en apparence — comme par dérision — pour mieux montrer à quel point elles restent étrangères à l'homme' (RG, 24). As literature follows the example of film in refusing anthropomorphism, 'la *surface* des choses a cessé d'être pour nous le masque de leur cœur' (RG, 27), and the novel achieves 'la destitution des vieux mythes de la "profondeur"' (RG, 26). Mito, in his description of his room, far more sensuous than anything in Robbe-Grillet, echoes the philosophy of the Frenchman: 'la sala existe para ser descrita, no vivida [...] el mundo externo debe vengarse de esa negación de años, de esa pretendida profundidad psicológica que se complace en negar la única realidad, la de las superficies' (116).

Robbe-Grillet's rhetoric is explicitly anti-humanist. Notions such as nature, humanism, tragedy (the title of a seminal essay) and even the absurd, much in vogue at the time, serve to 'récupérer' anything which is different from man, bring it back into the 'réalité profonde' and 'unité cachée' of a humanised world. If reality breaks out of the grid imposed by language and breaks the lens, the notion of the absurd is there 'qui absorbera cet encombrant résidu' (RG, 21). The notion of tragedy is similarly seen as the 'bénédiction du mal', 'Car la tragédie ne comporte ni vraie acceptation, ni refus véritable. Elle est la sublimation d'une différence' (RG, 67). While the notion of the tragic is explicitly important in *Cambio de piel*, a whole strand of *Zona sagrada* clearly denies it. The gaze in *Zona sagrada* is anti-humanist insofar as it dehumanises to the point of turning humans into an object among objects, though admittedly the process has more of witchcraft and magic about it than the bracketing out of meaning attempted by Robbe-Grillet. Guillermo wishes, for example, to trap his mother in his room and 'entonces, momia de polvo, podré contemplarla entre los demás objetos' (92), and enjoys in the same room, 'sentirme un objeto más' (30).

At another point, Mito's anti-humanism seems to echo that of the structuralism of the period in the wider sense: 'Se puede dejar de ser hombre y abrirse a un nuevo conocimiento. Conocer al hombre puede ser, dentro de muy poco tiempo, sólo una intención curiosa y envejecida' (165). In this he coincides with the Foucault of *Les Mots et les choses*: 'L'homme est une invention dont l'archéologie de notre pensée montre aisément la date récente. Et peut-être la fin prochaine.'[24] Claude Lévi-Strauss in his answer to criticisms by Sartre wrote in *The Savage Mind*: 'So I accept the characterisation of aesthete in so far as I believe the ultimate goal of human sciences to be not to constitute, but to dissolve man' (247). Octavio Paz, in an essay on Lévi-Strauss published in the same year as *Zona sagrada* and quoted by Fuentes in *La nueva novela hispanoamericana* in 1969, puts his ideas in an altogether more dramatic form: 'La naturaleza humana, ya que no es una esencia ni una *idea*, es un concierto, una *ratio*, una *proporción*. En un mundo de símbolos, ¿qué simbolizan los símbolos? No al hombre pues, si no hay sujeto, el hombre no es el ser significado ni el ser significante. Es hombre es, apenas, un momento en el mensaje que la naturaleza emite y recibe.'[25]

There are two rival forms of anti-humanism in *Zona sagrada*. One is akin to the accumulation of versions of a myth and the multi-directional readings of Lévi-Strauss, the versions of the myth of Ulysses, the multiple identifications of Claudia, the delirious metonymic chains that span continents, centuries and species, and which dissolve any identity: 'Disuélvete, Claudia linda, [...] disuélvete en todos los espejos de mi soledad' (156). The other is the discovery or fear, already alluded to, that beyond these mirrors there is a deep but animal or monstrous reality. As Mito towards the end of the novel follows Claudia and Giancarlo through the Garden of Monsters in the Orsini castle at Bomarzo near Rome, the large stone statues of monstrous forms are seen as announcements of a new mode of being: 'Las criaturas de Bomarzo, que aún no son nada, son, a pesar de todo, un anuncio, borroso, imperfecto, fatigado, de las otras realidades que nos esperan' (165).

The monstrous and the human, surface and depth, development against transfiguration are just a few of the many oppositions and contradictions in the novel. Perhaps the most basic of these is birth and death, which persistently haunts the text: 'los fetos y los cadáveres' (6, 98) are constant companions. Mito wanders his house obsessed with the extremes of 'Belén y Gólgota, [...] los claustros desnudos del principio y del fin' (41); Signorelli's figures in the murals of Creation and

---

[24] *Les Mots et les choses*, 398.
[25] *Lévi-Strauss o el nuevo festín de Esopo* (Barcelona: Seix Barral, 1993), 120.

Apocalypse 'dan la espalda al antiguo temor de morir y nacer' (164). Claude Lévi-Strauss's description of the role of myth may help us to see how Fuentes's text mediates these contradictions. For the anthropologist 'l'objet du mythe est de fournir un modèle logique pour résoudre une contradiction';[26] 'C'est une sorte d'outil logique, destiné à opérer une médiation entre la vie et la mort' (AS, 243). As the opposition is real and actually irreconcilable, new versions of the myth are constantly generated in a spiral movement until the point of exhaustion.

Lévi-Strauss's thought on myth provides the novelist with powerful strategies against authority, originality, influence, anteriority. A myth is seen as the sum of all its versions, none of which is seen as more primitive or authentic than another. Freud's version of the Œdipus myth takes its place alongside that of Sophocles:

> La méthode nous débarrasse donc d'une difficulté qui a constitué jusqu'à présent un des principaux obstacles au progrès des études mythologiques, à savoir la recherche de la version authentique ou primitive. Nous proposons, au contraire, de définir chaque mythe par l'ensemble de toutes ses versions. [...] On n'hésitera donc pas à ranger Freud, après Sophocle, au nombre de nos sources du mythe d'Œdipe. Leurs versions méritent le même crédit que d'autres, plus anciennes et, en apparence, plus 'authentiques'. (AS, 240)

The urge to break with the origin, to become one's own source can be detected in much of Fuentes's work. The dizzying accumulation of myth on myth in the novel contributes to the breaking of any notion of origin or anteriority: the versions of the Sirens and of Salomé for example. The master myth, which Fuentes takes as the symbol of narrative closure and at the same time of paternal authority is that of Ulysses, his escape from the transformations and dangers of Circe, his return to the faithful Penelope and his endless repetition of his story to his bored family. This story is endlessly fragmented and repeated throughout *Zona sagrada*, and reflected more or less grotesquely in most of the characters: Guillermo's father was a travelling salesman who returned home only to be abandoned by Claudia-Penelope; Giancarlo's father was a war hero who did not return home, but stayed

---

[26] C. Lévi-Strauss, *Anthropologie structurale* (Paris: Plon, 1984), 254, abbreviated hereafter as AS.

with his Circe: 'El viejo ha de haber aprovechado la guerra para quedarse con una puta en Trípoli y salvarse para siempre de la tradición, la familia, mi devotísima madre, un palacio destartalado...' (105). Claudia takes the roles of Circe, Penelope, Hermes, even Ulysses, often simultaneously. The most significant version is probably given in the ritual filmed in Italy, where in an alternative version to Homer's, given in Graves's *Greek Myths* and elsewhere, Telegonus turns Oedipus, slaughters Ulysses and marries Penelope. His halfbrother Telemachus marries Circe.[27]

Linked to the Oedipal murder, in its denial of paternity, genealogy, succession, is the obsessive presence of birth and especially selffecundation and immaculate conception. Claudia is insistently linked with immaculate conception: she brings Guillermo out of the housewomb in 'la época de los robachicos, tan puntual como la época de la Purísima Concepción' (18), while the connotations are more of witchcraft when Mito describes her voice as a 'concepción solitaria', adding that she is able to 'concebirme con su voz' (20). Michelet in *La Sorcière* talks of the witch's 'conception solitaire', whereby she conceives the devil.[28] The mouse, often associated with the demonic, which Claudia keeps in a glass container may be linked to this complex.[29] Hermione and Kirsten give a lurid mythological version of Claudia's self-fecundation: 'Se fecundó a sí misma para no estar sola. Se fornicó con el falo del viento, la perra madre, y parió a la serpiente y con la serpiente se dedicó a gozar y la serpiente creyó ser el verdadero creador pero ella [...] le hundió el cráneo con una patada [...] y lo exiló a las negras cavernas del negro mundo' (173). This complex is clearly linked to a denial of the past, of development, and to the affirmation of an absolute present. The already delirious Mito, at the beginning of the third part, has similar thoughts: 'El primer hombre, el verdadero, el todopoderoso, el que pudo concebirse a sí mismo, por fuerza debió der andrógino, fecundarse, parir a su primer hijo. No hay otra realidad de la génesis' (161).

[27] See also Lanin Gyurko, 'The Myth of Ulysses in Fuentes' *Zona sagrada*', *Modern Language Review*, 69:2, 1974, 316–24.
[28] Michelet, *La Sorcière* (Paris: Librairie Marcel Didier, 1952), I, 9.
[29] See J.E. Cirlot, *A Dictionary of Symbols* (London: Routledge & Kegan Paul, 1983), 272. This seems to be confirmed by the role of the 'mur' with Isabel in *Terra Nostra*.

Close to the androgyne is the notion of conceiving oneself from one's mother, becoming one's own father or perhaps the father of one's double. Something of this seems to be involved in a series of extraordinary sequences, involving Mito and Claudia in various chains of displacement. Two involve Mito's maid Gudelia and her lover Jesús, a parodic version of Claudia (further suggested by the similarity of the names Claudia and Gudelia) and Mito (often associated with Jesus Christ).[30] In an appropriation skilfully analysed by Severo Sarduy,[31] Mito borrows a sweater from Claudia which in its perfume brings Claudia's phantasmal presence, and gives it to Gudelia who passes it on to her coarse lover Jesús, who stains it on his bicycle delivery round, and delights Mito, who imagines him making love to Gudelia while wearing it with his prominent belly protruding from under it. It is curiously Jesús who receives Claudia's presence here, rather than Gudelia, but Mito is certainly a link in this bizarre network. When Mito becomes the canine witness of Gudelia and Jesús's love-making in his flat (replicating that of Claudia and Giancarlo), he is again deeply implicated. When he sees the photograph of Sarah Bernhardt (another avatar of Claudia), now trampled on the floor, with the dog at her feet, he addresses the dog as Baudelaire (now replaced in his frame by Elvis Presley) did his reader: 'Mon semblable, mon frère' (189). Gudelia attempting a reconciliation with her lover uses the term 'chucho', diminutive of Jesús and a slang word for dog, to effect an instantaneous identification of the two men: 'Ay Chucho, si ya sabes que soy tu vieja'.

More complex and more explicit is the Christmas day sequence in Madonna dei Monti. Mito rediscovers his ideal vision of Claudia, as 'la figura [...] querida, la de la silueta de reloj de arena' (91) in the old Italian posters of actresses like Francesca Bertini: 'las fotografías acartonadas de mujeres con figura de reloj de arena' (99). What could be read as a scene of sodomy between Giancarlo and Mito follows: 'Tu mano acaricia mi hombro, detrás de ti' (99). Immediately Mito is seen to have slept, sexually, with a female or male doll: 'La muñeca -o el muñeco- de trapo de color de rosa seguía durmiendo, despatarrado,

---

[30] For example, in the 'Y' shape he forms with his own legs (93), an image of the cross, while his mother is repeatedly identified as the Virgin Mary.
[31] See Severo Sarduy, 'Un fetiche de cachemira', in *Homenaje*, 261-73.

junto a mí' (100). As he wakes, where he would have expected an 'estampa religiosa', he finds a poster of Francesca Bertini in a leopard skin, whom he venerates as the Virgin Mary: 'Dios te salve, Francesca, llena eres de gracia: me hinqué en la cama y uní las manos cerca de la piel de leopardo que cubría el cuerpo de la Bertini.' As he mentions her virgin birth, Claudia-Francesca-Mary is again associated with Giancarlo: 'Y bendito sea el fruto de tu vientre... / Repetiste tu nombre desde el marco de piedra de la puerta' (100). As the sequence continues, Giancarlo, faun-like in a Napoleonic tunic, dances with and seems to penetrate a pregnant, overstuffed doll: 'esas muñecas preñadas' (102).[32] And yet it is Giancarlo who gives birth: 'Te alejaste de la muñeca, rodaste, permaneciste boca arriba, con las piernas abiertas, arqueado, apoyado en los codos. Y el parto —nunca sabré si pude decirlo— era [...]' (103). The maze of reflected penetration, pregnancy and birth between Claudia-Francesca-Mary, Mito, Giancarlo, and the masculine and feminine dolls is almost impenetrable.

The scene is similar to that in *Cambio de piel*, when la Pálida gives birth to a porcelain Infant Jesus,[33] but perhaps even closer to *Aura* where Felipe, having had his feet washed like Christ by Mary Magdalene, under the gaze of a dark crucifix, makes love to Aura, with arms spread like the Crucified. The next day, he realises that 'la concepción estéril de la noche pasada engendró tu propio doble'.[34] What was born in Italy to Mito-Giancarlo in *Zona sagrada* is clearly related: the 'ser que regresa cada vez que lo olvidan, del ser que antes ha muerto, y morirá siempre, de tarde en tarde, para no parecer un monstruo' (103). Mito through Claudia-Francesca-Mary-Giancarlo has engendered his own double, himself as double in Guillermo-Giancarlo.

[32] There are echoes here of Manuel Mujica Láinez's *Bomarzo* (Barcelona: Círculo de Lectores, 1973). Towards the beginning of the novel Pier Francesco Orsini relates how his brother Girolamo, next to naked and described as a 'fauno colérico' (31), dresses Pier first as a 'bufón' and then as 'Francesca' to feign marriage with him. Later, Silvio de Narni makes dolls, 'dos muñecas de estopa' (231), to gain the affection of Julia Farnesea and Porzia. See 249-54 and 316. Mito (165), shadowing his mother and friend, visits the garden of monstrous stone forms in Bomarzo described in Mujica Láinez's novel.
[33] *Cambio de piel*, 457.
[34] *Aura*, 51.

This self-genesis symbolically effects what the text throughout has sought: the liberation from the fixed signification of the paternal order, dependency, and depth. And yet, though Mito and the text gain a sort of autonomy, the reference to the monstrous again suggests the other side of the surface, the animal depth. Again Lévi-Strauss may provide a key to understanding the function of the duality engendered by Mito, his forming a pair of twins with Giancarlo: Romulus and Remus, Castor and Pollux, Cain and Abel, Telemachus and Telegonus and, most insistently, Apollo and Dionysus: 'Hermanos nacidos de una misma madre. [...] Gemelos, Guglielmo: Apolo dios del sol y su cuate antagonista, Dionisos, el conductor de almas' (107). For Lévi-Strauss the pair of twins, dual gods and other family pairings, form an essential function in the mediation between the poles of the contradiction which it is the role of the myth to resolve.[35] The duality engendered by Mito reflects that which fatally splits Claudia, in turn the repository of the oppositions which we have discussed as shaping the novel: Claudia as two-dimensional screen icon, self-made creation living in a perpetual present, and as a woman with the traumatic history of humiliation and struggle which she screams out behind a closed door and which Mito initially refuses to acknowledge and accept: 'renuncié al conocimiento de mi madre. No quise admitir lo que sabía' (156). But Mito comes to desire to reveal the soul behind the surface which he has been at pains to deny elsewhere: 'Puedo mostrar tu alma última, la que no te han robado las cámaras' (167). The missing or hidden dimension of Claudia is expressed in characteristically hyperbolic mythical language, as an amalgam of Beauty and the Beast and the Creator and Lucifer:

> la Bella se ofrece y reta al príncipe a descubrir a la Bestia, a la hermosura corrupta, al cadáver exquisito que se esconde en ella: al monstruo manchado y obsceno que, a su vez contiene la segura resurrección de la Bella [...] no hay acto de creación sin un hermoso ángel caído que refleje la belleza perdida de mi madre cuando ella se complete en la imagen de la muerte y asuma el horror probable. (154)

---

[35] See *Anthropologie structurale*, 248–51.

Giancarlo-Guillermo's giving birth to himself as the 'ser que [...] morirá siempre [...] para no parecer un mostruo' is a dramatisation of this process. The relation between the two reflects and mediates the duality in Claudia. Mito in an increasingly demented fashion takes on the responsibility of 'saving' Claudia: 'Yo soy, yo seré siempre, el ángel caído de tu creación' (156). As the beautiful Giancarlo becomes Claudia's lover, Mito is sadistically chased by him through the original labyrinths of the Paris metro network and takes on more and more animal, viscous, monstrous attributes: 'el terror físico de sentirme menos que un animal conocido y catalogado: el otro ser, nonato, de los laberintos originales' (162). His ultimate self-sacrifice for his mother, or his ultimate punishment at her hands as Circe, is literally to become the 'bestia' as he turns into a dog, replacing his mastiff Faraón.

III: NATIONALISM UNWRITTEN

Una familia lejana, 1980; *Gringo viejo*, 1985

Una familia lejana was published thirteen years after *Cambio de piel* and after the intervening decade of the monumental *Terra Nostra* and the spy thriller *La cabeza de la hidra*. Both *Una familia* and *Gringo viejo* take from novels like *La región más transparente* the theme of national or Continental identity and from *Cambio de piel* the question of the Other. National identities become a relationship, a mutual distortion in the gaze of the Other, a complex exchange of clichés, texts, reflections. From this point of view they look forward to *La frontera de cristal*. Both novels approach the relation between cultures, Spanish America and France, Mexico and the USA, through the mediation of writers. In *Gringo viejo* the North American writer Ambrose Bierce, in the shape of the Gringo of the title, crosses over to Mexico during the Revolution in search of death. In *Una familia lejana*, though a Gallicised figure called Carlos Fuentes is the last narrator, a whole series of French writers of Latin American or Caribbean origin serve as go-betweens: José-Maria de Heredia, Supervielle, Lautréamont, Alexandre Dumas. Intertextual games, reflections and echoes between historical events, characters and stories, migrations and movements have the effect in both novels of undoing the oppositions between the cultures, with their neo-colonial connotations.

Though the novels share a complex and ambiguous relaying of narrations, their styles are very different. *Gringo viejo* has hyperbolic, almost parodic figures and confrontations, especially between the 'greaser' and the 'gringo', the potent revolutionary Tomás Arroyo and Bierce. Men prove their worth by shooting holes through gold coins tossed into the air; the sex scenes reflect the prurient fantasies surrounding the mysterious alien. *Gringo viejo* is set in a burnt out *hacienda* and Arroyo's bordello-like railway carriage in the deserts of northern Mexico, while *Una familia lejana* develops from a stylised conversation with a French aristocrat in the elegant dining rooms of the Automobile Club de France overlooking the Place de la Concorde in Paris. *Una familia lejana* is a complex and rather mannered novel. It has an epigraph from M.P., Marcel Proust presumably, and is dedicated to Buñuel, and both are present in the style. The long, difficult sentences and the contrived, clever observations of its narrators are reminiscent of the Frenchman. So is the importance of memory and also analogy, between generations, geographical areas, sensations, so fundamental to *À la recherche du temps perdu*. The analogies of *Una familia lejana*, however, are those of a Proust rewritten by Buñuel, dislocated, malfunctioning, proliferating, uncontrolled. They partake of the wild continuities in the scene from *Un Chien andalou* described in the novel where a bourgeois living-room in Paris opens out onto the beach at Deauville.

Una familia lejana, 1980: Ballet trasatlántico, fandango en los sótanos de la muerte[1]

Una familia lejana has four major and various minor narrators who pick up each other's story and elaborate it. The story and the telling of the story are virtually indistinguishable. Branly will only find out what happens when he has finished narrating. The decentring of the narrative and the superimposition of voices has a disturbing effect on the reader, who cannot decide whose story he is reading, or indeed reconstruct much sense of a unitary or coherent plot. The major scenification of narration closest to the present is a conversation between the comte de Branly in an elegant Paris club and his interlocutor, in which he tells of two visits to Mexico and his virtual imprisonment in a house in Enghien-les-Bains, between these visits. Narrating the visits to Mexico, he recounts his conversations there with the Mexican archaeologist Hugo Heredia, who recounts conversations with a character usually referred to in quotation marks as 'Heredia', and a demonic plot involving him, and also the story of his family, recent and over various generations. Branly also recounts in the exclusive dining room of the Automobile Club de France the circumstances surrounding his confinement in the Parisian suburb of Enghien, and how he was tricked in a concerted plot by Hugo Heredia, his son Víctor Heredia, and 'Heredia'. He recounts his own dreams and his recollections of his childhood provoked in Enghien and the accounts by his host/sequesterer 'Heredia' of the past of his family, the French Langes and the Dominican-Cuban Heredias, over four or so generations in the Caribbean. Here the voices of two nurses, the French Félicité and especially the black Venezuelan Clemencita, are also incorporated into the network. The passing of the story from 'Heredia' to Hugo Heredia to Branly is accompanied by warnings of dire consequences if it is repeated.

The narration of Hugo Heredia centres on the death of his French-Mexican wife Lucie and their son Antonio in an air-crash and his

[1] *Una familia lejana* (Barcelona: Bruguera, 1980), 127 and 105.

subsequent relationship with his son Victor and their peculiar ways of mourning. The often contradictory and chronologically impossible story of 'Heredia' centres on the hatred of Francisco Luis Heredia for his French father-in-law Monsieur Lange, and his revenge on the latter's daughter Mlle Lange whom he prostitutes when young and later when very old in the various parts of the Caribbean where his corrupt and brutal career takes him. Mlle Lange, mockingly referred to as the Balzacian heroine the Duchesse de Langeais, is buried in a deep gorge or *barranca* later to be disinterred and devoured by vultures. Francisco Luis and a new French wife seem to live with their son 'Heredia' in the Paris of the Second Empire.

The fourth narrator, and internal author, is called 'Carlos Fuentes' by his interlocutor and friend Branly in the dining-room and at a later encounter at Branly's mansion in the Avenue de Saxe. This Carlos Fuentes is a writer of Mexican origin who spent much of his youth in Argentina and elsewhere in South America before settling in Paris in 1955, some twenty-five years before their conversation. He specifically did not return to Mexico to face up to the problematic reality of that country, did not write *Los días enmascarados* and *La región más transparente*, which becomes an alternative phantasmal past for him:

> Imagine si hubiese regresado a México […] y se hubiese arraigado en el país de sus padres. Imagine que publica su primer libro de cuentos a los veinticinco años y su primera novela cuatro después; habla usted de México y los mexicanos, las heridas de un cuerpo, la persistencia de unos sueños, la máscara del progreso. Queda para siempre identificado con ese país y su gente.
>
> —No fue así, Branly, digo sin demasiada seguridad. (213-14)

This Fuentes is not quite at ease with the role the confident French aristocrat condescendingly lends him. He associates Fuentes with the European mistrust of the encyclopaedic knowledge of certain Latin American intellectuals (16), with an aristocratic disdain of any form of resentment (61) associated with Hugo Heredia (221) and repeatedly with 'Heredia', and with an instinctive assumption of Gallic *politesse* as an essential code of behaviour (15). On the other hand, he is quick to remind Fuentes of his Latin roots when referring as a European to precisely those topics which might most enrage a Latin American: pointedly to bribery, described as 'pomada mexicana' (162), to the most varied forms of barbaric behaviour he recounts, associated with the emblematic figures of Rómulo Gallegos: 'esa impunidad del feudalismo latinoamericano, tan anacrónico como pintoresco como delicioso como suicida... Fermina Márquez en París, Doña Bárbara en los llanos del Apure...' (63). On such occasions he says with impeccable courtesy: 'Lamento informarle, mi querido amigo, puesto que usted es en parte de allá [...]' (157). One imagines that the resentment engendered by such comments is not alien to the occasional subtly grotesque aspects of Branly's behaviour as narrated by Fuentes as the final voice.

It is precisely the 'Fuentes' who has turned his back on Mexico who finally recounts the tropical horrors and vicariously visits the heart of darkness of the Caribbean and Spanish American world. He does so, however, amidst a wealth of contortedly subtle aesthetic and psychological disquisitions of a markedly Proustian style,[2] and from a milieu of refinement and symbolist cultural spirituality. From the window of the dining-room over the Seine, 'un minuto milagroso disiparía los accidentes de la jornada —lluvia o bruma, canícula o nieve— para revelar, como en un paisaje de Corot, la esencia luminosa de la Isla de Francia' (11). The conjunction on the same page of the epigraph from Marcel Proust and the dedication to the Spanish cineast Luis Buñuel, with all the echoes of the depiction of the Spanish grotesque of *Viridiana*, the Mexican social reality of *Los olvidados* and the surrealist satire of the French bourgeoisie in *Le Charme discret de la bourgeoisie* is a forewarning of various aspects of *Una familia lejana*.

Never far from Branly's mind and lips are the words of the poem 'La chambre voisine' by the French author of Uruguayan origin Jules Supervielle. Branly associates 'Fuentes' with this poet: 'Supervielle nació en Uruguay; es de allá, como usted'. This elicits from Fuentes the topos of the Latin American cultural emigré or tourist: 'Buenos Aires, Montivideo, son mis ciudades perdidas [...] La patria final de un latinoamericano es Francia; París nunca será una ciudad perdida' (29). While 'Fuentes' (the narrator and implied author, to whom I will give quotation marks), whose twin Carlos Fuentes had been Mexican Ambassador in Paris until 1977, three years previously, is not sure

---

[2] See Wendy Faris, '"Proustitución": *Una familia lejana*', in Merlin Forster and Julio Ortega, eds., *De la crónica a la nueva narrativa mexicana. Coloquio sobre literatura mexicana* (Mexico City: Oasis, 1986), 369-82, 376-7.

whether he is really from the 'allá' referred to by Branly (158), which another twin of his, the Argentinian Horacio Oliveira, calls 'acá', but he is certainly associated with a whole group of transatlantic writers represented by Supervielle. His 'neighbouring room' is on one level the ghostly presence of one side of the Atlantic in the other in most of the characters of the novel. Branly's use of Supervielle is interpreted by 'Fuentes' as French sublimation of the crudity of Spanish American history, selecting and aestheticising, retaining the fantasy and exoticism of the Americas, while disguising the colonial crimes of France:

> Reflexioné [...] en que éste era el poema de un uruguayo francés y que Branly, al recuperarlo, ejercía el supremo don de selección, síntesis y consagración que Francia se ha reservado secularmente. Supervielle era la manera de alejarnos suficientemente de ese enervamiento tropical en que lo sublime roza constantemente lo ridículo y los sentimientos de una culpa cruel se revelan con demasiada crudeza, sin los piadosos velos que los europeos sabemos arrojar, prontamente, sobre nuestros crímenes históricos para acercarnos al espíritu de la razón y el gusto, ambos discriminativos y exigentes, de Francia, pero sin perder el filo de fantasía, de desplazamiento, de locura reveladora, de las tierras anchas y vacías del nuevo continente.
>
> (130–1)

Branly counts a number of French Latin Americans like sheep jumping fences in a 'ballet trasatlántico'. Among them are Reynaldo Hahn (Caracas 1874, Paris 1947), the Venezuelan musician who was for some time the lover of Proust and is portrayed in *Jean Santeuil*, and the Uruguayan Jules Laforgue, author of the wittily detached *L'Imitation de Notre-Dame la lune*, the compatriot of Supervielle, whose lines from 'Whisper in Agony' (*Le Forçat innocent*) he redeploys to refer to the *pampa*: 'una gran plaza vacía entre dos ejércitos' (128). Another is the Parnassian poet of Cuban origin José-Maria de Heredia (Santiago de Cuba 1842, Paris 1905), whose aestheticising and romanticising lines from *Les Trophées* he quotes here (128) and uses as the epigraphs for two key chapters, reflecting the most brutal plot elements in the Caribbean, 'Clemencita' and 'La Mamasel' (clashing rather with the obscene connotations in Spanish of her title): 'La bête épanouie et la vivante flore' (108, from 'Le Récif de corail') and 'Fatigués de porter leurs misères hautaines' (115, from 'Les Conquérants').

Another far less reassuring figure, however, jumps over the fence with the others: Isidore Ducasse, Comte de Lautréamont (Montevideo 1846, Paris 1870), author of the brutally and deliriously transgressive *Les Chants de Maldoror*. His line 'c'est un cauchemar qui tient la plume'[3] is attributed to both Branly and 'Fuentes' as it becomes 'c'est un cauchemar qui tient *ma* plume' (128). Applied to the Montevideo which is the 'ciudad perdida' of 'Fuentes' it evokes a horror of dismemberment and massacre which could just as easily be the work of Juan Manuel de Rosas in the mid-nineteenth century or the Dirty War against the Tupamaros of the 1960s and 1970s: 'morir [...] en los miserables hospitales de París, cuando en Montevideo tenía ya su mal de aurora: las aguas del Río de la Plata amanecerían embarazadas de pellejos inflados, pieles de reses sacrificadas, de hombres mutilados' (127). For the European ancestors of Branly the pen of Maldoror combines with the dominating image from Kafka's 'Penal Colony' to evoke the horrors of colonialism and imperial intervention: 'Allá, nos convertimos en Heredias: en criollos enervados. Le diré que la cruel pluma de Maldoror escribió a latigazos su poema sobre demasiadas espaldas inocentes' (128). 'Fuentes' seems to make a conscious decision in his narration to favour the rational lucidity of Supervielle over the unthinkable in Lautréamont: 'excluyo para siempre de su narración a ese doble monstruoso del conde de Lautréamont [...] respiro involuntariamente cuando mi amigo libera el espacio de su sueño para otro francés de Montevideo, el lúcido y magistral Jules Supervielle' (127-8).

The whole novel could be seen as following this same rhythmical move into and out of sublimation. The word 'connotación' as used in a couple of sequences seems to mean hard historical referentiality against either mythification or loss of meaning in post-colonial kitsch or detritus. Branly dreams of a timeless woman who was somehow the promise of his lost youth and 'Heredia' places her in a brothel in Mexico in 1864 during the French intervention. A dirty 'tide' of connotation swallows up his pure vision: 'la invasión de su sueño prístino de la mujer situada ubicuamente en el umbral común del nacimiento y de la muerte por la marea connotativa, lodosa, de guerras

---

[3] Isidore Ducasse, Comte de Lautréamont, 'Poésies I', in *Les Chants de Maldoror. Lettres. Poésies I et II* (Paris: Gallimard, 1973), 290-1.

y pasiones, venganzas y rebeldías, tráficos de armas y de cuerpos' (125). On another occasion, Branly climbs the stairs to the *mansarde* of 'Heredia"s house. His reception of the smell of various leathers is translated into pictorial terms by 'Fuentes': an 'inmenso cuadro de trofeos' (101) (echoing J.M. de Heredia's *Les Trophées*) and booty brought back from the Eastern Mediterranean by the Napoleonic armies for the museums of Europe. The imagined painting, translated from smell, is characterised by re-painting, reworking of one style into another: 'un lienzo con temática de David pintado por un Delacroix menos áspero' (101). The meaningful works of art, experiences, history when exported and reappropriated, become empty murmurs, dead flowers woven into a phantasmal funerary wreath (101): 'todos trenzados en la ausencia absoluta de su propia connotación histórica, meros rumores, flores aplastadas, despojo de nombres' (101-2). The images culminate in the vision of a woman, the woman of Branly's dream, which turns out to be a painting for whom 'los trofeos avasallados por Masséna para Francia se trenzaban como flores de veneno en torno a joyas preciosas' (102). The female figure, which recurs throughout the novel, is of a lady of the First Empire associated with the portraiture of Ingres, perhaps his famous painting of Sabine Rivière, 1806. Within the theme of palimpsest, however, she is reworked from Ingres to Gustave Moreau, as she covers her face with poisonous, mercury-based golden nails, as Proust's previously quoted description of Moreau's work is also woven into the picture: 'flores envenenadas entrelazadas con joyas preciosas' (18).[4]

The lucid sublimation of Supervielle and the Parnassian aestheticisation by J.M. de Heredia of the American is taken to an almost delirious extreme here, where any sense of origin or originality is highly problematical. It is almost as if Fuentes undoes the distancing and appropriation of the Other by French culture by introducing a tropical, Caribbean storm of baroque analogies, using technology, architecture, painting, poetry and history. It is thus ironic that 'Fuentes' seems to mock the pedantry, the 'sonrisa llena de coquetería referencial' (78), of the Frenchman Branly, who likens the presence of the crashed

[4] 'la femme entretenue — chatoyant amalgame d'éléments inconnus et diaboliques, serti, comme une apparition de Gustave Moreau, de fleurs vénéneuses entrelacées à des joyaux précieux', *Du côté de chez Swann*, *A la recherche du temps perdu*, 218.

Citröen in the formal, Le Nôtre-inspired garden to a painting by Kurt Schwitters,[5] to Lautréamont's 'fortuitous encounter of an umbrella and a sewing machine',[6] and to the anachronistic inappropriateness of imagining Louis XVI's 1791 flight to Varennes happening in a helicopter taking off from the Petit Trianon. On the level of identity, both personal and national, binary oppositions are deployed by various characters as a sort of barrier to hold the line against contamination. But such oppositions seem to have a tendency quickly to become unstable and almost deconstruct themselves. The supposedly pure French aristocracy of Branly is opposed to the hybrid, new identity of 'Heredia' tainted by contact with the colonies: 'el contraste entre una vieja línea francesa y un transplante colonial era [...] demasiado grosero' (51). If the 'Heredias' are seen as unbalanced 'criollos enervados' (128), the Frenchman strikes a classical balance between sensuality and rationality. There are various allusions to Matthew Arnold's phrase in French 'l'homme sensuel moyen', originally embedded in an English sentence, but taken up by the French as 'l'homme sensuel moyen dont la patrie est la France et la ville Paris, et dont l'idéal est la vie libre, gaie, plaisante, de Paris'.[7] The sensuality of the original is tempered by Cartesian rationality. Hugo Heredia denies the Mexican monopoly of violence to avoid alarming 'la sensibilidad de un francés razonable, sensual seguramente, pero mediocre no, jamás' (14). 'Heredia' describes the precarious balance in Branly scathingly: 'De veras que es usted un buen francés racionalmente sensual' (123). The politeness of the conversation between Branly and 'Fuentes' is thus hopefully presented as a 'el remanso prolongado de la buena razón cartesiana' against the 'caos tropical de los Heredia' (147).

[5] Schwitters (1887-1948) belonged to an idiosyncratic brand of Dada called Merz, and was known for collages and constructions, making consciously aesthetic abstract designs out of junk and rubbish. See *The Encyclopedia of Visual Art* (London: Encyclopaedia Britannica International, 1989), V, 881.
[6] See Lautréamont, *Chants de Maldoror*, 'Chant sixième', 234.
[7] Othon Guerlac, *Les Citations françaises* (Paris: A. Colin, 1961), 236, gives this French translation from Matthew Arnold's *Mixed Essays*, 1870. I am grateful to Professor Peter Rickard of Emmanuel College, Cambridge, for the reference.

The underlying opposition evokes a nature-culture split, which is explored in terms of gardens and architecture. 'Heredia' puts it crudely. Spanish language brings his family 'sólo recuerdos de barbarie, revolución e impaciencia'. The French language he claims to prefer is like the order of his formal garden against the nature of the wood within which it is set: 'El francés es como mi jardín, elegante [...]; el español como mi bosque, indomable' (50). But, as Hugo Heredia had pointed out, architecture not only distinguishes itself from nature, but echoes it, contains it: 'El templo [...] es un lugar aparte, sagrado y distinto de la naturaleza. Pero también es un eco de ella porque fue creado para distinguirse de ella' (19). Both 'Heredia''s garden and Branly's courtyard seem to illustrate the way in which the oppositions melt. The order of the garden is set against the disorder of nature, but the continuity between the rose bushes, the beeches and the willow, and especially the symmetrical line of the white trunks of the birch trees neutralise the opposition:

> Más allá de los contraste soberanos del bosque y del jardín, el espíritu del orden que parecía gobernar a éste salía al encuentro de la mitad que lo negaba en aquél; orden y desorden se reunían sin conflicto entre los rosales, las hayas y un sauce solitario, pero, sobre todo, en el bosque de abedules que cercaba uno de los extremos de la mansión. (38).

Branly contrasts the solidity of his house and garden against the invasion from outside with the fragility of that of 'Heredia'. The oppositions he mentions, however, are far from stable. His courtyard has grass and a bed of sand in which a pine-tree grows. The sand is seen at once as sterile like the asphalt of the road outside, and yet it allows growth and protects against the invasion of the road which would kill the tree:

> el jardín de césped bien recortado, las urnas sin valor y un grueso pino marítimo contento de crecer en la arena gemela, en cierto modo, del asfalto igualmente estéril de la calle. No obstante, mi amigo insiste en concebirla como una defensa contra la posible invasión de la calle; invoca el hecho de que ese pino crece gracias a la arena y sería asesinado por el asfalto (38).

He goes on to correct himself, adding that the road would hate the 'falso oasis del jardín, reconociendo en él un desierto disfrazado' (38-

39). Such a complex and apparently rational process of oppositions and analogies could go on indefinitely, becoming a sign of its opposite in delirium. The play between rationality and madness, artifice and nature is taken to its most inextricable pitch in the Parisian Parc Monceau, which is a key space in the novel. Bought in 1778 by Philippe d'Orléans, nicknamed Égalité, it contains false ruins, Chinese pagodas and miniature windmills.[8] It is seen as the site where a secret unhinging of Paris and French culture is played out: 'un secreto desquiciamiento de la ciudad toda aflora y se apaga, se enciende de nuevo y se apoya en el gesto de la fantasía imprevisible antes de paralizarse, finalmente, en la piedra de las ruinas fingidas'. The park is the sign of the terminal madness of the eighteenth-century aristocracy before the Revolution: 'ese relámpago de demencia aristocrática final, desesperada y agónica'. And yet it is also see as an exercise of reason exorcising the divine insanity of nature:

> un siglo extrañamente obsedido por reproducir en miniatura, a escala, con exquisita delicadeza y amor del *trompe l'oeil*, pero también con un temblor secreto, la naturaleza entera, como si ésta no se bastase o nos bastase sino que, más bien, poseyese el pecado imborrable de un pasado, un origen no atribuible a la razón humana sino a la vesania divina. (84)

Hugo Heredia takes these paradoxical games with madness and order, parallel to those explored in *Cambio de piel*, onto a cultural and political plane, when he considers the consequences of importing French rational thinking into Mexico. French reason is both a palliative and a 'terrible furnace' to Latin American delirium, when Rousseau and Voltaire, Comte and then Bergson are seen to fuel a hundred years of turmoil from the Independence movement of 1810, the Positivism of the *científicos* of Porfirio Díaz, the Ateneo and the Revolution of 1910:

> la razón francesa es un buen correctivo del delirio latinoamericano; también es su terrible horno y Lucie se divertía en recordarme que mi país hizo una revolución de independencia porque algunos hombres leyeron a Rousseau y

---

[8] See *Baedeker's Paris and its Environs* (London: Dulau and Co., 1898), 202-3.

Voltaire, una contrarrevolución ilustrada porque otros leyeron a Comte y una nueva revolución intelectualmente inflamada por Bergson. Le permito manifestar sus dudas sobre los resultados de esos trasplantes ideológicos.

(172)

Set in direct contraposition to the flow and exchange, opposition and fusion, palimpsest and transplants sketched out here is the demonic demand for absolute unity. The unity is also one of narrative closure, symmetry, resolution, but the complex plot which links the destinies of Hugo Heredia, Branly and 'Heredia' and their families is that of the ghost story, Gothic tale, a story of pacts with the devil. 'Heredia' is a devil who has much in common with the 'diablo cojuelo' of *La región más transparente*, Ixca Cienfuegos, like him a powerful 'especialista en recuerdos' (178), able magically to manipulate the action of the novel, but with little personal fixity or identity of his own. In his demand for unity and the absolute he has much in common with Herr Urs from *Cambio de piel* and through him with the devil of Mann's *Doctor Faustus*, with whom he also shares an atrocious bad taste in clothes. In a later comment on the novel, Fuentes says of him: 'Me gusta el personaje del Heredia francés. Es el Diablo que quiere la unidad perfecta y el dominio absoluto. No lo logra, porque el lector es libre de continuar la historia.'[9] His plot to forge that unity, once reconstructed from the shifting frames and fragments of the novel, is incredibly precise and determined. 'Heredia' is described as 'unfinished': 'el confuso vástago de muchos lugares más que de tiempo alguno, este hombre cargado de historias inconclusas porque él mismo no tenía fechas ni orígenes' (153). His son André is described as literally unfinished, 'mal acabado'(148), in that his lower limbs are unformed and covered in shaggy hair. He is never seen at the same time as his son, who is to him much as was Aura to Consuelo in the novella *Aura*, a magical projection through which to forge or recover unity with a lost partner or even parent.

In an outline of the demonic plot, the first episode is when 'Heredia' appears to Hugo Heredia and his wife Lucie, from behind a statue of Balzac, at a party in Caracas. Some time later, Lucie and one of her sons, Antonio, are killed in an air accident. Hugo Heredia is left with

---

[9] Carlos Fuentes 'Cronología personal', in Julio Ortega, ed., *Retrato*, 112.

Víctor. In the Toltec ruins at Xochicalco, Víctor finds an object which represents absolute unity: 'contempló algo que no me podía describir, una unidad de tal manera excelente, sin fisuras, como una poderosa gota de oro cóncavo, que no necesitaba adorno, talla o añadido alguno' (182-3). Feeling an invincible hatred for the object and 'su belleza que era sinónimo de su unidad' Víctor breaks the object into two and throws the halves towards the precipice which the site overlooked. He falls a great distance, but is caught. The unity of the object was very much the embodiment of the world view of Hugo Heredia: 'la memoria de la unidad del tiempo' (183); 'Nada existe aisladamente' (184). Hugo and his son play identity games, combining parts of photographs from different periods, but especially one based on the notion of homonymy. Homonymy can point to a spurious sort of unity; sharing a name may or may not point to real family relationships or identity. They ring people with their own names in the cities they visit, and in Monterrey end up visiting 'Heredia', characteristically the same and not the same person Hugo had met in Caracas: 'este "Heredia" no era exactamente el otro; sólo me lo recordaba' (188). 'Heredia' proposes an ill-defined pact whereby Víctor seems to pass into his power, joining someone who is described as never having existed ('si yo podía desear el regreso de quienes fueron, él requería la presencia de quien nunca fue' (190)), and as having died: 'un espacio antiguo donde mi muerto y el suyo se encuentren a través del joven Víctor, que está vivo' (191). Víctor will somehow recover the memory of his dead brother Antonio. For Hugo the pact is equivalent to bringing together the parts of the object broken by Víctor, and restoring his unified view of life: 'Quisiera que las mitades de ese objeto se reuniesen para que esa unidad no falte en el arte, la historia, el pasado, la cultura, como usted guste' (191). 'Heredia' promises that Víctor will find half the object at Xochicalco and with that token will later recover the other half. In the early pages of the novel Víctor does find the half in the presence of Branly, who had been taken there and introduced to Hugo by a common friend, Jean, presumably in league with either Hugo or 'Heredia'. Víctor nearly falls again, and is saved by Branly (14). That evening in Cuernavaca Branly and the others hear from the depths of the *barranca* below the *tonada* which will become the refrain of the novel and Víctor whistles the same tune in response. The reader later understands that the singer is Andrés, who has found the other half of the object. Branly invites Hugo Heredia and his son to stay in his house in Paris and during that visit they look up their names in the telephone directory and Branly and Víctor visit a certain Víctor Heredia in Enghien les Bains. Various accidents are manipulated and Branly is injured and retained at the house of 'Heredia' or 'el Heredia francés', in his third incarnation after Caracas and Monterrey. In the garden, and in his crashed Citröen, he sees the 'brutal cópula' between Víctor and the 'son' of 'Heredia', André. As Víctor is sodomised he and his partner bring together the two halves of the object from Xochicalco: 'se unieron como un objeto de metal fundido a otro' (137). Víctor and André become one person, probably the waiter whom Branly and 'Fuentes' see in the swimming pool in the club. Hugo Heredia tells the authorities that his son has drowned in Normandy and returns to Mexico, where Branly visits him for the second time, and is told the story of the pact, which Branly in turn passes on to 'Fuentes'.

This plot, in both senses of the word, as conspiracy and narrative, is powerfully symmetrical, moving from separation to magical reunion and closure. Its simplicity is mocked by the almost uncontrollable complexity and ambiguity of a series of migrations, of people and stories between the New World and the Old, Mexico and the Caribbean and France. Textual, intertextual and extratextual analogies, a complex network of disturbing, often tenuous and perhaps fallacious links relate the four characters to each other, to a long family heritage, and to the life and works of transatlantic writers. They become ghosts, palimpsestic echoes of writers who themselves are set in similar family chains. These writers, especially José María Heredia, José-Maria de Heredia, and Alexandre Dumas, are marked by homonymy, as are the fictional Heredias.

The presence of the French Parnassian poet José-Maria de Heredia (1842–1905) is clearly signalled. His lines are used twice as chapter epigraphs, the collection *Les Trophées* is included in the list of titles from Branly's library which figure in the novel (206), Branly mentions him in the list of French intellectuals of Latin American origin and quotes the lines used in the epigraphs and others, in Spanish (128). When Branly meets 'Heredia' he asks '¿parientes del poeta?' to which 'Heredia' replies '¿cuál poeta?' before answering negatively and adding that his family had dropped the use of Spanish: 'no, concluyó con un aire de fatiga presuntuosa, había desterrado el uso de la lengua española' (50). The Spanish-language poet is clearly the Cuban poet José María Heredia (1803–1839) who was the cousin of his homonym

the French Heredia, though he died before the latter was born. When 'Heredia' apologises for not using the 'de' before Branly's surname, the allusion is to the 'de' affected before his name by the French Heredia, who had certain pretensions to nobility as seen in his poem 'L'Ancêtre' with its allusions to his ancestor the sixteenth-century 'Adelantado', don Pedro de Heredia. In one of his very few Spanish-language poems the French Heredia pays homage to the heritage of his cousin.[10]
There are references to Alexandre Dumas throughout the novel. Branly hears André ask Víctor if he has read *La máscara de fierro* (72), and remembers having read it himself when young (73). He links Dumas to his father 'Heredia' saying that both came from Haiti. Various references are made to information given in his *Mes mémoires* (169). More strikingly, Dumas actually appears indirectly as a character in the novel, when André refers to a visit by him to the house at Enghien (in 1870), and asks Víctor whether he remembers (in 1980), adding: 'Creo que escribió un libro. Pero se perdió' (97). The polysemia of the novel and the difficulty in reading and identifying characters definitively are nicely illustrated by the characters carved over 'Heredia's' house in Enghien: 'A.D. 1870', The chauffeur believes it to be an address, while Branly reads the A.D. more conventionally as 'anno domini', indicating a date. 'Fuentes' later reads that Alexandre Dumas had visited the house in 1870, the year of his death, and that the letters were the initials of his name. The initials offer other possible readings. In Fuentes's article on the writing of *Aura*, published in 1982, two years after *Una familia lejana*, he talks of meeting Maria Callas in 1976, the year of her death, listening to her recording of *La Traviata* and re-reading the book on which the opera is based, *La Dame aux camélias* by Alexandre Dumas *fils*, to write a film script. He writes: 'La novela se inicia con el regreso a París de

---

[10] 'Oh! Sombra inmensa que la luz admira!
    Yo que cogí de tu heredad la lira
        Y que llevo tu sangre con tu nombre,
        Perdón si balbuceo tu lenguage,
        Al rendir, en mi siglo, este homenaje
        Al Gran Poeta con que honraste al Hombre!'
José-Maria de Heredia, 'A José Maria Heredia en su centenario', in *Œuvres poétiques complètes* (Paris: Société d'Édition 'Les Belles Lettres', 1984), II, 195.

Armando Duval, A.D., el sosias de Alejandro Dumas [*fils*]'[11] Another two names, two readings are suprimposed on the first three interpretations. Fuentes had been most impressed by what he calls the 'necrofilia delirante' of the description of the exhumation of Marguerite Gautier's body and reproduces in the article the description of the face of the corpse. When 'Fuentes' in *Una familia lejana* pulls the hands from the face of the ghost of the dead Lucie, his horror is very similar. In a novel where, as we shall see, generations can be seemingly reversed, the remark of Alexandre Dumas *fils* about his father, reported by André Maurois, is pertinent: 'Mon père, disait-il, c'est un grand enfant que j'ai eu quand j'étais tout petit.'[12]

In the volume of Dumas's memoirs which 'Fuentes' takes from the shelf of Branly, he reads words which seem to fly from the pages 'para ganar un vuelo similar al de los pájaros migratorios' (207), the migratory birds Branly sees fly over Enghien, as names and destinies migrate across the Atlantic in the pages of the novel. He reads something the status of which is difficult to determine, and which 'no pertenecía, propiamente, a las memorias del poderoso escritor', logically so, as it recounts the writer's death. On his death-bed Dumas gave to his son a gold coin which he had brought with him to Paris in his youth and had never spent. By this page, presumably printed and apochryphal, there was a hand-written sheet, by the owner of the house in Enghien, presumably the father of 'Heredia', Francisco Luis, but of course a curious link is established by the fact that the book and the note are the property of Branly. Reminiscent of the note found by Faria in *Le Comte de Monte-Cristo*,[13] it records a visit by 'AD' in 1870 to Enghien to deliver a blond baby and take away in exchange a black baby born from a slave woman from the plantations lost in Haiti by Francisco Luis's father-in-law. The exchange of black and white babies also happens at the beginning of *La campaña*. The swapping of children is relatively common in the nineteenth-century novel. In Dumas's *The Man in the Iron Mask*, for example, the twin brother of Louis XIV is

---

[11] 'Como escribí algunos de mis libros', 3.
[12] André Maurois, 'Introduction' to Alexandre Dumas *fils*, *La Dame aux camélias* (Paris: Gallimard, 1991), 8.
[13] See Alexandre Dumas, *Le Comte de Monte-Cristo* (Paris: Le Livre de Poche, 1973), I, 247.

separated at birth and eventually confined to the Bastille before he is briefly substituted for the king by Aramis.

Family origins in Haiti link the Heredia family and that of Alexandre Dumas. Haiti is actually an ideal component of Fuentes's novel because of its confusing and ambiguous history and names. It was formed when the western part of Hispaniola was ceded to France in 1697 and renamed Saint-Domingue. About a hundred years later Spain ceded the rest of the island to France, by the treaty of Basel in 1795, but it never actually changed hands. In 1809 the whole island was declared independent as Haiti, but in 1809 Santo Domingo, the present-day Dominican Republic, was reunited with Spain, only to declare its own independence in 1821. The mulatto Boyer invaded Santo Domingo in 1822, but was expelled in 1844. Its history has been marked by a series of bloody slave rebellions, such as that of 1791, fictionalised in Alejo Carpentier's *El reino de este mundo*. The island is thus the dramatic site of a problematic and shifting relationship between French and Hispanics, and between white settlers and black slaves.[14]

A third writer is pointed to in an over obvious, almost parodic fashion, with something of the air of a red-herring. The Christian names of the son Víctor Heredia and the father Hugo Heredia give Victor Hugo. In terms of homonymy, two other names and phantasmal presences spring to mind. The first is Victor Hugues, the Haitian revolutionary from Carpentier's *El siglo de las luces*, who moved from Cuba to revolutionary France and thereafter the width and breadth of the Caribbean. The second is Hugues de Saint-Victor, whose meditations on belonging to a nationalism group and exile have been quoted by Fuentes on various occasions.[15] As to why the name of Victor Hugo should be highlighted, apart from the game of homonymy and the playful creation of a fuzzy labyrinth of echoes, the classic swapping of children in *Notre-Dame de Paris* comes to mind. There the beautiful Agnès, later called Esmeralda, is abducted by gypsies and replaced by the hideous hunchback Quasimodo, who later falls in love with the gypsy girl and is only united with her in death.[16]

---

[14] See *Encyclopaedia Britannica*, fifteenth edition (1992), XXIX, 745 and 749.
[15] For example, in the interview with Reyzábal, in Julio Ortega, ed., *Retrato*, 82.
[16] Dr Peter Whyte of the University of Durham kindly informs me that Hugo's daughter Adèle, who went mad in 1863 and remained so until her death in

Behind the names of José María Heredia, Alexandre Dumas and Victor Hugo, and the homonymy involved therein, there lies a key hidden homonymy: that of Carlos Fuentes, born in Panama in 1928, and his uncle, the poet from Veracruz, Carlos Fuentes Boettiger, who died from typhoid fever in Mexico City in 1914. This poet uncle, who died fourteen years before Fuentes's own birth, is vividly evoked in *Los años con Laura Díaz*. Fuentes expands on the significance of their homonymy in a speech given in Veracruz:

> Pero mi padre, a su vez, llevó siempre en su corazón la herida del hermano muerto. A mí me puso su nombre y si desde niño me rodeó de libros; fue, sin duda, como un homenaje a una esperanza para ese otro Carlos Fuentes, el segundo de ese nombre, como yo soy el tercero y mi joven hijo, cineasta, pintor y poeta, el cuarto.[17]

The character 'Fuentes' fits into the pattern of José-Maria de Heredia by becoming a predominantly French writer with a Hispanic relative writer based in Latin America.

If the Hispanic relatives of José-Maria de Heredia and Carlos Fuentes die before the latter are born, Branly and Víctor Heredia meet by chance when they are both alive, though Branly repeatedly comments that it would have been more logical if he had died before they had met, suggesting that Víctor is in a sense a reincarnation of Branly: 'Lo normal es que yo hubiese muerto antes de que él naciese' (96). The fact that the metempsychosis happens when both are alive is reminiscent of the short story 'Una flor amarilla' by Julio Cortázar, whose presence is felt strongly in many pages of *Una familia lejana*.[18]

The story of 'Heredia' in the novel is woven or rather loosely assembled from fragments of the real life story of the family of the

---

1915, was in the Caribbean.

[17] 'Regreso al hogar', in *Nuevo tiempo mexicano* (Mexico City: Aguilar, 1994), 190.

[18] Enghien-les-Bains is also the setting of Cortázar's short story/novella 'Las armas secretas'. Both Cortázar's story and Fuentes's novel share the motif of the dry leaves, metempsychosis, and a violent heritage from the past. 'Heredia''s house in the Clos des Renards is apparently modelled on a house lent by José Luis Cuevas to Fuentes, La Renaudière. See 'Cronología personal', 111.

Cuban José María Heredia and the Dumas family. One writer on the Heredia family asserts that 'sus principales miembros llevaron una vida ambulante, llena de peligros y trágico destino'.[19] The family can be traced to the the sixteenth-century 'Adelantado don Pedro de Heredia, Capitán General y Gobernador de Cartagena de Indias', and were established from the sixteenth to the early nineteenth century on the island of Santo Domingo. The brothers José Francisco and Domingo de Heredia y Mieses, the fathers, respectively of the Cuban and the French poets, were forced to leave Santo Domingo at the beginning of the nineteenth century after the cession of the Spanish part of the island to the French. The family moved to Cuba, and the lawyer José Francisco, an honest and principled *criollo* loyal to the Spanish crown occupied various difficult posts in Cuba, Florida and later Venezuela as 'Oidor de la Audiencia de Caracas' during the precarious period around 1812 when his movements and fate depended on the campaigns of Simón Bolívar. His health broken, he died in Mexico in 1820. His son José María was also a lawyer, and was exiled from Cuba to the USA in 1823 for conspiring against the Spanish government, but lived for most of the rest of his life in Mexico, often in Cuernavaca, as politician, magistrate and lecturer until his death in 1839.

The story of the Dumas family reads even more like a romantic novel. His unscrupulous and dissipated grandfather, from an old aristocratic French family, Alexandre-Antoine Davy de la Pailleterie, went in 1760 to Saint-Domingue where he left his brothers, took the name Delisle, and lived in obscurity with the black slave Louise-Césette Dumas, from whom he had four children. When his brothers died, he sold his half-cast children and returned to France in 1773 to claim his inheritance. In 1789 he maried his 'dame de charge', forty years his junior. He was joined by his son Thomas Alexandre, dissipated like himself, who on joining the 'dragons de la reine' in 1786 was forced to renounce the surname of his father and chose that of his black mother: Dumas. He had to face his young step-mother to claim the inheritance of his father, married a thirteen-year-old daughter of the 'petite bourgeoisie de commerce' and with her fathered the famous novelist

---

[19] Lomberto Díaz, *Heredia: primer romántico hispanoamericano* (Montevideo: Ediciones Geminis, 1973), 15. I have taken most of the information about José María Heredia from this work.

Alexandre Dumas (1802–1870). The son of the latter, another Alexandre Dumas, who first wrote under the name of his grandfather, Davy, was the author of *La Dame aux camélias*, 1848.[20] 'Heredia' tells the story of his family in two versions to Hugo Heredia and to Branly. To his account is added the voice of the mulatta nursemaid Clementina. In the first account, 'Heredia' explains to Branly that he belonged to a Cuban family which emigrated to Haiti during the struggle in Cuba at the end of the nineteenth century against the Spaniards, and made their fortune trading with France during the First World War (50). In a longer, more complex account, the story emerges of a French trader, M. Lange, who at the beginning of the nineteenth century fled from Haiti and black revolts and massacres to la Guaira in Venezuela, via Cuba (following José Francisco Heredia). His fortunes dwindle and when in 1812 the French imperial bonds lose their value, he is virtually ruined. His one asset is his beautiful daughter, admired by Bolívar, and won by Francisco Luis Heredia, a disinherited penniless rebel who married her believing her to be a rich heiress, while the Langes in turn believed him to be a rich heir. This is the origin of the hatred of Francisco Luis for his father-in-law and his wife, and much of the evil in the novel: 'el dinero puede ser la fuente de rencor, tragedia y mal' (112). The young Venezuelan follows the model of the Lange he so hates: 'siguiendo las huellas de tu detestado suegro repetiste su vida y fortuna a la sombra de la independencia republicana' (117). He made his fortune trafficking in goods and later slaves and prostitution between the islands of the Caribbean and Mexico. His revenge on his wife is to prostitute her and then abandon her in la Guaira when she is too old, looked after by the young mulatta Clemencita. José Francisco remarried a bourgeoise French wife (following Thomas-Alexandre Davy) with whom he had a son and lived in Paris at the Court of Napoleon III and Eugénie (1852–1870). The latter has a portrait by the Court painter Winterhalter, while Mlle Lange seems to have been painted by the painter of the First Empire, Ingres. He undergoes in the Second Empire what his father-in-law had suffered in the First as the bonds of Jecker devalue when they are not recognised by Benito Juárez (1862). The French Intervention in Mexico (1861–

---

[20] See Dumas, *Mes mémoires*, 1830–1833 (Paris: Robert Lafont, 1989), II, esp. 1264–70.

1867) gives him the chance to remake his fortune, setting up a brothel in Acapaltzingo, Cuernavaca, where he brings his elderly wife to vilify her even more by prostituting her under the name of Balzac's heroine the Duchesse de Langeais (from where Fuentes presumably derives the name Lange), burying her in the *barranca* in 1864 when she dies. Clemencita is the maid of José Francisco in Paris, and later the *nodriza* of Víctor, that is, 'Heredia' (117), to whom she transmits the story of Mlle Lange. If at this stage one factors in the black and white children exchanged later, a characteristically strange but clear enough link emerges between the black child picked up in the novel by Alexandre Dumas, the mulatta Clemencita and Dumas's real black grandmother, Louise Césette. Another presence here, given the mentions of Bolívar in the la Guaira passages, and Hugo Heredia dressing like him in the fancy-dress party, is Hipólita the black maid who brought up the Libertador, and of whom he wrote 'recuerda que no he conocido otra madre'.[21]

The uncontrolled, almost wild analogies, between courts, within families, between literary characters and the families of real writers, between literary characters and characters from other novels, etc., create a reading situation which hovers between the pleasurable and the nightmarish. The internal narrator-interpreters share the same hazy understanding and disbelief when confronted by the impossible chronologies offered by 'Heredia': 'abundaban en su historia las faltas de sintaxis histórica, las fechas no coincidían y al cabo era difícil saber si [...]' (192). Carnival, disguise and farce enacted within the novel contribute to this feeling. Lucie, the wife of Hugo Heredia, dresses up in fancy dress in the First Empire style of the Ingres portrait and Mlle Lange. Clemencita, who wishes in her old age to return to Venezuela, is sent via Gibraltar and Marseilles and then back to a room in Paris disguised as the tropics 'con hamacas y pericos y un invernadero con soportales y tejas' (109). A delirious baroque and tropical logic transforms the Old World.

'Heredia's' real story becomes indefinable. He is the 'confuso vástago de muchos lugares más que de tiempo alguno' (153). Indeed, he

---

[21] Quoted in Rufino Blanco Fombona, *Bolívar*, 3 vols (Caracas: La Gran Pulpería del Libro Venezolano, 1984), I, 72. See also *El espejo enterrado* (Mexico City: Fondo de Cultura Económica, 1992), 261.

reserves the right to rewrite his own genealogy, declaring himself repeatedly to be the son of José Francisco and Mlle Lange, rather than of the second wife of his father: 'Las verdaderas generaciones no tienen nada que ver con su cronología pedestre' (148). In this he echoes Dumas's father taking the name of his mother, old and abandoned in America, and his coinciding with his young bourgeoise step-mother in Paris. True freedom, he claims, would be 'nacer sin padre ni madre' (103). The closest thing is to choose one's parents, in which 'Heredia' is little different from Jaime Ceballos, Rodrigo Pola or Bernabé Aparicio: '¿No le extraña que la escogiese a ella como mi madre?' (123). Europe, claims 'Heredia', is certainly not free from the delirious fecundation which comes from tropical forests to the wombs of respectable French matrons: 'huracanes que arrastran hojas viejas y en pleno agosto pelan a una selva entera de ramas y frutos y se los llevan lejos, allende el mar, a preñar de puro polen tropical a las austeras esposas europeas que luego paren sin saber que las semillas viajan, el aire las lleva, se meten por las narices, las orejas, las bocas, los culos' (149).

'Heredia's' 'son' André is at the centre of this reversible logic. Never seen together with his father, he is in a sense 'nonato', unborn, a potential. But unborn children join their parents: 'a los jóvenes amantes [los une] el nonato que, él sí, exige su propia creación a través del alma de los jóvenes padres' (104); generations are not linear: 'todos somos padres de los padres, e hijos de los hijos' (147). André is 'Heredia', the fruit of his will to give birth to all that which might have been: 'mi voluntad de darle vida a todo lo que no fue y pudo ser' (149). He is associated with a time of absolute simultaneity of birth and death in the Parc Monceau and the house off it, where the young Branly saw him, and Mlle Lange seems to remember him. His somehow faceless person seems just to have been born: 'sin rostro imaginable, torpe, nervioso, lento [...] todo, dice, era nuevo para ese niño; ni ignorancia ni misterio [...] la aparición del ser encerrado en su perfecta agonía' (86–87). The Parc Monceau becomes a sacred zone in the novel, a place of salvation and at the same time absolute horror, not dissimilar to the rooms of Ludivinia, Consuelo, and Claudia, or the *hacienda* of the Mirandas.

The most glaring contrast in the novel and the most fascinating duel is that between the aristocratic comte de Branly and the grotesque and vulgar 'Heredia'. The excessive oppositions between France and Latin America, civilised rationality and barbaric delirium, are embodied in the two men in a such a way as to render any stability unlikely: 'el contraste entre una vieja línea francesa y un trasplante colonial era [...] demasiado grosero' (51). From an early stage, Branly himself realises that he is projecting his own prejudices onto his enemy: 'el hombre burdo era yo, incapaz de arrojar sobre mi anfitrión otra luz que no fuese la de mis propias normas' (83). His traumatic dealings with the Heredias constituted a form of self-knowledge: 'No conocí a los Heredia. [...] Me concocí a mí mismo' (141).

Strange, disturbing links between the two men gradually emerge throughout the novel in a nebulous, nightmarish fashion. A good image of the logic of the links may be the recurring *barranca* or gorge, a break in the landscape and in logic and chronology, an entrance to a demonic underworld, and a communication between places, generations and planes of signification: 'el barranco sin fondo de una vieja memoria ajena que solicitaba un alma nueva donde anidar su pozoña peregrina' (136).[22] It is the *barranca* where Mlle Lange is buried and disinterred by 'perros y buitres' (146), into which Víctor Heredia is repeatedly on the verge of falling, and suddenly an unlikely ravine in the woods near Vervins, near Branly's grandfather's house, where the body of a female suicide 'amaneció devorado por los lobos' (96). The *barranca* seems to work almost like the covered galleries which link the Paris of Lautréamont and the Buenos Aires of Perón in Cortázar's story 'El otro cielo'.

Towards the end of the novel Branly admits that three elements in his house linked him mysteriously to the Heredias: a photograph of his father, an Empire clock, the gilt on which had poisoned various artisans in the workshop of Antoine-André Ravrio, with the figure of a woman playing the harpsichord (199). The tune played by the clock resonates throughout the novel as a haunting linking motif, while the woman playing the harpischord is repeated in the figure of Mlle Lange playing the harpsichord in la Guaira.

The portrait of the father evokes, as had 'Heredia', the paradoxes of time and genealogy, as the old Branly looks at a photograph of his

[22] At another point, the 'precipicios' do actually communicate with the underworld described by Dante in *Inferno* Canto 3, lines 19–23: 'esa ciudad doliente que 'Heredia' parecía arrastrar consigo, abriendo los precipicios que son las cicatrices de esta historia para dar voz a un universo insoportable de duros suspiros, lenguas extrañas y horribles jergas [...]' (198).

father who died at the age of thirty: 'El, un hombre de ochenta y tres años, mira a un joven de veintinueve que fue su padre' (21). The title *capitán* serves to link and blur the identity of father and son. The father in the picture is called 'capitán de Branly' and described as an 'oficial de reserva' though he had never been to war (28). When Branly, on leave in 1914 from the First World War, faints in the house in Avenue Velázquez, the woman exclaims '¡Oh, Dios mío, señor capitán, qué tiene usted!' (97). This phrase is repeated following a similar phrase directed at an officer involved in the French Intervention in Mexico: '¿señor capitán, qué le parece?' (121). Only much later does Branly admit something very important told to him by his nurse Félicité, the French double of Cemencita, but seems somehow unsure of the memory, which is perhaps apocryphal: 'mi abuelo también fue militar, primero con la Monarquía de Julio y luego con el Segundo Imperio. Pero él nunca me contó nada de eso. No sé' (210). A similar pattern of repetition emerges in Branly's family as elsewhere. Branly's way of approaching the memory of his father is through recitation of the poem 'La Chambre voisine' by the Uruguayan Supervielle.

Another link emerges in a different fashion, in the dream-memories that Branly has in Enghien when retained by 'Heredia' and which may have been somehow provoked by him. They concern childhood memories of the strange boy in the house by the Parc Monceau, who approaches the young Branly with a ball, but Branly is embarrassed and fails to recognise or acknowledge the boy, or take his outstretched hand.

Perhaps the most important link, far-fetched and grotesque, but underlying much of the logic of the novel, is made rather brutally by 'Heredia'. Branly's father, he asserts, had been present at the Cuernavaca brothel and had paid for fellatio from the 'Mamasela', M[lle] Lange, the Duchesse de Langeais, the 'mother' of 'Heredia'. He had mockingly given her half a gold coin. The link is made very elliptically: '¿Le parece una gran coincidencia la homonimia, conde?' (122), asks 'Heredia', but no name appears on the page in the account we read of the conversation. Hugo Heredia has already heard Branly's surname from 'Heredia' when he meets Branly for the first time in Cuernavaca (194). Branly protests that his father had never been at war and had only been born in 1870, but, of course, later half-heartedly admits that his grandfather had fought for the Second Empire of Napoleon III, who had intervened in Mexico. The suggested logic of all this is again bizarre. The symbolic copulation between the French officer and the decrepit Mlle Lange, especially given the notion of transatlantic fertilisation, makes her the possible mother of Branly's father. His father died in 1900 of 'un microbio que no hubiese resistido una inyección de penicilina' (206), which rather suggests syphilis contracted in the Mexican brothel. Syphilis is widely believed to have come from the Indies, and is treated by penicillin. The picture develops when we consider that Branly's father was born in 1870, the year of the death of Alexandre Dumas (and Lautréamont) and the year the blond baby was brought to Enghien, as we learn from the page inserted in the copy of Dumas's memoirs in the possession of Branly. Much is made of the hair of Branly's father, 'cabellera rubia larga y ondulante' (278), echoed in the exchanged baby, 'niño rubio y hermoso' (207), that of 'Heredia's' son André, 'cabellera rubia y rizada' (137), and that of the final waiter who is the synthesis of André and Víctor: 'cabellera rizada y broncínea' (205). (The black baby, born from M. Lange and 'una esclava de las plantaciones', echoing Louise Césette Dumas and Clemencita, suggests Dumas himself.) The link would explain why the woman whom 'Fuentes' calls Lucie, but who is clearly also Mlle Lange, is seen kneeling and sobbing by the portrait of Branly's father at the end of the novel (215). Within this logic, Branly and 'Heredia' would be something like brothers. André is not only 'Heredia' but to an extent Branly himself.

'Heredia's' designs on Branly are thus revenge: for the humiliation of his supposed mother by Branly's supposed father, and for refusing to recognise him in the boy he remembers shunning in the Parc Monceau: 'quién era inferior, la mamadora o el mamado, eh?, ¿quién debió pagar a quién, Branly, tu padre a mi madre o tu madre a mi padre [sic]?' (146). Here 'Heredia' is answering Branly's insistence on paying André for the sexual service of sodomising Branly's ward Víctor: 'hay que saber distinguir si el *partenaire* es de la misma clase o de una inferior; a éste, se le paga.' (145). While Branly stays at Enghien and the mental, oneiric and fantastic elaboration of the fusion of the two men, Branly and 'Heredia', is taking place, Víctor and André are bonding outside Branly's room and in his black Citröen. André is dressed in the same sailor's suit that the boy in Parc Monceau was wearing in 1906 (77, 85) and the memory games Victor and André play evoke the Sarajevo of 1914 where the First World War was unleashed (91). It was in that year that Captain Branly entered the house of the strange boy he had gazed at to gaze in turn across the park to the balcony of his Nervalian lover Myrtho, whom he had left some months earlier for the front. The space becomes the whitewashed, tomb-like room of the demonic 'Heredia' in Enghien ('encalada' (143), 'enjalbegado' (95)), and Branly faints at the unspeakable, presumably hellish, vision he sees. From the house in Avenue Velázquez, the complexity of the crossed gazes evokes the *Meninas* that Fuentes analyzes in *El espejo enterrado* (189–92).

Branly emerges, then, from the house at Enghien to witness Víctor being sodomised by André in his black Citroën. The half object which Víctor brings for André, and which becomes whole on fusing with the other half, echoes the half coin given by the French officer to Mlle Lange. André and Víctor fuse into one person; the *nonato* André is recognised and reborn whole, the humiliation of Mlle Lange is reversed and avenged. What was separated and unfinished becomes as whole as the gold coin unspent by Dumas and passed on to his son.

Again we come up against closure, the 'unidad perfecta y el dominio absoluto' sought by 'Heredia'. But as Fuentes goes on to say, any supposed narrative closure is quickly undone: 'No lo logra porque el lector es libre de continuar la historia. Pero de cierto modo, todos estamos poseídos por otros, el autor o el lector.'[23] The time of absolute simultaneity, where birth and death coexist in the same moment, and which is the only time when Branly, as *nonato*, can dream of and remember the woman of his youth, must necessarily cede to 'el tiempo dulce y lento de los hombres y las mujeres que se aman sobre la tierra' (74), the time repeated evoked by Branly in the line of Lamartine's 'Le Lac': 'Je dis à cette nuit: "Sois plus lente"' (93).

Analogy in *Una familia lejana* is replaced with continguity, metaphor with metonym. Branly seems to be recalling the chapter of Foucault's *Les Mots et les choses* quoted in *Cambio de piel*, when he talks about the loss of a classical unity, and the play between analogy and difference in the novels of Cervantes, Proust and others:

> Ve usted, yo también he perdido el poder de analogía entre las cosas, esa relación entre todo lo que existe que fue el signo profundo de nuestra cultura de fundación a la que se refiere Hugo Heredia. Quizá algún antepasado mío, en el siglo catorce, podía entender sin pena la homologación entre Dios, un

---

[23] 'Cronología personal', 112.

ciervo de astas nacientes y la aureola de una luna roja. Mi antepasado del siglo diecisiete ya no sabía esto; nada se parecía entre sí. El arte, ve usted, sobre todo el arte de narrar es un desesperado intento por restablecer la analogía sin sacrificar la diferenciación. Esto es lo que se le ocurrió a Cervantes y Balzac. Dostoievsky y Proust no han hecho otra cosa. (200)

The delirious analogies, half correspondences, bizarre echoes of the novel, the relaying of narrators and the complex web of palimpsest, attest to this joust between analogy and differenciation. What emerges is a necessarily unfinished story, haunted, forged and disrupted by many other contiguous stories. Branly's intimate story had already been told in the words of the poem of Supervielle about the 'chambre voisine', the 'contiguous room': 'Es extraño: todas [las palabras] habían sido dichas antes, por el poeta o por su lector, mi amigo Branly' (131). Branly tells his story but it will be incomplete and contiguous with that of Hugo Heredia, which he will try to repeat faithfully:

> la historia no había concluido porque la naturaleza de lo narrado es que sea incompleto y sea contiguo. [...] Toda narración es contigua de otra, repitió mi amigo. Quiero ser lo más fiel posible a la de Hugo Heredia. [...] se trata de una figura creada por la imaginación narrativa, pues sólo ella es capaz de reproducir algo verbalmente, así sea incompleto, así sea aproximativo. Esa proximidad incompleta será, de todos modos, la única verdad posible.
> (164-5)

The notion of contiguity applies equally to individuals and their ghosts, their unfulfilled possibilities, alternative destinies, the others, be they ancestors, children, or simply homonyms who enrich their supposed singularity. The French 'Fuentes' is haunted by the Carlos Fuentes we actually read and which he could have become, by his uncle Carlos Fuentes from Veracruz, the pupil of Salvador Díaz Mirón; his novel had already been written by Alexandre Dumas:

> Toda novela es algo inconcluso pero también es algo contiguo. Tome su propia vida. [...] [Usted] se convirtió en un ciudadano del Río de la Plata y en 1955 pasó a vivir en Francia; [...] Imagine si hubiese regresado a México al terminar la guerra y se hubiese arraigado en el país de sus padres [...] Por su otra vida, Fuentes, por su vida adyacente. Piense en lo que pudo ser y celebre conmigo su aniversario [...] Piense que lo mismo sucede con toda

novela. Hay otra narración contigua, paralela, invisible, de cuanto creemos debido a una escritura singular. ¿Quién ha escrito la novela de los Heredia? [...] la novela ya fue escrita. Es una novela de fantasmas inédita [...] Su autor, sobra decirlo, es Alejandro Dumas. (213-4)

National and continental identities, France and Spanish America, are no more isolated entities, or terms in reassuring oppositions, than are individuals; each one takes up, appropriates and rewrites the stories of the other. Neither is immune from the gaze of the other, from the migratory waves of definitions, prejudices, histories and distant relations.

Gringo viejo, 1985: Over the Rio Grande

Gringo viejo is the story of the imaginary last days of the American journalist and writer Ambrose Bierce who entered Mexico in 1913 at the height of the Revolution, apparently in search of death. On a *hacienda* in Chihuahua he meets a prim Washington schoolmistress, Harriet Winslow, who has entered Mexico through the U.S.-occupied port of Veracruz as governess of the children of a family which has already fled the country. The two are held virtually captive by a young revolutionary officer, Tomás Arroyo, who finally kills the Old Gringo for burning the papers which certify his ownership of the *hacienda*. Arroyo is executed in turn by no less than Francisco Villa. Harriet returns with the memories of all these actors to Washington, and it is to a great extent in the darkroom of her mind that the novel is developed.

The aesthetic of the novel is mischievous and ambiguous. National clichés are immediately rehearsed: 'los lugares comunes del machismo mexicano', for example, as the Old Gringo is invited to eat whole green chiles and *tacos* of bull's testicles.[1] There is a sly, disruptive presence of Anglicisms running through the Spanish of the Anglos: 'no les daban el beneficio de esta duda' (21); 'sin tratar de sonar argumentativa' (76). Many of the scenes have the Hollywood air of a Tortilla-Western: 'La línea del encuentro se alejó a medida que el viejo avanzó, con sus piernas largas colgando bajo el vientre de la yegua y el maletín negro anidado en el regazo' (19). Villa himself collaborates by putting off an execution until the light improves for a U.S. film crew. In 1989 a Hollywood film version of the novel was released starring Jane Fonda and Gregory Peck. The intellectual framework of the novel seems almost parodic: a North/South political border which quickly translates into a whole series of clear oppositions: New England puritanism is set off in an absurd contrast with the steamy sex offered by the brooding, dark, violent Mexican.

---

[1] *Gringo viejo* (Madrid: Fondo de Cultura Económica, 1985), 32. The test echoes a similar ordeal, this time by liquor, sprung on the American journalist John Reed during the Revolution, and recounted in his *Insurgent Mexico*.

An excellent clue to the most interesting dimensions of the text is given by a very strident and vehement attack on Fuentes and especially *Gringo viejo* by the historian Enrique Krauze in Octavio Paz's *Vuelta*. Lightly veiled accusations of plagiarism were combined with allegations that Fuentes juggled irresponsibly with historical fact;[2] that 'usa el tema de México distorsionándolo frente al público norteamericano con credenciales que no ha querido o sabido ganar' (15); and that 'la clave de Fuentes no está en México sino en Hollywood' (16). The presence of the United States is obvious in the novel, but even the title reveals that the interest lies in a relation and a perspective, a reciprocal distortion: 'gringo viejo' contains two terms which evoke opposites like 'young greaser', which might easily have been applied by the Old Gringo to the foreign revolutionary.[3] The 'distortion of facts' alleged by Krauze points to the significant displacements effected by Fuentes. Krauze complains that Fuentes had Bierce-Gringo Viejo killed by an Arroyo who has many of the characteristics of Emiliano Zapata, specifically the land deeds with which the latter was entrusted by the elders of Anenecuilco in the southern state of Morelos,[4] when in fact the gringo's death is that of the Englishman William Benton, who was executed on the orders of the northern revolutionary leader Francisco Villa. Such displacements are central to the working of the novel. Closer attention shows that the *gringo viejo* has come to live out in Mexico the drama of the American Civil War some forty years earlier, the Spanish-American War fifteen years earlier, and the U.S. invasion of Mexico and annexation of Texas some seventy years before. Any notion of unmediated historical referentiality is mocked.

[2] See Enrique Krauze, 'La Comedia Mexicana de Carlos Fuentes', *Vuelta* 139 (junio 1988), 15–27, 26.
[3] Note the titles of some U.S. films of the period on the Revolution: *Tony the Greaser* (1911), *The Greaser's Revenge* (1914), *Broncho Billy and the Greaser* (1914). See Margarita de Orellana, *La mirada circular. El cine norteamericano de la Revolución mexicana* (Mexico City: Joaquín Mortiz, 1991), 163, 175.
[4] Fuentes's source is presumably John Womack, *Zapata and the Mexican Revolution* (Harmondsworth: Penguin, 1972), esp. 21, 508, which Fuentes reviewed in *Tiempo mexicano*, 131–46. See also Gastón García Cantú, *Utopías mexicanas* (Mexico City: Fondo de Cultura Económica, 1987), 168–70.

The strong cinematic presence in the novel stresses both the problematic nature of unmediated referentiality and the force of the U.S. construction of a Mexican identity as its own dark other fitted to the purposes of Manifest Destiny and its high conception of its own valour and morals. In the novel Villa puts off executions until the light improves for the U.S. cameramen, and indeed Villa, as Margarita de Orellana tells in *La mirada circular* (73), had a lucrative contract with the Mutual Film Corporation and did allegedly change the timing of battles to suit filming schedules. He posed for a fictional film on his life. Orellana shows that the techniques for fictional films were derived from newsreel techniques, not vice-versa as one might have imagined (29). This is mainly due to the fact that the newsreel account was perceived as much more real when 'maquillada', that is, faked in a studio (38). The North American has gained his knowledge of Mexico and Latin America mainly from the cinema.

Carlos Monsiváis explains that in Mexico, too, the nationalist celebration of the epic of the Mexican Revolution by politicians and in national cinema produces a congealing of historical meaning:

> la Revolución deviene en acontecimiento fílmico. Y en medio de una enseñanza histórica superficial (fechas y discursos con el mapa de la República de fondo), la versión oficial o pública termina siendo la del cine. [...] De modo contradictorio pero inexorable tiene lugar el despojo: en el robo de realidades se evapora el sentido político (radical o no*)* de la Revolución. No importa demasiado. Se ha encontrado el camino para aprovechar finacieramente el interés mundial y nacional por la violencia de un país exótico.[5]

The confusion between film and reality in this example and in the U. S. newsreels was already foreshadowed in Martín Luis Guzmán's *El águila y la serpiente* where *villista* soldiers shoot at a cinema screen when they see the image of Venustiano Carranza.[6] Such examples and

---

[5] Carlos Monsiváis, 'Notas sobre la cultura mexicana en el siglo XX', in *Historia general de México* (Mexico City: Colegio de México, 1981), II, 1512.
[6] See Martín Luis Guzmán, *El águila y la serpiente*, in *La novela de la Revolución Mexicana*, ed. by Antonio Castro Leal (Mexico City: Aguilar, 1974), 372.

the presence of Hollywood is nicely signalled by Fuentes in the Gringo Viejo's repeated wish: 'Quiero ser un cadáver bien parecido' (139), echoing James Dean's famous: 'I want to live fast, die young and be a good-looking corpse'.

The historical displacements mentioned by Krauze, in fact clear, systematic transpositions, are related to the accusation of plagiarism. Fuentes took the scene of the execution and disinterment of Benton-Bierce-Old Gringo from Martín Luis Guzmán's *Memorias de Pancho Villa*.[7] Intertextuality and the notion of intellectual property form one of the most explicit motifs of the novel and are inseparable from major historical and symbolic clusters in the novel: land tenure, property, questions of paternity and legitimacy within the context of the Revolution and the ideologies and identities of the USA and Mexico.

There is a nice misunderstanding when the Gringo Viejo imagines being asked by customs officers about three books he carries, which include two by Ambrose Bierce: ' —¿Y los libros, señor? / —Son míos. / — Nadie insinuó que se los hubiera robado' (18). The other volume he is carrying is a copy of the *Quixote*, the story of the squire who went mad trying to read the complex world of seventeenth-century Spain through the simple texts of chivalresque romance. As Fuentes has expounded in *Cervantes o la crítica de la lectura* and elsewhere, any univocal reading of reality in the *Quixote* is dissolved into plural readings, the integrity of the literary character is shattered by the readings which he knows he is being subjected to, as is the stable wholeness of the author. Who wrote the *Quixote,* he asks: Cervantes, Don Quijote, Avellaneda, Cide Hamete Benengeli, Pierre Menard, Borges? (*Cervantes*, 95).

The importing, translating and transposing of foreign texts has been important for Latin American literature. Any mention of the *Quixote* now almost automatically evokes the writing of Jorge Luis Borges in a twist of anachronism and a redeployment of literary tradition which he would have greatly enjoyed. The practice of Borges is paradigmatic in a continent much of whose culture originated in various elsewheres and which has by its history and geography a constitutionally critical notion of originality and the 'naturalness' of any cultural construct. There are,

---

[7]   See Martín Luis Guzmán, *Memorias de Pancho Villa* (Mexico City: Compañía General de Ediciones, 1981), 256–68.

of course, various types of critical relation to tradition and to history and history writing in Latin American letters. In Alejo Carpentier's 1956 novella *El acoso*, within an extremely complex context of Cuban history, the terrorist protagonist tries to order his life according to heroic, sacred and classical models.[8] While a complex web of irony and inappropriateness is created, it is the very proliferation of such foreign codes and their equivalents in foreign architectural styles imported into the Caribbean, recombined and putrescent in its unsuitable climate, which offers the beginnings of a new autochthonous baroque. Another very important paradigm for *Gringo viejo* is the so-called 'new historical novel' as represented by the Paraguayan Augusto Roa Bastos and his 1974 novel on the dictator Dr Francia, *Yo el Supremo*. Here, together with the question of the representability of the past, the notion of authorship is questioned by a text which claims not to have an author but a *compilador*, to be a compilation of a wide range of historical documents, personal testimonies, letters to the dictator and literary texts plagiarised, modified and returned to their communal origin. The text, claims Roa, inverts the traditional hierarchy in having been 'leído primero y escrito después';[9] on being infiltrated by the plural voice of the people, he comments, 'la voz del Poder Absoluto queda al servicio de lo que domina.'[10]

The equivalent in *Gringo viejo* to the univocal readings and filiations subverted by Borges and Carpentier, and to the 'Absolute Power' emptied out by Roa's compiler, are national stereotypes couched often unconsciously in hierarchical oppositions, easy certainties about identity, historical mythification, and the notion of an absolute, unmediated representation of historical reality. In a radio interview Fuentes commented that the characters of *Gringo viejo* were stereotypes, but that 'they have finally to be seen as creations of literature, which is the very denial of the stereotype.'[11] The first certainty is the conviction of the United States of its superiority over

[8] See my article 'Making Sense in Carpentier's *El acoso*', *The Modern Language Review*, 85 (July 1990), 612–22.
[9] Augusto Roa Bastos, *Yo el Supremo* (Buenos Aires: Siglo XXI, 1974), 467.
[10] Roa Bastos, 'Algunos núcleos generadores de un texto narrativo', *L'Idéologique dans le texte (Textes hispaniques)* (Toulouse: Université de Toulouse-le Mirail, 1978), 93.
[11] In interview with Natalie Wheen, BBC Radio 3, 27 June 1989.

Latin America and its right to intervene in its internal affairs. Harriet Winslow puts it succinctly: 'Mírelos, lo que esta gente necesita es educación no rifles. Una buena lavada seguida de unas cuantas lecciones de cómo hacemos las cosas en los Estados Unidos, y se acabó este desorden' (46). This she then translates into political terms: President Woodrow 'Wilson [and Winslow is an anagram of W. Wilson] habló de la Nueva Libertad y dijo que les enseñaría la democracia a los mexicanos. Hearst [Randolph, Bierce's employer] exigía: Intervención, Guerra, Indemnización' (28). This refusal to see the other as different but equal is translated into a whole series of black / white oppositions, which Fuentes associates in the novel with the Calvinism of the father of Bierce-Old Gringo, as García Cantú does with that of Wilson.[12]

Fuentes's novel works to decentre and deconstruct these oppositions and myths, and the notions of originality and legitimacy associated with authoritarian conceptions of the self. His decided intent to displace the established is announced in all the paratextual apparatus of the novel: title, dedication, epigraphs and final 'Nota de Autor'. The dedication is 'A William Styron, cuyo padre me incluía en sus sueños sobre la guerra civil norteamericana': a clear geographical and temporal transference. The first epigraph, from the dedicatory preface to Thomas Browne's *Hydriotaphia* ('Mas, ¿quién conoce el destino de sus huesos, o cuántas veces va a ser enterrado?') pluralises what is expected to be a unique happening, questioning and postponing what is assumed to be a final resting place. The second epigraph, from Bierce's story 'Parker Addison, Philosopher', is a comment on death.[13] The 'Nota del Autor' tells us that the 'gringo viejo' protagonist of the novel is the writer who wrote the epigraph. Such short-circuiting already nudges the narrative hierarchies of realism.

The oppositions which Fuentes sets up between the Mexican and North American cultures and their representatives are not always intended to be subtle, especially that between the Old Gringo and Arroyo: puritanical / debauched, tall / short, fair / dark, old / young, head / heart, knowledge / memory. More complex oppositions are derived from a long, more cultured tradition, some important ones from

---

[12] See *Utopías mexicanas*, 162.
[13] 'What you call dying is simply the last pain', in Ambrose Bierce, *In the Midst of Life*, *The Collected Writings* (London: Picador, 1974), 166.

the essays of Octavio Paz. In *Conjunciones y disyunciones*, Paz uses the terms of Norman O. Brown to contrast the sublimation of excrement into money in capitalism and the markedly non-bodily spirituality of Protestantism with the far more corporeal nature of Latin Catholicism, and what he calls 'el barroco excremental' of Mexican church architecture: 'un soberbio desperdicio excremental de oro, sangre y pasión'.[14] Fuentes takes this up with gusto in the description of the altar which so scandalises Harriet Winslow: 'el altar centelleante, autodevorador, excrementicio' (103).

Oppositions like the one suggested here between North-head-upper-abstract / South-body-lower-physical are however constantly displaced by being reproduced as an internal complexity of one character, or reproduced on both sides of the geographical frontier. Harriet Winslow, for example, has both a real, very physical and whoring father with a negress lover in the cellar and another in Cuba, and a symbolic father in the puritanical and perfumed Old Gringo who chooses platonically to love the nice safe WASP girl. A similar example is a parallel between the houses of the American Harriet and of the Mexican lover of Arroyo, known as the 'mujer de la cara de luna'. Harriet's respectable family life in Washington took place in the upper quarters of the house, later inhabited just by her mother, while in a *sótano*, her father's sex with the negress is described in aggressively physical terms: 'el olor agridulce del amor y de la sangre, las axilas húmedas y los temblores púbicos' (54). La Luna lives in a house in provincial Durango with her repressed and sexually repressive money-lending husband. The *sótano* of her house, 'el vientre de la casa' (155), comes to represent her own physical liquids and odours and the fear of her husband, who threatened to send her down there for talking to a man in the street (Doroteo Arango-Villa): 'poblado de terrores, rumores, fantasmas, bestias, voces tarareantes' (155). Arroyo is enclosed there for some days with a couple of fierce animals, enormous dogs, which he shoots and possibly eats.

Another formulation by Octavio Paz in 'Literatura de fundación' colours one of the most powerful structuring concepts of the novel, permanence and essence against change, plurality and future:

---

[14] *Conjunciones y disyunciones* (Mexico City: Joaquín Mortiz, 1978), 32.

> Nosotros somos hijos de la Contrarreforma y la Monarquía universal; ellos, de Lutero y la Revolución Industrial. [...] El llamado realismo angloamericano es el pragmatismo [en el cual] la realidad deja de ser una substancia y se transforma en una serie de hechos. Nada es permanente porque la acción es la forma privilegiada que asume la realidad. Cada acto es instantáneo; para prolongarse necesita cambiar, ser otro acto. La América española y la portuguesa fueron fundadas por la civilización que concebía la realidad como una substancia estable. [...] Encarnación de la voluntad de permanencia, las obras se erigen para resistir al cambio.[15]

A major manifestation of this opposition in the novel is that between the deeds which legitimise Arroyo's claim to permanent possession of the land and the shifting, corrosive stories and articles of the Old Gringo-Bierce.

The use of intertextuality in *Gringo viejo* is extensive and very varied, from the generalised historical canon, through the model of the epic, that is, the *Odyssey*, to other very specific transcriptions. Fuentes himself stressed the mediated nature of his novel and specifically of his character Harriet Winslow by explaining in the BBC interview that she comes from a novel by Edith Wharton, *False Dawn*. The story that Harriet tells about the paintings of her uncle certainly does come from that 1924 novel. 'La historia de su familia era curiosa,' he drolly has Harriet comment in the novel, 'parecía inventada' (68).

The most striking quotation, however, is Fuentes's rewriting of the life and works of Ambrose Bierce himself. Fuentes uses other people's works to subvert the pact between reader and author, text and referent, author and originality, on which the oppositions and clichés mentioned above are grounded. Fuentes uses three sorts of generically well defined material with subversive indiscriminacy: biography, correspondence, fiction. The many biographies of Bierce follow his life until he disappears into Mexico in 1913. For some years thereafter there were several fanciful reports of his death: in Arizona by his own hand, in

---

[15] 'Literatura de fundación', in *Puertas al campo* (Barcelona: Seix Barral, 1981), 17–8. Many other statements by Paz on United States-Mexican relations are relevant to the novel, for example,, 'Si se me preguntase: ¿podrán los Estados Unidos dialogar con nosotros?; yo contestaría: sí, a condición de que aprendan antes a hablar con ellos mismos, con su propia *otredad*: con sus negros, sus chicanos sus jóvenes' (*Posdata* (Mexico City: Siglo XXI, 1982), 17).

Mexico at the hand of Villa, at the battle of Ojinaga, in Europe in the trenches of the Great War. An unfinished biography and an unfinished character of the sort that well suits Fuentes's conception of literature. Fuentes quotes the letters that Bierce sent to various relatives in the 'Nota de Autor', and uses them sparingly in the text as unmarked quotations, as with Bierce's much quoted 'To be a Gringo in Mexico — ah, that is euthanasia.'[16] In Mexico, however, Fuentes has him live out not only a fantasised continuation of his own biography, but also the stories that Bierce himself wrote about the American Civil War (*In the Midst of Life*), and a fictionalised biography by another author: Guzmán's *Memorias de Pancho Villa*.

Bierce-Gringo Viejo, then, the character of Fuentes, lives out stories about another civil war fifty years earlier just as Don Quixote tries to live out the stories of his knight-errant heroes. The seven stories which are quoted and used are all about death: actively seeking it out, execution or parricide.[17] Bierce's real biography is contaminated by his stories, when, for example, a phrase from the story 'Chicamauga' ([Su padre] fue un soldado, luchó contra salvajes desnudos y siguió la bandera de su país hasta la capital de una raza civilizada, muy al sur' (77)) comes to mean that the Gringo Viejo's father had been in the

[16] Cited by Richard O'Connor, *Ambrose Bierce, A Biography* (London: Victor Gollancz, 1968), 299. Also quoted in *Gringo viejo*, 139.

[17] The following phrases from Bierce's *In the Midst of Life* are quoted or adapted in the novel. (Bierce's *Collected Works* = B, *Gringo viejo* = GV): 'In his younger manhood the father had been a soldier, had fought against naked savages and followed the flag of his country into the capital of a civilised race to the far South ('Chicamauga', B, 18, GV, 15, 77); 'I have never been dead in all my life' ('Parker Addison, Philosopher', B, 61, GV, 26); 'Consciously or unconsciously, this writhing fragment of humanity, this type and example of acute sensation, this handiwork of man and beast, this humble, unheroic Prometheus, was imploring everything, all, the whole non-ego, for the boon of oblivion. To the earth and sky alike, to the trees, to the man, to whatever took form in sense or consciousness, this incarnate suffering addressed that silent plea' ('The Coup de Grâce', B, 57, GV, 31); 'Well, go, sir, and whatever may occur do what you conceive to be your duty'; 'Cumplan con su deber. Disparen contra los padres' (B, 5, GV, 79); 'Try always to get yourself killed' ('Concerning the Wish to be Dead', B, 66, GV, 90); '[He saw]the leaves and the veining of each leaf — saw the very insects upon them. [...] He noted the prismatic colors in all the dewdrops upon a million blades of grass' ('An Ocurrence at Owl Creek Bridge', B, 14, GV, 139).

United States invasion force in Mexico in 1847 (78). The Gringo (an inextricable amalgam of Bierce and his characters) finds it ironic that he should be following in his father's footsteps. This structure of repetition of the parental model forms a significant combination with a central story which haunts the Gringo and which he lives out in the Mexican battles. 'Horseman in the Sky', an image which is used on the front cover of the Fondo de Cultura Económica edition of *Gringo viejo*, tells of an involuntary parricide when a young Unionist soldier is honour-bound to shoot his Confederate father. The two stories can readily be taken as a commentary on the drama of intertextuality: repetition of a model, destruction of its originality, displacement of geography and time, multiplication of reference and connotation.

The duplication and mirroring involved in the quotation of 'Horseman in the Sky' is significantly echoed throughout the text and becomes one of its main generative features. Just to give one example: the Gringo Viejo does not kill his father for a second time and neither does his Mexican double Arroyo manage to kill his *hacendado* father. Nevertheless, the pairing of the American and the Mexican is replicated in Arroyo's southern Mexican twin who does kill Arroyo's father, an act which is in turn repeated when Arroyo kills his symbolic father, the Gringo.

A large number of readings is generated in this way. One is particularly enjoyable. 'Horseman in the Sky' is repeatedly translated in the novel as 'jinete del aire'. This is the title of an essay by Octavio Paz on Alfonso Reyes (both very much literary mentors of Fuentes) in which he talks of Reyes's dramatic poem *Ifigenia cruel* where, through a variant on the story of Iphigenia and Orestes, Reyes dramatises a traumatic area of his own life. Although his father, General Bernardo Reyes, had been shot down by revolutionaries, Reyes opted to place himself at the service of the Revolution. The difference between the United States and Mexico and their respective civil wars is poignantly dismantled by the use of such intertextual echoes.[18]

The second repetition is not only of plots or symbolic structures, but of the very intertextual practice and sources on which *Gringo viejo* is

[18] Paz takes the title of his essay from a poem by Reyes himself. See 'Jinete del aire', in *Puertas al campo*, 57. Fuentes discusses the importance of *Ifigenia cruel* in 'How I Started to Write', in *Myself with Others*, 18-19. See also his 'Alfonso Reyes', in *Casa con dos puertas*, 93-98.

constructed. Fernando del Paso explains in the 'Nota final' to his 1977 novel *Palinuro de México*: 'El capítulo "Una bala muy cerca del corazón" fue inspirado por una narración del escritor y periodista Ambrose Bierce y por lo que pudo haberle sucedido a este escritor en las últimas horas de su vida.'[19] In del Paso's chapter, a grandfather relates to the narrator events in the Revolution where Bierce's retelling / reliving of his own story 'Parker Addison, Philosopher' is reported to Francisco Villa, while all the characters play out the plot of the story. The seamless Diderot-like self-referentiality which characterises del Paso's short and pointedly contrived text is far more pronounced than that of *Gringo viejo*. A reading of the later text in the light of the earlier one, however, serves to stress the latter's critical self-awareness.

Closely related to the effect of intertextual play are three other areas. In each case an opposition is established between North American and Mexican attitudes towards meaning, the written and spoken word, and the family, which are then dismantled in one way or another. The oppositions are played out in related themes of textual legitimacy, genealogical legitimacy and the notion of origins.

The contrast between movement and stability manifests itself in many ways in the novel. Mexican tradition and immobility, for example, are repeatedly contrasted with North American movement towards the Western frontier and beyond. The opposition, however, is typically reproduced on one side of the political / geographical frontier. For Harriet, it is the fixed light on the table of her mother as opposed to a light which moves from window to window in a dream-like mansion which she sees from outside and seems to be associated with her father. As in *Zona sagrada* and elsewhere, the contrast translates itself into the terms of the *Odyssey*, travelling as against two sorts of immobility: absorption by myth with the Sirens or Circe, or return to the patriarchal home and self-consciousness, 'unos de los más viejos mitos de la humanidad' (124), as Fuentes mockingly describes his own theme through Harriet. As in earlier texts, the return is an image of the final grasping of meaning, of textual closure.

The opposition is comically dismantled by the experiences of various characters. Captain Winslow, Harriet's father, fights in the Spanish-

---

[19] *Palinuro de México* (Mexico City: Joaquín Mortiz, 1977), 649. The story about Bierce is told on pages 466-77.

American War of 1898, and fails to return home, staying instead with a mulatta in the Caribbean. There is in fact a mock, spurious return in that his wife declares him dead in action, so that she can receive a widow's pension, and has an empty grave awaiting him. The normativity and legitimacy of the hearth was, however, already compromised in the black Circe figure installed in the Washington cellar, the internal analogue of the external U.S. 'back yard' of Central America.

The Gringo follows his father's tracks abroad and receives the death he wishes for at the hands of Arroyo, giving his ambiguous life its final meaning. The corpse is however disinterred on orders from Villa and executed post mortem. It is fraudulently claimed by Harriet to be the corpse of her amnesiac father, returned to America and buried in the awaiting grave at Arlington.

Turning to Arroyo, the Revolution is seen as breaking the immobility of the Mexican people (and, as he says to the Gringo, of making them more like North Americans), and the train becomes its favourite image. When Arroyo, who is the illegitimate son of the landowner Miranda, takes and sacks the *hacienda* of his father, from which he had always been excluded, he is almost physically caught by its influence and finds it impossible to regain the momentum of the push south towards the capital city. Movement and petrification, moreover, become one in him insofar as the road to power and corruption means being absorbed by the political father figure Porfirio Díaz, whereas staying in his (false) origins means to betray the Revolution and his violated mother, and ultimately leads to his execution.

Harriet returns home, but to a home which becomes the place where she elaborates the memories of Mexico. The prostitute, la Garduña, who had so disgusted Harriet, will emulate her deceptions by returning to her native village to gain burial in sacred ground by claiming to be her virgin aunt Josefa Arreola.

The origin, then, as final truth, legitimate values, confirmation of identity, is repeatedly emptied, its sign inverted. Adorno and Horkheimer have very dramatically illustrated the paradoxical nature of the nostalgia for the homeland in 'Ulysses or Myth and Enlightenment'. It is homesickness which gives rise to the adventures through which man passes from myth to enlightenment, yet it is that very homeland (the order of property and the renunciation of nomadic life) which produces the alienation and the longing for a lost primal state which is associated in turn with the homeland.[20] In a similar way, Fuentes's text evokes original models which are emptied and mediated. The supplementarity of his work is reflected in the shifting, plural patterns of paternity in the novel. Texts, Fuentes says with reference to his novella *Aura*, are never orphans.[21] But, one might add, they are nearly always bastards.

Americans and Mexicans are presented as holding opposite conceptions of language, written and spoken. Arroyo possesses the papers which certify his inalienable ownership of the land; indeed they 'legitimised' (144) his search. The papers are more real than speech: 'En vez de voz, yo tengo un papel', he claims (65). The Gringo does not have legal documents but corrosive, sardonic countertexts: *The Devil's Dictionary*, *The Parenticide Club*. Language, like property for the son of capitalism, only signifies in motion, in exchange: 'El viejo sólo contestó que la propiedad cambia de manos, así operan las leyes de mercado; no hay riqueza que nazca de una propiedad que nunca circula' (37). The opposition that Fuentes is playing on is one which he has theorised elsewhere: that between Hispanic Roman law and Anglo-Saxon common law. '¿Una ley que no está escrita en papel? ¿Entonces para qué demonios aprender a leer?', jokes Fuentes's Villa to American journalists (163).

The utopia behind the tendency Fuentes labels Hispanic is the absolute correspondence between word and reality: sacred meaning, absolute reality. In *Tiempo mexicano* Fuentes argues that Zapata fought 'a fin de que, finalmente, el texto y la realidad fuesen una sola, inseparable entidad';[22] he adds that 'sería tentador interpretar la hstoria de México como una lucha entre textos sagrados y realidades profanas' (125). Possession of the text signifies an annulment of Mexican orphanhood and bastardy; the text is the father, 'una génesis impoluta' (127). In the essay as in the novel, however, the duality between what is represented by the United States and Mexico is reproduced on one side of the opposition, thus decentring it. Possession of the text in Mexico, he argues, may imply either the revolutionary struggle to make it reality, or else the tyrannical (Aztec or Imperial) paternalism granted

[20] See Theodor Adorno and Max Horkheimer, *Dialectic of Enlightenment*, trans. by John Cumming (London: Verso, 1986), 78.
[21] See 'How I Wrote One of my Books', in *Myself with Others*, 38.
[22] 'La historia como toma de poderes', in *Tiempo mexicano*, 131.

by divine right. This dualism was present in the papers from the beginning when, despite their being a symbol of permanence, we first see them moving, like the patriarchal bed of Miranda, perhaps the supreme sign of legitimacy and fixity, in a luxury carriage across the deserts of northern Mexico.[23]

When we consider the Gringo, moreover, and remember that he has been placed clearly in the position of Don Quixote, Fuentes's description of Cervantes's novel becomes significant: 'la novela y el poema del Caballero de la Triste Figura en su lucha por hacer que coincidan las palabras y las cosas' (*Cervantes*, 110). Where there had been an opposition between the two men, there is a coincidence. What else is the Gringo doing but trying to make his own texts, profane ones this time, and reality coincide? Note also the paradox that possession of the texts signifies death for Arroyo, executed by Villa, whereas the Gringo's destruction of Arroyo's deeds signifies the death that he had been looking for and a meaning for his life.

When the Gringo burns the sacred text and the ashes fly across the desert he seems to liberate the words and the movements of Arroyo's men:

> cayó muerto el gringo viejo y los compañeros hablaron porque ahora los papeles con su historia ya no hablarían más por ellos [...]; murió el gringo viejo y las palabras de los papeles se fueron volando por el desierto, diciendo nos gusta pelear, nos sentimos como muertos si no peleamos. (145)

This would seem to reflect Fuentes's idea of his own literary practice in the novel: to liberate the words of the sacred texts, setting them on fire, unleashing the many tongues they contain or control. Mexican language and American language, normative text and rewriting are released from a rigid hierarchy, the opposition between them is deconstructed, a dynamic dialogue is initiated.

The all-pervading textuality of *Gringo viejo* is productively ambiguous. Does it liberate its subject from cliché, from the alienating, petrifying view of the Other, or does it obscure and mythify Mexico

---

[23] The bed of Javier's parents is treated in an analogous fashion in *Cambio de piel*, appearing in the orgy scene in the brothel in Mexico City and containing the corpse of Herr Urs in Prague.

and its history? Fuentes, having been brought up for some years in the United States, saw Mexico as 'the imaginary, imagined country, finally real but only real if I saw it from a distance that would assure me, because of the very fact of separation, that my desire for reunion with it would be forever urgent, and real only if I wrote it' (*Myself*, 18).

Edward Said and Todorov, whose studies of the Western approach to foreign cultures would seem to be a strong presence in *Gringo viejo*, illustrate how a text or especially a community of like-minded texts can alienate reality. In *Orientalism*, Said sets out to show that 'European culture gained in strength and identity by setting itself off against the Orient as a sort of surrogate and even underground self.'[24] As the discipline developed 'Orientalists after Sacy and Lane rewrote Sacy and Lane; after Chateaubriand, pilgrims rewrote him. From these complex rewritings the actualities of the modern Orient were systematically excluded' (Said, 177). Fuentes turns the gaze of the Orient, Mexico or USA, back on the West and dissolves both mirrors in a labyrinth of reflections.

Fuentes likes to quote the statement of Hugues de Saint-Victor quoted by Said: 'L'homme qui trouve sa patrie douce n'est qu'un tendre débutant; celui pour qui chaque sol est comme le sien propre est déjà fort; mais celui seul est parfait pour qui le monde entier est comme un pays étranger.'[25] Tzvetan Todorov picks this up and adds in a spirit not alien to Fuentes and novels like *Una familia lejana* and *Gringo viejo*: 'moi qui suis un Bulgare habitant en France, j'emprunte cette citation à Edward Said, Palestinien vivant aux États-Unis, qui l'avait trouvée lui-même chez Erich Auerbach, Allemand exilé en Turquie.'[26]

---

[24] Edward Said, *Orientalism* (Harmondsworth: Penguin, 1985), 3.
[25] Said, 253; see Fuentes's interview with Reyzabal, 82.
[26] Tzvetan Todorov, *La Conquête de l'Amérique. La Question de l'autre* (Paris: Seuil, 1982), 253.

IV: NOVELLA CYCLES

Agua quemada: cuarteto narrativo, 1981; *Constancia y otras novelas para vírgenes*, 1989; *La frontera de cristal: una novela en nueve cuentos*, 1995

After the second of his early collections of stories, *Los días enmascarados* (1954) and *Cantar de ciegos* (1964), Fuentes went on to publish six consecutive novels. Between 1981, however, and 1995, four out his eight works of fiction belonged to a hybrid genre which was new to him. Though the four narratives of *Agua quemada*, the five of *Constancia y otras novelas para vírgenes* and *El naranjo o los círculos del tiempo* (1993), and the nine of *La frontera de cristal* may be read as independent fictions, they form at the same time a floating and decentred unity, a mosaic which partakes both of the novel and the short-story, or novella genre.

Fuentes described *Agua quemada* as 'en cierto modo una elegía, una oración fúnebre' to his first novel *La región más transparente* and the Mexico City it depicted.[1] García Gutiérrez describes its fragmented form as a faithful representation of a fragmented city: 'una de las posibilidades de adecuar los medios de expresión a un objeto de naturaleza difícil, casi no aprehensible'.[2] Indeed, the fragmentation of the novel form into semi-independent novellas may be seen to reflect the geographical dispersal of Mexico City and the fracturing of any social cohesion through inequality and the violence exemplified in the Tlatelolco massacre of 1968. Though the language of the novellas is sharply inventive, it is forged from the real language of the people and their songs, and the historical framework underpinning the narratives is as meticulous as that of the early realist novels.

In *Agua quemada* the Virgin of Guadalupe is a recurrent, fiercely satirised presence pointing melancholically to an empty nationalist cult

---

[1] In an interview with Sylvia Fuentes, in Reina Roffé, ed., *Espejo de escritores* (Hanover N.H.: Ediciones del Norte, 1985), 91.

[2] In the 'Postscriptum' to the Introduction to her edition of *La región más transparente*, 67.

offering a spurious unity. In *Constancia y otras novelas para vírgenes*, however, eight years later, the vertiginous proliferation of Virgins, the creation of a cosmopolitan network of them from Madrid to Mexico City, Seville to Savannah, Georgia, seems to be a motive for literary celebration. Unity and the 'feliz identidad del sujeto y el objeto' are a source of terror, 'una idea totalitaria' to be contested by difference.[3] In the essays of *Valiente mundo nuevo*, published a year after *Constancia*, Lyotard, whose appeal to 'activate differences' echoes here, is cited as a champion of multinarratives against the metanarratives of liberation: 'Se ha agotado lo que Jean-François Lyotard llama "los metarrelatos de liberación" de la modernidad ilustrada. Pero el fin del metarrelato, por definición abstracto y absolutista, ¿no promete la multiplicación de los *multirrelatos* del mundo policultural [...]?'[4]

La frontera de cristal belongs to a more sombre and sober world. After the signing of the North American Free Trade Agreement in 1994 and the financial disaster in December of the same year, with the enormous outflow of capital, which joined Mexico and the USA like two grotesquely unequal Siamese twins, the urgency of studying the new Mexican reality was stressed in works like Fuentes's *Nuevo tiempo mexicano* and Jorge Castañeda's *Sorpresas te da la vida*. Fuentes reiterates this duty in January 1995: 'Terminó la época de las ilusiones, la grandilocuencia y la soberbia. Llegó la hora del trabajo, de la modestia y del *alka seltzer* colectivo.'[5] *La frontera* sometimes reads almost like a textbook of the themes and problems of bilateral relations with Mexico's Northern neighbour. The style is a tricky combination of didacticism and scepticism, stereotyped expression and a sharp critical edge. The deceptive transparency of the style does, however, conceal some of the fun and games enjoyed in *Constancia*.

---

[3] *Constancia* (Madrid: Mondadori, 1989), 336–7.
[4] *Valiente mundo nuevo*, 25.
[5] *Feliz año nuevo* (Mexico City: Aguilar, 1995), 32.

Agua quemada, 1981: Violence with Impunity

All four stories of *Agua quemada* open with images of loss and absence. In the title 'El día de las madres', 'madres' refers both to real mothers (the dead grandmother Clotilde, raped in her youth, her daughter Evangelina, murdered by her husband, the maid Manuela, raped and expelled), and in Mexican Spanish to violent blows, and to *desgracias*, misfortunes. As the story opens, the aged and once priapic General Vincente Vergara drinks instant coffee because nobody knows how to make the traditional stuff: 'Ya nadie sabía hacerle su café de olla, sabor de barro y piloncillo, de veras nadie, ni la pareja de criados traídos del ingenio azucarero de Morelos. Hasta ellos bebían Nescafé.'[1] In 'Éstos fueron los palacios', the preterite tense in the title alludes to the colonial palaces in the centre of Mexico City now subdivided and converted into *vecindades* or tenements. It alludes to the disappearance of the city celebrated by Bernardo de Balbuena in the early seventeenth century in *Grandeza mexicana* and by Salvador Novo in the twentieth, the city once known as the 'ciudad de los palacios', a name evoked as the title to a chapter of *La región más transparente*. In the first line of 'Las mañanitas', as the aristocratic Federico Silva gazes out from the balcony of his house in the Colonia Roma district, we have a similar evocation of a lost past: 'Antes, México era una ciudad con noches llenas de mañanas. [...] Eso era antes, ahora su casa quedaba a una cuadra de la gigantesca plaza a desnivel del metro de Insurgentes' (71). In the fourth story, 'El hijo de Andrés Aparicio', where the father of the title is as absent as Pedro Páramo for his son Juan Preciado in Rulfo's novel, the loss extends to the act of naming: the squatters' camp where Bernabé and his family live 'no tuvo nombre y por eso no tuvo lugar. Otras colonias fueron nombradas. Ésta no. Como por descuido' (97).[2]

[1] *Agua quemada* (México: FCE, 1981), 11.
[2] Speaking of the Mexican poor, Elena Poniatowska comments: 'nunca han tenido derecho a nada, ni siquiera a que se les designe con un nombre, toda su vida ha sido un largo y continuo soportar que se les haga a un lado' ('Prólogo' to *Fuerte es el silencio* (México: Era, 1987), 11).

205

The breaking of unity is already announced in the epigraphs of the collection, from two literary forebears of Fuentes: Alfonso Reyes and Octavio Paz. The first is from Reyes's 'Palinodia de polvo': '¿Es ésta la región más transparente del aire? ¿Qué habéis hecho, entonces, de mi alto valle metafísico?'. Fuentes through Reyes sadly evokes the dictum of von Humboldt on the Central Valley of Mexico, which Reyes had already used as the epigraph to his 'Visión de Anáhuac', and which Fuentes appropriated as the title to *La región más transparente*. The epigraph from Paz comes from the poem 'Vuelta', one of the three poems which make up the sequence 'Ciudad de México': 'se quebraron los signos / atl tlachinolli / se rompió / agua quemada'. The fragment gives *Agua quemada* its title, an ancient nahua name for México-Tenochtitlán, while at the same time alluding to the breaking and fragmentation of Mexican language. The next lines of Paz's poem express a dispersion which echoes the form of Fuentes's stories: 'No hay centro / plaza de congregación y consagración / no hay eje / dispersión de los años / desbandada de los horizontes.'[3] It is interesting to note the significance that Paz, in another of the poems, 'Petrificada petrificante', attributes to political violence in this 'dispersión': 'Imágenes reventadas / imágenes empaladas / salta la mano cortada / salta la lengua arrancada / saltan los senos tronchados / la verga guillotinada / tristrás en el polvo tristrás / en el patio trasero / podan el árbol de sangre / el árbol inteligente.'[4] This is the same violence which fractures the world of *Agua quemada* at the same time as it gives it is appalling unity: the massacre of students in the Plaza de las Tres Culturas in Tlatelolco on 2 October 1968, the 'Jueves de Corpus' slaughter of 10 July 1971 carried out by a paramilitary fascist group known as 'Los Halcones',[5] the guerrilla struggle and the dirty war of the seventies.

Alluding to the difference in Mexico City and its representation between Fuentes's first novel and *Agua quemada*, García Gutiérrez says: 'la ciudad dispersó ese haz de vidas humanas todavía reunido en *La región más transparente*.'[6] In the earlier novel, despite the huge

[3]   *Poemas*, 601.
[4]   *Ibid.*, 609.
[5]   See Poniatowska, 'El movimiento estudiantil de 1968', in *Fuerte es el silencio*, 69-71, and Bethell, ed., *Mexico since Independence*, 366.
[6]   García Gutiérrez, 'Introducción' to *La región más transparente*, 67.

number of characters and the complex plot, there still exists a community and a meta-narrative or symbolic scheme which generates scenes which would no longer be conceivable in *Agua quemada*. The patriarch Federico Robles (the counterpart of General Vergara, the fascist boss Mariano Carreón and the absent father Andrés Aparicio) crosses Mexico City in a sort of trance and ends up at the wake of a poor worker, *macehual* and 'wetback', where he experiences an anagnorisis which brings together many threads and characters of the novel and produces a sort of totalising memory in himself and the text which lends some global meaning to his life. On the last page of *Agua quemada*, in the Spanish Cemetery in Azcapotzalco, Bernabé Aparicio catches a glimpse of his long-lost father. But here there is no recognition, the thread is broken: 'Bernabé sintió vergüenza. Que no regrese. Basta una memoria vaga un desconocimiento.'

Geographically, there is a generalised tendency towards dispersion in the four families of the four stories of *Agua quemada*. The landlord Federico Silva and General Vergara live in Colonia Roma after the Revolution, but while Silva resists the encroachment of skyscrapers on his twenties mansion, Vergara moves to the new elite residential area of the Jardines del Pedregal, in the south of the city. After the death of the General's wife, Clotilde, Manuela, the maid of the Vergaras, is dismissed and expelled from the house together with her daughter, who was possibly the fruit of Clotilde's violation by the General or his son. The family of the crippled boy Luis and the Aparicio family live after the Revolution in a tenement building in calle Guatemala, near the central square, el Zócalo, in a house owned by Federico Silva. While Luis and his family stay on, the Aparicios are forced to move away by the *licenciado* Carreón, a political enemy of Andrés Aparicio. His family ends up in a decrepit shack in a shanty town on an anonymous dusty plane, without water or sanitation, near the airport.

The intermittent contact between the members of the families from their scattered neighbourhoods serves paradoxically to highlight their isolation. One day Bernabé takes his fiancée to meet his ex-friend Luis; his uncles get a job at a petrol station belonging to Tin, the son of Vergara, because their father had worked as stable boy to the General; one of them similarly is offered a place in an Acapulco band through Carreón, who is keen to recruit Bernabé as a member of his fascist brigade, *Los Gavilanes*, clearly *Los Halcones* in reality. These are contacts which simply belong to the network of *patrimonialismo*.

Elsewhere the text gives the illusion of contacts which are actually inexistent: Plutarco, Vergara's grandson, has a phallic red Ford Thunderbird and el Güero, the *guarura* or bodyguard of Carreón, also has one, this time second-hand. Plutarco goes to the Panteón Francés to visit the family crypt and Bernabé makes love with Martincita in an almost identical crypt in the Panteón Español. These are no more than simulacra of unity.

As happens later in *Constancia* the recurrent presence of the Virgin of Guadalupe lends a dubious and parodic continuity to the stories. For Vergara, 'la guadalupana es una virgen revolucionaria [...] una virgen a toda madre pues' (18). The daughter confined by Manuela throughout her youth to a wheel-chair to protect her from the predatory seductive instincts of Agustín is called Lupe Lupita, a double contraction of Guadalupe and thus 'doblemente virgen, dos veces amparada' (63), but is reduced simply to Lupe when deflowered by the brother of Luisito. One medallion of the Virgin of Guadalupe allows Martincita to recognise her lover Bernabé, while another fulfils a grotesquely amusing role in the love-making of Carreón and his wife:

> la señora Carreón encuerada salvo las medallas religiosas, sobre todo una en forma de concha de mar con la imagen en oro de la Virgen de Guadalupe sobrepuesta que la señora se puso sobre el sexo mientras el Jefe Mariano se acercó a levantársela con la lengua y la señora rió con una voz coqueta y tipluda de quinceañera y dijo no amito mío no mi rey respeta a tu virgencita y él en cuatro patas encuerado con las pelotas moradas de frío [...] ay mi gorda cachonda ay mi putita santa mi huilita perfumada mi diosa bucles de nácar deja a tu papacito bendecirte a tu virgencita mi amor. (129)

According to Vergara, Mexicans are united by their 'amor a la Virgen y el odio a los gringos' (16). A fragile link indeed.

The theme which most effectively links the stories of *Agua quemada* is the same one which ensures their fragmentation, in turn a reflection of the damage done to the fabric of Mexican society in the sixties and seventies: the transmission and inheritance of 'la violencia impune', violence with impunity. Each story features a son, a 'delfín', who depends on a father figure from whom he receives an identity which he must in turn forge anew; these are Plutarco Vergara, Luisito, the hippies from the Insurgentes underground station (El Artista, Pocajonta, El Barbero), and Bernabé Aparicio. One emblematic father figure is

Vicente Vergara. In the Revolution he famously castrated a man; he raped Clotilde who later, in an apparent parody of the relationship between Artemio Cruz and Regina, became his loving wife; he helped to kill his son's wife for her infidelity and probably raped his maid Manuela: 'amor de criada, a oscuras, a tientas, rehusado, nocturno, hecho de una sola palabra repetida mil veces. / —No...no...no...no' (66). In an era which does not offer the possibility of heroic military feats, he issues a challenge to his son and his grandson: 'a ver si son capaces de hacer lo que yo hice, ahora que ya no se puede, a ver si saben heredar, además de mi dinero, algo más difícil. / Mi violencia impune' (41). Plutarco willingly takes up the challenge of violence with impunity: he roughly twists a prostitute's arm and has sex with her while a hired mariachi band in the same room plays the *corrido* 'Camino de Guanajuato'. His grandfather, impotent and castrated in his turn by age and alcohol, must be content to look on. He has 'pasado la espada' to his grandson.

As in the stories and novel of Juan Rulfo, violence is contagious and omnipresent, but it unties bonds, dissolves identity, denies any sense of community. The 'violencia impune' unmentioned in the novel is that of 1968, traumatic to the national community, and that of the Halcones/Gavilanes in 1971. The real culprits of both massacres were never brought to trial. The figure of Mariano Carreón in 'El hijo de Andrés Aparicio' refers us to the head of the Departamento del Distrito Federal, the Governor of Mexico City at the time, Alfonso Martínez Domínguez. Fuentes associates the notion of 'violencia impune' with the Venezuelan novelist Rómulo Gallegos and especially with his 1935 novel *Canaima*, where it embodies *la barbarie,* the barbarism explored by Sarmiento in his 1845 study *Facundo*, to which the characters of Gallegos constantly fear regressing: 'la tempestad de los elementos infrahumanos'.[7] It is this same irresponsible 'violencia impune' which is omnipresent in *Agua quemada* and corrodes the fabric of society. The head of the *Gavilanes* expresses it in a chilling fashion:

[7] Rómulo Gallegos, *Canaima* (Madrid: Espasa-Calpe, 1977), 185. See Fuentes's essay 'Rómulo Gallegos: la naturaleza impersonal' in *Valiente mundo nuevo*. See also the passage from *Canaima* : 'Guyana era un tapete milagroso donde un azar magnífico echaba los dados y todos los hombres audaces querían ser de la partida. Y eran, juntos con los de presa —mayorazgo de la violencia que allí encontraría impunidad— los segundones de la fortuna o del mérito' (13).

> ustedes son la mera brigada de los gavilanes [...] lo importante es que cuando se los encuentren se suelten el alma, chinguen sin piedad [...] si le sacan un ojo a un cabrón rojete de esos no le hace, [...] aquí los protegemos [...] la policía los va a conocer por los moños y los brazales. (132-3)

The fear of this violence has been present in the work of Fuentes since his early stories, such as 'Por boca de los dioses', from 1954, where the protagonist is killed and violence takes on a mythical form as the disguises of civilisation are stripped away:

> el monstruo de piedra labrada de un país inútil, impotente, bien mostrenco que sólo subsiste mientras las fuerzas del éxito ajeno quieran respetarlo... Disfraces de Galilea, disfraces de Keynes, disfraces de Comte, disfraces de Fath y Marx; todos los trituraremos, todos quedarán desnudos, y no habrá más ropa que la piedra y la escama verde, la de pluma sangrante y ópalo de nervios...'.[8]

In his article on Héctor Aguilar Camín's 1991 novel *La guerra de Galio*, about the same period of Mexican politics as *Agua quemada*, Fuentes takes up a characteristically animalistic vocabulary: 'El reférí se llama la modernidad. Pero debajo del ring esperan, inquietos, gruñentes, los salvajes, los bárbaros, los caníbales... [...] Se teme al "México bronco", al "tigre desatado".'[9] The character Galio from Aguilar Camín's novel is the same fascistic intellectual known as Ureñita in 'El hijo de Andrés Aparicio': Emilio Uranga, who once belonged to the Hiperión group and later became a Marxist.[10]

Porfirio Díaz, in the words of Enrique Krauze, 'would sometimes speak of the revolutionary potential of the poor as the "sleeping tiger" of Mexican history — an animal that should not be awakened'.[11] The 'tigre' is perhaps the clearest sign of the infra-human, animalistic

---

[8] *Los días enmascarados* (Mexico City: Era, 1982), 68-9.
[9] 'Héctor Aguilar Camín: la verdad de la mentira', in *Geografía de la novela* (Mexico City: Alfaguara, 1993), 117-18.
[10] See Francisco Larroyo, *La filosofía iberoamericana* (Mexico City: Porrúa, 1978), 162-63.
[11] Enrique Krauze, *Mexico: Biography of Power. A History of Modern Mexico, 1810-1996*, translated by Hank Heifetz (New York: Harper Collins, 1997), 220.

vocabulary which runs through all the stories. When General Vergara and his grandson Plutarco, together with their hired mariachi band, wreak havoc in the Club de los Aztecas, walking away from the scene with impunity after leaving 'ese reguero de centenarios para pagar los desperfectos' (33), their violence is a re-run, a grotesque repetition of the founding revolutionary violence of the battle of Celaya:

> a ver, al asalto, mis tigrillos, [...] puros jotos envaselinados con corbatita de moño y esmokin brillante de tanta planchada, planchados te voy a dejar los güevos, vejestorio, órale mis muchachos, ya me bravearon y eso no, por la santísima virgen que no, cápalos, abuelito [...] sáquenle las tripas al piano como a los caballos de Celaya [...] descontón a la panza [...] patada al culo.
>
> (32-33)

This is the same language which Bernabé received from licenciado Carreón, who brought him up with the purpose of humiliating his real father: 'ustedes son la mera brigada de los gavilanes [...] pateen, descontón y a los güevos [...] luego a la fiesta, a pegar recio, a venirse de gusto pegando recio' (132-3).

The infra-human and the non-social are embodied in the omnipresent dogs. The dogs are virtually indistinguishable from all the dispossessed of the city, and indeed are described in remarkably similar terms. Plutarco describes the inhabitants of the urban sprawl as 'legiones de desempleados, inmigrantes del campo y millones de niños concebidos [...] entre un aullido y un suspiro' (37). The dogs which fill the pages of 'Estos fueron los palacios' are 'perros paridos quién sabe dónde, perros nacidos del encuentro callejero entre otros perros igualitos a ellos' (49). The dogs fornicate and move on just as Andrés Aparicio had to leave his son without his memory, at the mercy of values radically at odds with his own. The street kids hack off the tail of the dog in the same way as the tram breaks the legs of young Luisito. Shared social links are dissolved: in a scene reminiscent of Buñuel the priests in the Cathedral use crucifixes to expel Manuela and her dogs from the Cathedral; Luisito has to leave his school because of the cruelty of the other pupils. Only at the end of the story, and then in a dream-like, fantasy sequence, are separations undone and absences filled: the crippled boy and Manuela waltz round the courtyard of the palace-tenement magically restored to its original splendour, while the old woman manages to transform Luis into her absent lover, perhaps

General Vergara, in the same way la señora Consuelo in *Aura* transforms Felipe Montero into the absent, long-dead general Llorente. The Mexico of these stories is riddled with absence and gaps: the gaps between the families and the stories and the absence within them. In 'Las mañanitas', the bachelor Federico Silva is emptied out, separated from himself firstly by the castrating tyranny of his grotesque mother, and then by the scalpel which cuts out his possible paternity in the abortion he pays for: 'te has visto obligado a llevar a una muchachita al doctor para que la operen o, peor tantito, le mandas el dinero con tu criado para que se haga abortar' (92). But in *Agua quemada*, as elsewhere in Fuentes, paternity is not straightforwardly biological. Silva associates his absent child with an animal force within him. He associates the humidity from the subterranean Aztec lake with a force that might make him 'reaccionar visceralmente, como un animal [...] Temo que regrese [...] el fantasma de un animal que pude ser yo o el hijo que nunca tuve' (93). And indeed these children do appear in the story: they are the 'nacos', the 'méndigos chamagosos', the 'jipiza', the youths that he had always refused really to see on Insurgentes: 'los ojos de resentimiento, los tigres enjaulados dentro de los cuerpos nerviosos' (76). These same children burst into his house one night and cut his throat with a razor: '—Ah que la chingada, ora sí... ya la regamos' (90). Silva's obsession with the guillotine, which was the fate of the character to whom Silva is compared in the story, Monsieur Verdoux as played by Charles Chaplin in the film of that name, the severing of his own head, all inflict further laceration of the gangrened body of Mexico City.

The bundle of terms associated with 'violencia impune', violence with impunity, gaps and absence, are essential to the stories and their very structure. Their most dramatic expression is perhaps the penis of the Mexcian *macho* and its absence in castration, the real and metaphorical gap which it leaves. The very name of the first patriarch, General Vergara, hyperbolically flags up his phallic power: 'Verga rara y alabío, alabau, alabimbombá, Verga, Verga, ra, ra, ra. [...] Vergara Plutarco, presente y parada' (14). The General's fame is derived from the fact that he killed a man: 'el General Tompiates, cuídate los aguacates, ríete pero no me mates' (15).[12] Despite the amusing

---

[12] In Mexican slang, *verga* means penis, while *tompiates* and *aguacates* refer to

wordplay, the reality of the Mexican sun eating up the castrated man is not pretty: 'Ese hombre desangrándose al amanecer sobre el polvo del desierto. Luego se lo comió el sol y los zopilotes lo velaron' (24). Bernabé's life in 'El hijo de Andrés Aparicio' is defined by the paternal absence, which in turn was the consequence of previous violence. His father, an agronomist, probably from the Escuela de Chapingo, and a supporter of Cárdenas like Fuentes's own father,[13] had crossed a local *cacique* from Guerrero, Mariano Carreón, when he attempted to investigate a massacre at an agricultural cooperative. Carreón systematically humiliates Aparicio and destroys his life until finally Aparicio kicks one of Carreón's thugs to death and disappears. Violence generates absence and silence, which in turn generate violence: '[A Bernabé] las palabras le costaron mucho [...] porque ya no recordó la voz de su padre' (98); 'las palabras nomás no le salían y por primera vez supo oscuramente [...] que si no había palabras entonces había cates [blows]' (101). The original paternal heritage, the social justice of Lázaro Cárdenas, is exchanged for its opposite, the violence with impunity of his other *jefe*, his substitute father the fascist Carreón. On the last page of the collection, the penis no longer belongs to the individual, to the real father whom Bernabé glimpses and chooses to ignore, but is rather institutionalised in the cruel solar deity Huitzilopochtli: 'un viejo distraído orinando detrás de un ciprés, calvo, sonriente, como un bobo, sonriendo sin parar que luego se fue caminando con la brangueta abierta bajo ese sol picante como un gran chile amarillo [*chile* is Mexican slang for penis] del mediodía en Azcapotzalco.'

One word well characterises both the situation of Mexican man, the coherence of his society, and the form of the stories which represent them: *inconcluso*, 'unfinished'. Federico Silva orders the Unfinished Symphony of Schubert to be put on the record-player on his death and a copy of the unfinished novel of Charles Dickens, *The Mystery of Edwin Drood* to be left open on his bedside table. While in prison for murder, Bernabé remembers fragments of 'Alturas de Macchu Picchu' which Ureña had read to him: 'tuvo un sueño en el que él se iba rodando en

testicles.

[13] On the role of Fuentes's father in the diplomatic defence of the policies of Cárdenas, see the interview with Sylvia Fuentes, 84.

silencio, muriéndoso, rodando como un pedacito de hombre ¿qué? ¿de hombre qué?' (136). The verse of Pablo Neruda which he imperfectly remembers is 'el pedacito roto del hombre inconcluso'. The 'cuarteto narrativo' *Agua quemada* combines continuity and discontinuity, an irremediable chaos and an implacable order. By reflecting the universality of 'violence with impunity' and the no less universal dislocation it produces, it is perhaps the literary form which most faithfully captures the social reality of Mexico City in the sixties and seventies as seen by Carlos Fuentes.

Constancia y otras novelas para vírgenes, 1989: A Post-Modern Baroque

The five novellas of *Constancia* weave a network which is at once minutely symmetrical and deceptively unstable. In a labyrinth of echoes its pages are traversed by a single virgin, or a whole clan of virgins, made of wood, porcelain, flesh and bones, reflected in the blinking of traffic lights, giving birth each year to a new infant Jesus, in the shape of a vampiress from Seville in Savanna, Georgia. There are virgins, bullfighters and a whole forest of *cuates*, twins, brothers, whose family lineage is indescribably ambiguous, mobile, reversible: perhaps Saint Joseph and Jesus, then Quetzalcoatl, perhaps Cain and Abel. They inhabit complex, hallucinatory architectural spaces, with much of Piranesi, the 'invisible cities' of Calvino, subterranean convents only intermittently in existence, and rooms of the purest *art nouveau* style. The circulation and recycling of meaning between the novellas reflects the practice of Sterne in *Tristram Shandy* as described by Franscisco de Goya: 'escribe a base de digresión, negándole autoridad al centro, [...] rebelándose contra la tiranía de la forma' (244).

The raw material of the stories is densely cultural: the most obvious and notorious icons and simulacra of the Hispanic world, both Spanish and Mexican. They share, for example, with Bigas Luna's film *Jamón, jamón,* the conjunction of the bull-advertisement for Osborne brandy, strangely fixed on a television screen, and a well-known painting by Goya which has become a custom in an Andalusian village: 'los señores de su pueblo se divertían enterrando a los mozos del lugar hasta los muslos en arena y dándoles garrotes para combatirse hasta la muerte' (249). The vampiress Constancia crosses the Atlantic to meet a husband who shares a name with the seaport where Dracula's coffin arrives in Bram Stoker's novel: Whitby. A headless Goya in nineteen eighty something chats away happily with the same anachronism as the head of Dr Francia from its noodle tin in *Yo el Supremo*. His characters seem to know that they are characters of a mischievously strident, postmodern Fuentes. Nicolás Sarmiento laments not having been able to seduce 'las dos Elenas', who belong to the story from *Cantar de ciegos*, and discusses the house of his friend Federico Silva, straight from the pages of *Agua quemada*. Indeed, the whole of 'El prisionero de las lomas' can be read as a parodic rewriting of *La muerte de Altemio Cruz*. This aesthetic, however, does not free the text from a vein of mysticism, a clear fascination with mystery and enigma. Fuentes said of it: 'Quién sabe si lo logré, pero en estas historias me propuse darle a la ficción el valor de hacer visible lo invisible, predecir la ausencia y apostar a que, en la novela, es más importante lo que se ignora que lo que se sabe.'[1] Fuentes's texts usually have some point of absolute unknowability. The three voices of Artemio Cruz will be reunited only in the ineffable moment of death; it is impossible to attribute a coherent reality to characters like Freddy Lambert from *Cambio de piel*. In *Constancia*, there are fundamental facts which cannot be known or are clearly contradictory: When did Constancia first die? Who is the mother of the Vélez brothers? Are Dimas Palomero and Lala brother and sister? Who usurped the identity of Prisciliano Nieves? The angels in the chapel where the bullfighter Rubén Romero prays before going out to die (predictably repeating 'dejarme solo' (262)) in the bull-ring at Ronda are excellent representatives of the intriguing aesthetic of the work, where icons seem to be demystified through fumigation:

> Pensó en todo esto, hincado ante una virgen ampona, color de rosa, con el niño en las rodillas, en la capilla de la plaza. Los ángeles en vuelo eran la verdadera corona de esta reina, pero su función desconcertó a Rubén Oliva: éstos eran ángeles con fumigadores, y en sus rostros había una sonrisa burlona, casi una mueca, que los excluía de toda complicidad irónica, poniéndolos aparte de la figura ¿virginal? ¿materna? (259)

There is a second angel, however, in this novella otherwise haunted by the fear of the tyranny of the centre, which embodies a fundamental underlying nostalgia: the origin, the sacred, full meaning, and the catastrophic expulsion from this space. In Seville, the North American Whitby Hull discovers that his lifelong wife, whom he married in 1946, had been machine-gunned to death in Cadiz in the Spanish Civil War, and that in the register which contains the details of his marriage, Constancia's data have disappeared, leaving absolute nothingness:

---

[1] 'Cronología personal', 114.

Mi nombre, mis fechas, mi genealogía, aparecían ahora huérfanos, sin la compañía, ésa sí desde siempre capturada en la orfandad, de mi Constancia. Frente a mi columna escrita, había una columna vacía. [...] el original del archivo de Sevilla era *la nada*. (60)

On the plane back home, Hull reads the famous passage of Walter Benjamin on Paul Klee's 'Angelus Novus':

> Da la cara al pasado. Donde nosotros vemos una cadena de eventos, él contempla la catástrofe única que acumula ruina sobre ruina y luego las arroja a sus pies. El ángel quisiera permanecer, despertar a los muertos y devolverle la unidad a lo que ha sido roto. Pero una tormenta sopla desde el Paraíso; azota las alas del ángel con una violencia tal que ya no puede cerrar sus alas. La tormenta, irresisitiblemente, lo arroja hacia el futuro al cual él le da la espalda, en tanto que las ruinas apliladas frente a él crecen hacia el cielo. La tormenta es lo que nosotros llamamos el progreso. (65-66)

This expulsion, orphanhood, exile, underlies all the stories. Benjamin died on the border between Spain and France fleeing the holocaust; Plotkinov, the Russian husband of Constancia, dead but present in Savannah as a vampire, is exiled from communist Russia; when Hull returns home, he finds that his house has been occupied by a family of refugees from El Salvador; the architect Santiago Ferguson feels exiled in Mexico from the Scotland of his ancestors. This loss is associated with the figure of Kafka, whom the barren Constancia assumes mentally as adopted son. According to Constancia, if Kafka had taken charge of the Spanish railway system with his uncle, 'los trenes habrían llegado a tiempo, pero sin pasajeros' (28); according to one Mexican critic, if Kafka had written in Mexico he would have been considered a realist writer.

If Klee's angel is expelled, other angels seem to annnounce the return: those on the façade of Wells cathedral, where Santiago Ferguson is buried. Again an aeroplane acts as an intermediary and as a mocking echo of the transcendental return: 'saboreamos [sendos Bloody Marys ...] para compensar la transitoriedad de este refugio por trece horas [...] el vientre materno de aluminio y hule espuma que nos conduce' (350). The fever of analogy compares the nave of the late English Gothic church with the interior of the Boeing 747:

> el doble ojal de piedra al fondo de la nave abre perspectivas comparables a las del interior de un avión pero, también, recuerda la cueva primigenia: dos ingresos al refugio —los motores del 747 no se dejan escuchar, más ruido hace un gato regalón— que nos protege; pero que, quizás, también, nos aprisiona. (350)

The angels announce the two poles of the world of *Constancia*: the expulsion and the return to the origin, to the womb of the stifling cultural community. The ideal poem, novel, or building combines inside and outside, expulsion and absorption:

> el lugar que nos salve [...] del dilema que nos persigue desde que nacemos, expulsados del vientre que nos dio la vida, condenados al exilio que es nuestro castigo [...] pero también la condición de nuestra vida, [...] adentro o afuera, ése es todo el problema, adentro vives, pero si no sales, mueres: afuera vives pero si no encuentras un refugio, mueres también. Sepultado adentro, desnudo afuera, condenado siempre, buscas tu lugar exacto, un afuera/adentro que te nutra. (301)

Hence the importance of architecture in all the work of Fuentes: the inclusive, all-containing construction of El Escorial in *Terra Nostra*, and of the pyramid and the concentration camp in *Cambio de piel*, the hallucinatory house in *Cumpleaños* and the opposition between original space and mediated, palimpsestic spaces in the same novel, and, in *Zona sagrada*, the house of Claudia and that of Mito.

Outside and inside, unity and dispersion, *parálisis* and *desenfreno*. The ever-changing architecture and the agile shifts in perspective in the novellas of *Constancia* preclude any final resolution of the dilemma, unless it be a constant activity: 'El arte propone un enigma, pero la solución del enigma es otro enigma' (67). The novellas are external one to the other, but also reflect each other *en abyme*, like Toño behind his friend Bernardo in the mirror; like the city of Savannah and the dreams of Hull, which 'se parecen como gemelos a la ciudad de Savannah, que es una ciudad dentro de otra dentro de...' (15); like the house of Rennie Mackintosh inside a museum inside a concrete building. In the first novella, Constancia dreams that she incarnates the characters from all the other novellas (35–36). A similar effect is created when container and content, actress and role, reading and performance are shuffled on Hull's video player. The sequence culminates in another opposition explored in *Constancia*: the hard and lasting against the instantaneous and shifting:

> Le doy la vida cada vez que aprieto el botón. Está muerta Vivien Leigh; Vivien Leigh vive. Muere y vive interpretando el papel de una mujer rusa del siglo pasado. La película es una ilustración de la novela. La novela vive cada vez que es leída. La novela tiene el pasado de sus lectores muertos, el presente de sus lectores vivos y el futuro de sus lectores por venir. Pero en la novela nadie interpreta el papel de Anna Karenina. Cuando muere Anna Karenina en la estación de Moscú no muere la actriz que la interpreta. La actriz muere después de la interpretación. La interpretación de la muerte sobrevive a la actriz. El hielo del cual habla el actor Plotnikov se convierte en el mármol del arquitecto Plotnikov. (46–47)

Here there is no inside or outside, original and representation, but Moebius strip, reproduction and vertigo.

The alternation between inside and outside sometimes takes on a symmetry which is the sign of horror and death. Constancia flees the heat of Savannah inside the house, Hull on the veranda. In the house of Constancia's dead husband Plotnikov, facing the house shared by Constancia and her living husband Hull, a sinister symmetry reigns: one room with all the clichés of Russian culture is reflected in another which is stereotypically Spanish: with *mantones de Manila*, paintings in the style of Romero de Torres, of gypsies and bullfighters. This room in the South of the USA has a pretty close copy in that of Sonsoles in Mexico City in 'La desdichada'. In the Russian room there are two paintings:

> El primero reproducía una escena sumamente externa, una troika, una familia que sale de excursión [...]. El otro cuadro, totalmente interno, era una recámara apenas iluminada, una cama de agonía, donde yacía muerta una mujer joven. (51)

Ferguson, the architect, yearns for symmetry and detests it in equal proportions:

> Ferguson coqueteaba [...] con la visión, tentadora y abominable a la vez, de una perfecta simetría que sería tanto el origen como el destino del universo (336). Un edificio me permite, simplemente, recuperar la diferencia entre

las cosas, apuntando hacia la simetría como la idea que contiene tanto similtud como diferencia. (337)

Implicit in his fear and fascination is the horror of the *Doppelgänger*, which he conceived on realising, when he visited Mackintosh's house in Glasgow, that Mackintosh was his ghost, or double, or vice-versa, that his family was that of Mackintosh and that he was responsible for them. As in a painting by the Belgian surrealist Paul Delvaux, the architecture opens up to the exterior and a series of figures echo each other as far as the horizon: 'El primero grupo sólo ocultaba al segundo, pero ambos estaban relacionados, lejanos en el espacio, pero cercanos en el tiempo. Simétricos' (339). The city of Savannah also partakes of this symmetry, which is clearly associated with the totalising visions of rationalism, in the misquotation of Goya's caption, and the nightmarish labyrinths of Borges, the labyrinth promised by Lönrot to Red Scarlach, which consisted of a straight line (the paradox of Zeno), and the interminable galleries of the Library of Babel:

> El misterio de Savannah, de este modo, es su transparente sencillez geométrica. Su laberinto es la línea recta. De esta claridad nace, sin embargo, la sensación más agobiante de pérdida. El orden es la antesala del horror y cuando mi esposa, española, revisa un viejo álbum de Goya y se detiene en el más célebre grabado de los *Caprichos*, yo no sé si debo perturbar su fascinación, comentando:
> —La razón que nunca duerme produce monstruos. (16)

Passageways and courtyards combine outside and inside, and serve as a mediating space as in Julio Cortázar's story 'El otro cielo' where the Pasaje Güemes and the Galerie Vivienne act as an ambiguous, intermediate space between Buenos Aires and Paris. Hull meets Plotnikov in a shopping mall described as 'un falso interior (y también un falso exterior): es una calle de vidrio' (31). The courtyard of the house in 'La desdichada' is 'esa gracia mediadora entre el ruido de la calle y el abandono del apartamento' (87). It links the private with the public, the din of social discourse and the silence of the individual. Speaking of the house of Mackintosh, Ferguson describes 'una secuencia espectacular de ausencias, un pasaje de ingreso blanquinegro, como la división ideal entre la luz y la sombra, la vida y la muerte, el afuera y el adentro' (299).

The communication between novellas, periods and texts suggested by these passages is saved from the threat of cold geometry by an aggressive, savage, contaminating energy. It works through liquid, subterranean flows, like 'la fuente de Neptuno, el manantial de donde corrían las aguas invisbles de la Castellana' (183). The streets and waters of Seville and indeed the whole world yield to the vision of a fluid paneroticism:

> la ley del agua, universalmente comunicada, manantiales con arroyos y riachuelos [...] con el pozo más oscuro. [...] todas las recámaras del mundo comunicadas entre sí, sin una sola puerta cerrada, ningún candado o traba, ni un solo obstáculo para el deseo, el texto, la satisfacción de la cama. (228)

Goya, speaking about the trinity formed by himself, Pedro Romero and Elisia Rodríguez, denies the perfect independence of the individual:

> Imaginad tres espacios [...] tres círculos perfectos que jamás debieron tocarse, tres orbes circulando cada uno en su trayectoria independiente [...] Quizás son así los mundos de los dioses. Los nuestros, por desgracia, son imperfectos. Las esferas se encuentran, se rechazan, se cruzan, se fecundan, rivalizan, se asesinan entre sí. (190-91)

This flux pollutes, and the double function of the moon is to control tides and menstruations. The *matador* Rubén Oliva faces the bull absolutely still; in his *traje de luces* he is an immobile, central sun, while his wife menstruates in the kitchen and cuts her finger, like so many of the characters, when opening a tin. The moon seems to bring the sea to Madrid in August: 'lo traía impulsado por los imanes secretos de la luna, [...] convirtiendo a Madrid en playa estival de mareas y drenajes y menstruaciones cotidianas, cloaca y fuente lustral' (186).

Within this flow and spectacular proliferation, any notion of originality loses its grip. La desdichada is a dummy which is at the same time the mother of God and an artefact mechanically reproduced and mass-produced for the whole world from a European racial model. The Virgin Mary does not give birth once but repeatedly: 'una concepción inmaculada la primera vez, corrupta y pecaminosa la segunda vez' (357). Various characters try to impose a unique perfection on the world, but the world evades them: dwellers in a house subvert the ideal conception of its architect; readers the formal, univocal perfection of a poem; the Oedipal drama the independence of an individual; peasants from Morelos occupy the house of Nicolás Sarmiento and impose their dense network of memories and genealogies in the very place where they had previously been denied a past. Francisco de Goya, a jealous voyeur ('Espiaba a los amantes por las cerraduras de sus cuadros' (227)), tries to fix Elisia Rodríguez for ever on canvas: 'De ahí no te mueves. Así eres y así serás eternamente.' But he knows that as soon as other people see the picture, 'la sacarían de la prisión del cuadro y la lanzarían a hacer de las suyas, acostándose con quien se le viniere en gana, desmayándose *à son plaisir*, entre los brazos de éste y aquél' (202–3).

The culmination of the paralysis which Goya wishes on 'la Privada' is the icon or statue. From *La muerte de Artemio Cruz* we know that 'Entre la parálisis y el desenfreno está la línea de la vida' (206). In *Constancia* the virgins do not stay in their niches but wander freely through the texts, pursuing a long series of Saint Josephs and Jesuses in multiple metamorphoses considered by Toño to be simply a Mexican surrealism which has become innate:

> todas las bromas a que aquí hemos sometido al cristianismo, trastocando los sacrificios de carne y hostia, disfrazando a las rameras de diosas, moviéndonos a nuestras anchas entre el establo y el burdel, el origen y el calendario [...] jugando charadas con el más exquisito cadáver [*cadavre exquis*] de todos, Nuestro Señor Jesucristo, en nuestras jaulas de cristal sangriento. (95)

The spirit of López Velarde's Fuensanta has passed from *Cristóbal Nonato* to *Constancia*: 'Nardo es tu cuerpo y su virtud es tanta / que entre tus brazos beatíficos me duermo / como sobre los senos de una Santa.'[2] In 'La Desdichada' Toño and Bernardo leave their 'noviecitas santas' back in their native provinces without expecting to meet the wooden holy virgin which they come across in a shop window in calle Tacuba, Mexico D.F.

The move between the animate and the inanimate is not uncommon in the work of Fuentes: the crippled Amilamia in 'La muñeca reina' and

---

[2] Ramón López Velarde, 'Elogio a Fuensanta', in *Obras* (Mexico City: Fondo de Cultura Económica, 1986), 63.

the grotesque doll in which her parents have tried to capture her lost childhood; the statuette of Chac Mool bought in the Lagunilla market with fatal consequences; the Christ which talks to Jaime Ceballos in *Las buenas conciencias*; the composite royal mummy in *Terra Nostra*, etc. In 'Viva mi fama', the Virgin, with her court of Santas Mártires, snatches the child from the woman with bushy eyebrows, an avatar of La Privada, who has suckled the child and turned it from black to white, and climbs with him onto the float which will carry them in procession. In 'Gente de razón', Christ is an irreverent young lad who mocks the holy martyrs like Saint Agatha and Saint Lucy: 'A veces porta panecillos, a veces campanillas, la muy simbólica: tilín de tetas tostadas, ¿oyes? Y mira a la que sigue, Lucía [...] preferiste quedarte ciega a ser fornicada, ¿no? pues ahora cómete tus ojos puestos como huevos fritos sobre tu plato' (316). At the end of the story, doña Heredad shows off the miraculous child round the rich houses in Lomas de Chapultepec in exchange for 'las sobras de un banquete, revoltijos de cerdo y langosta, tortillas secas o manojos de ensaladas desmayadas' (360). The god-child in his shopping basket is a 'muñeco de hulespuma con sus rizos dorados y sus ojos azules y su ropón blanco con filete dorado y sus dedos sangrantes, caridad, caridad para el niño' (361). The wooden immobility of the plump Macarena to whom Constancia prays is reproduced in the repeated deaths suffered by Constancia, or in the erotic swoons of La Privada at the moment of orgasm, and in the sleepiness of the *chiapaneca* lover from 'El prisionero de la Lomas' who falls asleep in mid-coitus and has to be awakened with buckets of water, at which point she starts to perform regional dances. In 'La Desdichada', the dummy which comes to life as Saint Mary, or Bloody Mary considering the scratches she inflicts on Toño, at the end of the story, after a night of orgy goes back to her niche in the Metropolitan Cathedral from where 'sus párpados alargados, como de saurio, nos miran entrecerrados [...] como si fuésemos muñecos inanimados' (125).

It is difficult to avoid mention of Felisberto Hernández's short story 'Las hortensias' here, but the figure of Pygmalion is even more important. Pygmalion falls in love with Aphrodite and makes a statue in her image, which the goddess deigns to bring to life, with the name of Galatea. The theme rings a bell for Elisia when her Catalan husband launches her stage career: 'su marido haciéndola de pirmaleón y tú mi galletera, o algo así' (194). The Mexican Nicolás Sarmiento 'les daba atole con el dedo' to each 'potencial Galatea', 'enseñándolas cómo caminar' (139-40). The North American Whitby Hull meets the beautiful Andalusian Constancia and enjoys his role of Pygmalion, that of George Bernard Shaw and *My Fair Lady*, rather than that of Ovid:

> Yo el hombre seguro de sí mismo, de su país, su tradición, su lengua, y que por eso podía tomar a esta muchacha casi iletrada, que no hablaba inglés: por una vez —lancé una sonrisa en dirección del fantasma de Henry James— el norteamericano sería el Pigmalión de la europea. (55)

More than twenty years later, Hull discovered that Constancia was a sort of succubus or vampire and visited the funeral room of the Russian Dracula to whom she had been transferring the vitality of Hull. On the sculpted tomb he saw 'la figura yacente de una mujer, el perfil más dulce, los párpados más largos, el ceño más triste', Constancia turned into a recumbent statue. Hull touched the cold forms not without a degree of necrophilia: 'Recorro con mis dedos ávidos las cornisas del atroz monumento, palpando sin querer los pies de la mujer, sus hombros, sus facciones heladas' (57). There are reminiscences here perhaps of the scene from Carpentier's *El reino de este mundo* when the masseur Solimán caresses the marble body of Canova's Paolina Borghese.

Both in the case of Whitby Hull and in that of Nicolás Sarmiento, to refer to the woman as a Galatea implies cutting her off from her past, turning her into a projection of the man. Nevertheless, in both cases the memory, the past and the varied circumstances and dependencies of the dead woman invade the men's private, exclusive space: Whitby feeds the Russian and his skeleton baby, and at the end a family of refugees from Central America; the mansion of Sarmiento is invaded by Lala's vast family from Morelos, while he is condemned to immobility as the 'prisionero de las Lomas', the title of the novella. When he brings the statue to life, the apparently untouchable and independent demiurge becomes inextricably implicated in his creation.

In 'La desdichada' and 'Gente de razón' two pairs of 'twins' or *cuates*, Toño and Bernardo, and José María and Carlos María, the Vélez brothers, adore in a pretty fetichistic way an iconic form. They drift between the roles of Saint Joseph and Jesus, Quetzalcoatl and his twin, Apollo and Dionysos, brothers, father and son, rivals and lovers. José María worships the wedding dress of Catalina Ferguson, his sister or the incestuous daughter of his teacher, the dress which later (in fact fifty years earlier) dresses the dummy adored by Toño and Bernardo, in the same way as the latter's mother venerates the memory of her dead husband in the simulacrum of his uniform, spread out on the bed. 'La desdichada' is a shop display dummy bought by Toño for his friend Bernardo for the student apartment they share in calle Tacuba in the old centre of Mexico City.³ The story nostalgically brings back to life the Mexico of Cárdenas experienced by the young Fuentes, a world which ends with a Quevedo-inspired elegy to 'la región más transparente del aire': 'éramos lo que éramos, escritores, periodistas, burócratas, editores, políticos, negociantes, ya no éramos un será, sino un fue, en estos años, y el aire era tan...' (126). It revisits a close group of friends and a series of supposedly long-resolved existential and family dilemmas. The Waikiki cabaret revisited by Bernardo at the end of the story has all the atmosphere of the *milonga* where Dr Hardoy and Mauro glimpse the dead Celina in her 'duro cielo conquistado' in Cortázar's story 'Las puertas del cielo'.⁴ La Desdichada's ring finger is missing, an imperfection which lends her more life, but associates her with other impossible lovers like Rubén Darío's Venus, 'al abrazo imposible de la Venus de Milo',⁵ or with her younger sister from Céasar Vallejo's poem 'Pugnamos ensartarnos por un ojo de aguja'. The Mexican *cuates* are even less polite: '¿Por dónde?'. The severed finger also evokes Fuentes's great-grandmother, Clotilde Vélez de Fuentes, a brave lady who 'se deja cortar un dedo con machete [...] antes que entregar voluntariamente sus anillos de bodas'.⁶ At the same time, this Clotilde Vélez is the mother of the 'veloces Vélez' brothers from 'Gente de razón', ensconced in the secret underground convent. The virgin in the convent, with 'un bozo prominente sobre los labios'

[3] 'Paz y [José] Alvarado habían compartido una buhardilla del centro cuando estudiaban derecho en San Ildefonso, y allí se llevaron a vivir a una maniquí bautizada "La Rígida" y que me sirvió de tema para el cuento, La desdichada, en la que el papel de Bernardo corresponde a un retrato imaginario del joven Octavio', 'Mi amigo Octavio Paz', in *El País* (Edición Internacional), 18–20 May 1998, 7–8, 8.

[4] Julio Cortázar, *Bestiario, Cuentos completos* (Madrid: Alfaguara, 1994), I, 163.

[5] Rubén Darío, 'Yo persigo una forma...', *Prosas profanas, Poesías completas* (Madrid: Aguilar, 1968), 622.

[6] In 'Cronología personal', 104. See also *Los años con Laura Díaz* (Mexico City: Alfaguara, 1999), 21–23.

(316), is the Vélez brothers' and Catalina Ferguson's mother, who has a 'notable bozo en el labio superior' (358), and also 'la Privada', from 'Viva mi fama', 'esa soberbia mujer cejijunta y de no malos bigotes' (221) and all the other virgins associated with her. The dummy gradually comes to life for the two friends to a different extent and in a different manner; they lay on a formal dinner for La Desdichada, dress her with clothes stolen from the cabaret hostesses or the washerwomen, and finally Toño murders her by immersing her in boiling water, perhaps so as not to compromise his friendship with Bernardo. For Bernardo, she is mute, ideal and perfect in a way, whereas for Toño she is loquacious, violent, prey to continuous metamorphoses: she is Penelope and Circe, immobility and mutability, *parálisis* and *desenfreno*. Toño fears the scratches or infections that her 'perversidad polimórfica' might inflict on the purity of his friend:

> ¿Crees que ella tiene derecho a interponerse entre tú y yo, destruir nuestra amistad, hechizarte, entorpecer tu voluntad, liberarte para el mal, frustrar tu romanticismo monogámico, introducirte en su perversidad hambrienta de formas? No sé qué opinas. Yo la he visto de cerca. Yo he observado sus cambios de humor, de tiempo, de gusto, de edad, es tierna un minuto y violenta el que sigue; nace a ciertas horas, parece moribunda en otros cuadrantes; está enamorada de la metamorfosis, no de la forma inalterable de una estatua o de un poema. (115)

La Desdichada as a statue, unalterable for Bernardo, constantly changing for Toño, is inseparable from a poem which Bernardo is translating, Gérard de Nerval's 'El desdichado'. Here the poet, 'le ténébreux, — le veuf, — l'inconsolé, Le prince d'Aquitaine à la tour abolie' speaks of two contrasting women, 'les soupirs de la sainte et les cris de la fée',[7] similar perhaps to those who seem simultaneously to inhabit La Desdichada. The feminisation in the latter's name of the title of the poem echoes the androgyny of Arturo's fiancée-twin, 'casi sin pechos pero con un vello púbico abundante' (110), of Madreselva, the substitute mother of the bullfighter Rubén Oliva, of Rubén himself like all the young strollers on the Castellana in Madrid: 'como ellos, como casi todo español majo, tenía algo de andrógino' (185).

---

[7] Nerval, *Les Chimères* (Genève: Droz, 1966), 5.

If La Desdichada is a wooden statue, the poem is a statue of air: 'El poema de Nerval es, literalmente, el aire de una estatua. No el que la rodea, sino la estatua misma hecha del puro aire de la voz que recita el poema' (84). The statues and the poems come to life as they are spoken. The perfection of a poem before it is spoken is a paralysis, an imperfection, an imperfection already inscribed on the body of La Desdichada in her lost finger:

> un poema de Gérard de Nerval en el que la desdicha y la felicidad son como estatuas fugitivas, palabras cuya perfección significa fijarse en la inmovilidad de la estatua, sabiendo, sin embargo, que semejante parálisis es ya su imperfección, su mal-estar. La Desdichada no es perfecta: le falta un dedo y no sé si se lo mocharon adrede o si fue un accidente. Los maniquíes no se mueven, pero son movidos con descuido. (101)

We are reminded of Vallejo's *Trilce* XXXVI on the Venus of Milos, who 'manquea[s] apenas': 'Rehusad, y vosotros a posar las plantas / en la seguridad dupla de la Armonía. / Rehusad la simetría a buen seguro.'[8]

Bernardo amuses himself by playing with the meanings of *decir* and *desdecir*, *dicha* and *desdicha* in the context of the poem and the statue which come to life:

> Las palabras de un poema sólo vuelven a *ser*, imperfectas o no, cuando fluyen de nuevo, es decir, cuando son *dichas*. [...] decir no es sólo romper un silencio, sino también exorcizar un mal. El silencio es des-decir: es desdicha. La voz es decir = es dicha. El silencioso es el des-dichado, el que no dice o no es dicho —dichoso él—. Y ella, La Desdichada, no habla, no habla... (121)

The word-play opens Fuentes's reference beyond Nerval to poems like Xavier Villaurrutia's 'Nocturno en que nada se oye', or Octavio Paz's 'La palabra dicha':

> La palabra se levanta / de la página escrita. / La palabra, / labrada estalactita, / grabada columna, / una a una letra a letra. / El eco se congela /

---

[8] *Los heraldos negros, Trilce* (Barcelona: El Bardo, 1972), 129.

en la página pétrea. / Ánima, / blanca como la página, / se levanta la palabra. [...] Lo que dice no dice / lo que dice: ¿cómo se dice / lo que no dice? / Di / tal vez es bestial la vestal. / [...] / Lo que se dice se dice / al derecho y al revés. / Lamenta la mente / de menta demente: / cementerio es sementero, / simiente no miente. / Laberinto del oído, / lo que dices se desdice / del silencio al grito / desoído.⁹

In an essay on Borges Fuentes uses similar terms when he speaks of the activity of reading as an undoing of totalising projects: 'El lector es la herida del libro que lee: por su lectura (...) se desangra toda posibilidad totalizante, ideal, de la biblioteca en la que lee [...] El lector es la cicatriz de Babel. El lector es la fisura, la rajada, en la torre de lo absoluto.'¹⁰ Toño is the reader of Bernardo, and his effect recalls the way in which the versions of Javier in *Cambio de piel* dismantle the totalitarian, prison-like constructions of Franz. This is perhaps why Bernardo runs away from the readings and the gaze of Toño, and takes refuge in the pseudo-Andalusian residence of his aunt and uncle and the doll's house of his cousin Sonsoles. Bernardo, on the point of taking his leave of Mexico, exhausted by the complex demands of his family and others, is tempted by immobility, by literature as an absolute, or as a statue:

> ¿Me salva La Desdichada de la obligación de la familia? La muñeca inmóvil podría liberarme de las responsabilidades del sexo, los hijos, el matrimonio, liberándome para la literatura. ¿Puede la literatura ser mi sexo, mi boda y mi descendencia? ¿Puede la literatura suplir a la amistad misma? ¿Odio por esto a Toño, que se da a la vida sin más? (113)

Bernardo associates literature with the gaze of the Medusa, with immobility. The play between and within the stories generates a threatening Oedipal instability. The Vélez brothers, who saw their teacher Ferguson as an incestuous father and a rival, discover that his young lover is their sister; Nicolás Sarmiento in 'El prisionero de las Lomas' establishes a false family relationship with the usurper of General Prisciliano Nieves, based on complicity in deceit; Arturo has a

---

[9] Paz, *Poemas*, 326–7.
[10] 'Jorge Luis Borges: la herida de Babel', *Geografía de la novela*, 65.

lover who is identical to him, a false twin for whom he had long searched. Toño's Desdichada, that is, the one who changes and speaks, always a potential lover, begins as a mother and ends up as a daughter. When he was a boy she called him 'retoño', bud or son, but now it is she who is the infant: 'La cama está orinada. Ella no me reconoce, no reconoce a su Toño, mi re-toño, como me decía de niño. (...) La tomé, la arrullé, ahora me corresponde a mí, niña, ahora eres mía' (114). We are reminded of the lines of 'Piedra de sol': 'mirada niña de la madre vieja / que ve en el hijo grande un padre joven, / mirada madre de la niña sola / que ve en el padre grande un hijo niño'.[11]

For Bernardo, the figure of his father, who was killed after the Tlaxcalantongo massacre, is, like La Desdichada, a frozen effigy, fixed in an impotent immobility which nevertheless hides a latent threat. As in the case of Harriet Winslow in *Gringo viejo*, or Rosenda Pola in *La región más transparente*, for Bernardo's mother, the absent husband, dead or presumed dead, is an unresolved trauma, or a trauma to be resolved through the son or daughter. For many years she kept her husband's uniform spread out on the bed like a grotesque military fetish and family altar: 'La túnica con botonaduras de plata. El kepí con dos estrellas. (...) Éste era su perpetuo Te Deum doméstico. (...) Como si la gloria y el réquiem de una batalla desaparecida la acompañasen siempre a ella. Como si esta ceremonia de luto y amor fuese la promesa de que el esposo alguna vez (el padre) regresaría' (92). The display of La Desdichada's clothes is a precarious repetition of his paralyzing consecration.

As with Vivien Leigh on Whitby Hull's video machine, here again it is cinema which introduces movement. Some fifteen years after the death of his father, Bernardo's mother writes to him from Guadalajara to say that she has put the uniform away because she has seen her husband, alive and moving, in a silent film recording: 'con el mismo uniforme que yo he cuidado tan celosamente, tu padre, hijo mío, moviéndose, acicalándose el bigote, descansando la mano en el cinturón, mirando, mirándome a mí, hijo mío, a mí, Bernardo, me miró a mí. Lo he visto. Puedes regresar' (113). The longed for return of the dead young husband is inseparable from that of the distant son. Faced

---

[11] Paz, *Poemas*, 267.

with the threat of the 'simulacro móvil del cine', as he calls the film, Bernard opts for 'la muñeca inmóvil' of literature (113). While Bernardo might opt for that immobility, the author of *Constancia y otras novelas para vírgenes* clearly does not. The Vélez brothers also opt for closure, the ideal and the immobile in order to exclude the demands of others:

> ¿Cuáles eran los límites de la creación? No hay artista que, en su ánimo más íntimo, no se haya hecho esta pregunta, temeroso de que el acto creativo no sea gratuito, no sea suficiente, sino que se prolongue en las exigencias de quienes habitan una casa, leen un libro, contemplan una pintura o asisten a una representación teatral. ¿Hasta dónde llega el privilegio individual de crear; dónde empieza la obligación compartida con los demás? La única obra consumida en el puro *yo*, despojada de su potencial *nosotros*, sería la obra sólo concebida, nunca realizada. (...) Pero en este universo apriorístico, reinaba la muerte. (349)

Whitby Hull's house is occupied by the refugees from El Salvador; Nicolás Sarmiento's by the Morelos peasants, the pages of *Constancia* by us readers and by dozens of chaste and randy virgins. 'Apagaré la llama de la vestal intacta,' says Darío, '¡y la faunesa antigua me rugirá de amor!'[12] ¡Viva la Virgen!

---

[12] 'Ite, Missa est', *Prosas profanas*, 571.

La frontera de cristal. Una novela en nueve cuentos, 1995: Frontier Realism

The main frontier in this collection is the one which runs from Tijuana to Matamoros, from San Diego to Brownsville: between Mexico and the United States of America, the latter a 'ubicación fantasmal', according to Daniel Cosío Villegas in the text, 'que era como llamarse [...] "el Borracho de la Esquina" or [...] "Tercer Piso a la Derecha".'[1] The characters are constantly crossing the border, and perhaps the most emblematic of them is the powerful businessman Leonardo Barroso, the king of the Mexican frontier, the owner of a Tudor-cum-Norman style mansion, assembly plants (*maquiladoras*), extensive real estate, endless business in foreign currency, drugs, hired labourers. In the first story, 'La capitalina', he abducts his god-daughter on the day of her wedding to his son, and takes her off to a luxurious hotel on the other side, perhaps in El Paso, driving towards the mirage of 'esa ciudad encantada del otro lado de la frontera, torres de oro, palacios de cristal' (26), evoking the fabulous 'Siete Ciudades de Cíbola' seen and invented by Cabeza de Vaca and his companions in the sixteenth century. Leonardo is omnipotent for the characters who depend on his favours, the crumbs of his power: his god-daughter Michelina Laborde, the medical student Juan Zamora, the chauffeur Leandro Reyes and the labourer Lisandro Chávez (Leonardo, Leandro, Lisandro). In the final pages, as he crosses the same frontier, he has his brains blown out by assassins hired by US drug barons because he had presumed to split profits fifty-fifty with his northern colleagues.

The didactic and allegorical realism of the novel[2] focuses on three main thematic areas: immediate social and political reality, the clichés and myths of national identity, and the history of what is now 'La Frontera', 'el Suroeste' or 'Aztlán' from the journeys of Cabeza de

---

[1] *La frontera de cristal* (Mexico City: Alfaguara, 1995), 77.
[2] For an interesting discussion of the realism of the novel, see Florence Olivier, 'Une littérature *d'actualité* légère et engagée: *La frontera de cristal* de Carlos Fuentes', in *les nouveaux réalismes. América (Cahiers du CRICCAL)*, 25, 2000, 77–82.

Vaca, the conquest by Juan de Oñate, the independence of Texas and the American-Mexican War of 1846–1848, until the present day. The social themes are myriad: the emigration to the north of all the generations of a Guanajuato village from the time of the Mexican Revolution until the controversial Proposition 187 of the State of California; work in the *maquila*, in the Chicago steel mills, in Woolworths stores, as a maid; the *coyotes* who smuggle workers without papers across the border; the bandits who attack trains; the racism of the agents of 'la Migra', the Migration Service and the border patrols, like Michael Elmer, who in 1992 shot the Mexican worker Darío Miranda and was acquitted by an Arizona court;[3] the violence of the skinheads who set out to hunt down Mexicans; the surreal flying of workers from Mexico to New York for a weekend to clean the windows of a skyscraper.

Lisandro may leave the windows shining clean, but the transparency of reality is perhaps not as straightforward as the reader is initially led to believe. A 'crystal frontier' may reveal everything, or, alternatively, by dint of being invisible, hide everything, starting with itself. The *maquila* is perhaps the best emblem of the real in the novel, the image of a reality and an identity assembled on a production line with imported components like the televisions aimed at the market in the North. Reality is cross-border, inter-linguistic, mobile, the effect of speculation and exploitation. In the fifth story, 'Malinzin de las maquilas' the factory is another image of Cíbola: 'un espejismo de vidrio y acero brillante, como una burbuja de aire cristalino' (136), but the financial mechanism is far more banal:

> las maquiladoras que le permitían a los gringos ensamblar textiles, juguetes, motores, muebles, computadoras y televisores con partes fabricadas en los EE UU, ensambladas en México con trabajo diez veces menos caro que allá, y devueltas al mercado norteamericano del otro lado de la frontera con el solo pago de un impuesto al valor añadido. (136)

For Margarita Barroso the assembly process parallels her construction of a North American identity:

---

[3] See *Nuevo tiempo mexicano*, 108.

LA FRONTERA DE CRISTAL, 1995

allí estaba su chamba y en su chamba ella era buena, ella se conocía de pe a pa el trabajo en serie del ensamblaje, del chassis a la soldadura a la prueba automática al gabinete y la pantalla al warm-up [...] al alineamiento para aislar a la televisora del campo magnético del mundo para tener un aparato libre de interferencia, ¿qué tal?, ésa se la soltaba a los compañeros de baile y hasta perdían el paso porque sabía más que ellos y no la querían, la dejaban en paz y les hablaba del test del aparato ante espejos, el gabinete plástico, el empaque en styrofoam y el cajón final, el féretro del televisor listo para el K Mart, dos horas dura todo el proceso, once mil aparatos por día, ¿quihubo?, ah qué vieja más enterada, si a ella le tocaba cerciorarse de que cada etapa estaba correcta adjudicándole estrellas verdes a los aparatos con problemas y estrellas azules cuando no había problema, ella se merecía una estrellota de oro en la frente, en la mera frente, como las niñas buenas en las escuelas de monjas, como las drum majorettes que manejaban el bastón y marchaban mostrando los calzones y se disfrazaban de coroneles para encabezar los desfiles y que los chicos le silbaran, la llamaran Margie y dijeran no es pocha, no es chicana, no es mexicana, es como tú y yo... (260)

Margarita respects the system and turns herself into Margie, a good US citizen; Serafín Romero inverts and subverts the flow of trade and is turned into a hero, Joaquín Murieta reborn as a Mexican:

Cuántas noches como ésta recuerda Serafín Romero, alejándose en su troca del tren detenido en el desierto, la troca llena de objetos robados, el tren lleno de paisanos necesitados de trabajo, los objetos robados nuevecitos, empaquetados, relucientes [...] todo antes de convertirse en basura yendo a dar a una montaña de desperdicios en Chalco... [...] lo único que le faltaba para ser un héroe, era un caballo relinchón. (265)

Heroic bandits and drum majorettes: the cultural expectations of the characters also seem to be packaged in styrofoam. They speak, as Isabel accuses Freddy Lambert in *Cambio de piel*, 'como con luz neón' (60). The author himself, approaching a realist depiction of a whole geographical area in which he must necessarily look for representative figures and events, cannot avoid stereotype and cliché. Indeed, he embraces them, stylises them and tosses them into the air with all the skill of a drum majorette in a Kansas City parade. Infantilised images from television comedy shows are clearly filtered through the English language: 'El jefe de la casa, Tarleton Wingate, es un simpático gigantón con menos arrugas en su fresca cara juvenil que una vieja silla de montar' (44). Mexicans, of course, are predictably impenetrable for Miss Amy Dunbar: 'Eran impenetrables. Sintió que miraba un muro de cactos, punzante, como si cada uno de esos seres fuese, en realidad, un puercoespín' (179). Presumably for the same reason he does not avoid the most saccarine television soap sentimentality when, for example, the intelligent, altruistic and sweet Mexican maid and the thorny and cruel Miss Dunbar embrace tenderly at the end of 'Las amigas': 'un abrazo que aunque nunca se repitiese, duraría una eternidad' (183).

Frontiers do not lend themselves well to classical realism. Realism to a great extent implies the naturalisation, normativity or invisibility of the narrating voice. In an interlingual and bicultural border literature such impartiality is no longer possible. The frontier does not only divide the land, but also physically seems to split people, as can be seen in Michelina Laborde's attractive cleft chin, seemingly announcing 'los intersticios mismos del pudor' (12), the monstrous hare-lip of her husband Mariano Barroso, or the photograph of the late husband of Miss Dunbar: 'la cicatriz le atraviesa la cara como un rayo parte en dos un cielo tormentoso' (174).

Each side of the border has internalised the other side as a sort of double, and characters like the *chicano* poet who crosses every day with papers have, in a way, two beings on each side:

> — Lo que es de acá y también de allá. Pero, ¿dónde es acá y dónde es allá, no es el lado mexicano su propio acá y allá, no lo es el lado gringo, no tiene toda tierra su doble invisible, su sombra ajena que camina a nuestro lado como cada uno de nosotros camina acompañado del segundo yo que ignora?
>
> Por eso escribía José Francisco, para darle una oportunidad a ese segundo José Francisco que tenía, por lo visto, su propia frontera interior. Quisiera ser simpático con sí mismo, pero no se dejaba. Estaba dividido en cuatro.
>
> (278-9)

The alien, interiorised voice appears when least expected. Tarleton Wingate is the epitome, the grotesque incarnation even, of Middle America, middle-class white, xenophobic and homophobic, a go-between in arms deals, devoid of any hint of doubt about the innate morality of his homeland. When the Mexican student lodging in his house asks why young Americans work on paper rounds, etc., Tarleton responds: 'Es para inculcarles la ética de trabajo protestante —dice con solemnidad Mr. Wingate' (45). Though these may well be his motives, it is unlikely that Mr Wingate had read Weber or would apply his terms to himself. Another is speaking within him. Archibaldo in 'Las amigas', a Chicago lawyer, bizarrely displays knowedge of works of 'filosofía de lo mexicano' such as 'Tiempo de fundación': 'A ella les [sic] parecen repugnantes nuestras iglesias vacías, sin decorado, puritanas' (173). In the title story, 'La frontera de cristal', a Mexican labourer and an American executive fall in love in a phantasmagorical encounter from opposite sides of a plate glass window on the fortieth floor of a modern New York office building. Audrey writes her name in lipstick on the glass, while Lisandro Chávez, embarrassed but probably more clear-sighted, simply scrawls, in back-to-front block capitals: MEXICAN. It is as if he had guessed the process of idealisation and mythification in the head of the blond executive: 'Lo encontró con un relampagazo mental. Cortesía. Lo que había en este hombre, en su actitud, en su distancia, en su manera de inclinar la cabeza, en la extraña mezcla de tristeza y alegría de su mirada, era cortesía, una ausencia increíble de vulgaridad' (207). Dionisio Rangel, to alleviate the tedium of his culinary lecture tours around the US, revisits the fantasies about Mexican-Latin spirituality, aristocracy and courtesy, which, since the time of Rodó and the Rubén Darío of 'A Roosevelt', have served to value Hispanics favourably against Anglos:

> Buen mexicano, les concedía a los gringos todo el poder del mundo salvo el de una cultura aristocrática. [...] Pero en México hasta un bandido era cortés, hasta un analfabeta, culto, hasta un niño sabía decir buenos días, hasta una criada sabía caminar con gracia, hasta un político sabía comportarse como una dama, hasta una dama sabía comportarse como un político, hasta los tullidos eran alambristas y hasta los revolucionarios tenían el buen gusto de creer en la virgen de Guadalupe. (78)

The encounters and clashes between cultures very self-consciously take on a didactic or semi-allegorical role. They are usually championed by a pair of emblematic antagonists. Dan Polonsky, a fifth-generation North American Jew, who is racist and violent and obsessed with the night-vision technology for detecting illegal immigrants, clashes with his subaltern Mario Islas, a US citizen of Mexican origin, whom he sees as being suspect and certainly less American than himself. In the story 'Las amigas', reminiscent of Elena Poniatowska's 'Love Story' (from the collection *De noche vienes*), the sadism of the old lady Amy Dunbar turns in an exemplary fashion into tenderness. The homosexual relationship between Juan Zamora and Jim Reynolds, in Cornell, Ithaca, is similarly tender. From the passion between the Mexican and the American comes a utopian dream and a spatial dislocation which would eliminate any difference:

> la barranca es más honda que el firmamento y convoca a los dos jóvenes amantes con una promesa mentirosa: el cielo está allá abajo, el cielo existe boca arriba [...] hay que merecer el cielo entregándose a él, poniendo de cabeza la mentira que desubica el paraíso y lo exalta hasta las nubes: el paraíso, de existir, está en la entraña misma de la tierra, nos aguarda con su abrazo húmedo, donde se confunden carne y arcilla [...] su androginia perfecta, su identidad siamesa, su bellísima anormalidad, su monstruosa perfección. (63)[4]

The aged and crippled Emiliano Barroso, speechless after a stroke, a left-wing activist abandoned by his children who consider him a burden and whom he considers 'pochos', that is, sold out to the Americans, traitors to their culture, also yearns for the warm embrace of the land, of oneness: 'Regreso a tientas a la tierra. Ella es como mi mirada ciega. Ella es negra. Esta vez la parte oscura del mundo que llamamos tierra me recibe' (116). This *tierra* saves him from the time of his children and his brother Leonardo Barroso: 'Y qué diferente del tiempo de mis hijos, refrigeradores y televisiones, el día sin naturaleza, la noche iluminada, la comida preparada sin manos, la envidia del bien ajeno' (117).

The antagonist brothers fight for the soul and the aesthetic of the frontier. Emiliano Barroso, the representative of *chicano* social movements such as that led in the sixties by César Chávez, the Sindicato de Labradores Agrícolas, faces his brother Leonardo, the Tzar of the Frontier: 'un desigual combate con un hermano pobre. Una lucha entre hermanos por el destino de nuestros hermanos. Hermanos

---

[4] Lisandro feels a similar disorientation: 'Lisandro ascendía al cielo de cristal, pero se sentía sumergido, descendiendo a un extraño mar de vidrio en un mundo desconocido, patas arriba (201). There is a curious echo here of the words of Michelet in *Aura*: 'El cielo no es alto ni bajo. Está encima y debajo de nosotros al mismo tiempo' (*Aura*, 48).

anónimos' (119). We are reminded of the relation between the 'hijos del conquistador' in *El naranjo*: the two Martíns, the *mestizo* son of Cortés and Marina and the *criollo* son of Cortés and Juana de Zúñiga. The cousins Gonzalo and Serafín Romero function respectively as *coyote* and bandit. In 'El despojo', as we will see, the *cuates* belong to a different order and embody the aesthetic heterogeneity of the work: 'el charrito genio, su alter ego naco, cabrón, pinche y pintoresco, chanchanchanero, todo lo contrario de su alter ego simbolista, francés, baudelairiano, era también su semejante, su hermano' (98). In a nice set-piece on simulation and hyperreality, the elegant, cultured lecturer on culinary themes, Dionisio Rangel, goes into a travel agency in an anonymous shopping mall in California to protest at the racism shown by exhibiting a dummy representing a Mexican peasant sleeping a siesta under his enormous *sombrero* while leaning on a cactus. He finds to his horror that the dummy is in fact a real Mexican who had been lost in the mall for ten years without being able to find his way out. Realising perhaps that he has a lot in common with the peasant in that he too is little more than a picturesque curiosity for his US university audiences, he joins forces with his countryman. What follows is a surrealist or carnivalesque *despojo* in the sense of relinquishing or shedding, mirroring the *despojo* in the sense of plundering, carried out by the North Americans who took about half the original territory of Mexico in 1848. Leaving his Mustang in the Colorado desert, Dionisio and his companion walk towards the frontier shedding not only their clothes, but all the consumer items that the lecturer had accumulated in his stay in the North:

> 'Baco' y su escudero, el Don Quijote de la buena cocina y el Rip Van Winkle mexicano que dormitó la Década Perdida en un shopping mall, avanzaron hacia el sur, hacia la frontera, hacia México, regando a lo largo del desierto norteamericano, por tierra que un día fue de México, las aspiradoras y las lavadoras, las hamburguesas y los Dr. Pepper, las cervezas insípidas y los cafés aguados [...]. (100)

Beyond the seemingly single-minded insistence on 'content' in the work, there is a less obvious engagement with the question of representation. Any realism in a culture like the *chicano* or Mexican-American, necessarily interlingual and hybrid, must face a real sense of intertextuality and the consciousness of its history as a web of textual constructions. In the final pages there is even a list of young *chicano* writers, and not so young ones like the influential poet Alurista. The title, *La frontera de cristal*, can be read to contain a reference to Crystal City, Texas, the homeplace of Tomás Rivera, a representative figure of classic *chicano* literature and the winner in 1970 with ...*y no se lo tragó la tierra* of the first Quinto Sol prize.[5] When the action moves to a Spanish town in Extremadura, the young protagonist does not repress an improbable wink to the master of Spanish realism, Pérez Galdós: '¿El doctor Centeno se tiñe el pelo?' (221). Carlos Fuentes himself has said that the most important aspect of *La frontera de cristal* was the 'ruptura de géneros'.[6] Hence his adoption in many stories of the language of certain highly self-conscious realisms, and of certain highly stylised literary trends. From the Almodóvar of *Mujeres al borde de un ataque de nervios*: 'pero la mirada, otra vez, era de un apasionamiento irresistible, me enamoro en serio, le decía, sé pedirlo todo porque también sé darlo todo' (13). From Pedro Camacho in Mario Vargas Llosa's *La Tía Julia y el escribidor* : 'Era un hombre de cincuenta años de edad, [...] robusto, patilludo, medio calvo, pero con un perfil perfecto, clásico, como de emperador romano' (12). From the Puig of *Boquitas pintadas*: '¿Qué sentía Leonardo Barroso un minuto antes? [...] ¿Dónde estaba Leonardo Barroso un minuto antes?' (292). From Samuel Beckett: 'Estoy sentado. Al aire libre. No puedo moverme. No puedo hablar. Pero puedo oír. Sólo que ahora no oigo nada' (103). From the Neruda of 'Alturas de Macchu Picchu': 'hijo de la altura, descendiente de la nieve, los hielos del cielo lo bautizan cuando brota en las montañas de San Juan, rompe el escudo virginal de las cordilleras' (243).

In 'El despojo' Fuentes opts to explore US consumer culture and the mentality of various female figures through a Mexican and Spanish American sub-genre to which he contributes in turn: the culinary novel, based on recipes and eating. Dionisio Rangel politely mentions the founder of the dynasty: 'Llevado y traído por los Estados Unidos de América (sobre todo después del éxito de la novela de Laura Esquivel, *Como agua para chocolate*), Dionisio decidió que ésta era la cruz de su

[5] See Juan Gutiérrez Martínez-Conde, *Literatura y sociedad en el mundo chicano* (Madrid: Ediciones de la Torre, 1992), 71, 76.
[6] In conversation, 5 May, 1995.

existencia: predicar la buena cocina en un país incapaz de entenderla o practicarla' (68). *Como agua para chocolate. Novela de entregas mensuales con recetas, amores y remedios caseros*, where the recipes of Tita produce miracles and disasters, came out in 1989. Four years later, in 1993, Sealtiel Alatriste published *En defensa de la envidia. Calumnias de amor y sexo*, about the imaginary rivalry between Alfondo Reyes and Salvador Novo for the services of the cook Tía Chole. Fuentes's story was followed in 1997 by the irremediably commercial *Afrodita*, a recipe collection and manual of Californian life by Isabel Allende. Dionisio 'Baco' Rangel, the famous Mexican gastronome, is for some obscure reason researching American food and is sitting, not too comfortably, in an American Grill. As he absent-mindedly rubs the bottle of chilli sauce, he is amazed to see emerge 'un pequeño hombrecito, diminuto pero distinguible por su traje de charro, su sombrero de mariachi y sus bigotes zapatistas' (85). The genie from the chilli bottle at the order of his master Dionisio shoots his gun and a series of American women appear, each corresponding to a dish in the $22 menu chosen by the gourmet.

Another important mediating aspect of frontier realism, inseparable from compromise and negotiation, is translation and interlingualism. If in the case of the 'evangelistas' who transcribed the letters of the illiterate in the Plaza de Santo Domingo in Mexico it was necessary to 'tener fe', or 'confianza' as Jim translates (from what into what is not clear), here in the novel the question is much more problematical. Translation is everywhere. Dionisio Rangel's name is even translated from Greek into Latin: Dionisio 'Baco' Rangel. The river which separates the two countries, and which is the protagonist of the last story, always receives its two Spanish names, the one used by the Anglos and the one used by the Mexicans: Río Grande, Río Bravo. The double name reminds us of the titles of so many *chicano* works such as Gloria Anzaldúa's *Borderlands / La frontera*. The Mexican workers mix the two languages with a degree of promiscuity: they speak of 'jaraseros sexuales en la fábrica' (133), 'en la escarcha, no en el summer' (135). Elsewhere we have 'las inmensas bubis' (95). Sometimes the literal translation of sayings simply produces humour, as with the following phrase in English, which sounds absurd without the rhyme of the absent Spanish: 'You don't have a mom or a dad or even a little dog to bark at you' (68). (The Spanish phrase is 'No tiene ni padre ni madre ni perro que le ladre.') Conversely, the following phrase in

Spanish sounds extremely strange if one does not know the English from which it is translated: 'Te cortas la nariz para vengarte de tu cara' (181). (The English is of course 'You cut off your nose to spite your face.')

More interesting is the abuse of translation which foregrounds the manipulation of conventions. In the following example Josefina translates from Mexican Spanish into Spanish Spanish for her mistress when they are actually speaking in English:

—En México hay muchos güeritos —dijo impasible Josefina, sin bajar la mirada.
—¿Muchos qué?
—Gente rubia, señorita. (172-3)

Jim translates from Mexican Spanish to English, but actually mistranslates: 'Explícame sin pena y vergüenza [...] son algo así como pity y shame en inglés' (56). In English, 'pena' would be more likely 'embarrassment'. Measures are also used in this game. Talking about the obesity of a woman, Dionisio say 'si pesaba un kilo, pesaba 326' (95), clearly moving from kilos to pounds in mid-sentence. Something similar happens to the lad from Extremadura in 'La apuesta'. Some pages earlier we see Leandro driving at two hundred per hour, very fast in kilometres for the Cuernavaca road, but feasible. In Spain the lad drove at ninety per hour so that the police would stop him for speeding, passing from kilometres to miles on the road between Madrid and the Cordillera Cantábrica.

To mention translation and even more so translation with an element of duplicity in the Mexican or *chicano* context is to evoke Malintzin, Doña Marina, la Malinche, the *lengua* or *faraute*, translator of Hernán Cortés. But in the story where one would logically look for her, 'Malintzin de las maquilas', she is not to be found. Marina Alva Matínez is called Marina because her family had always wanted to see the sea. Marina hardly fits into the 'masculine' model of la Malinche as 'chingada' which we see in the 'Los hijos de la Malinche' chapter of Paz's *El laberinto de la soledad*, nor is she a translator or intermediary. The women workers in the *maquila* do not depend economically on a husband or lover, but the cynicism with which the factory owner explains to his American partner the liberation of the women as a contribution to democracy makes us doubt their exemplarity as feminist models. Their liberation seems mainly to consist in going out with their workmates to dance and see the Chippendale Boys do striptease, and watch often half-naked Mexican women modelling bridal wear. The figure of la Malinche has been taken up and revindicated in recent years by Mexican writers such as Rosario Castellanos and especially by *chicana* women writers including Adelaida del Castillo, Norma Alarcón and Gloria Anzaldúa. While the figure is still seen as problematical in the context of the relationship between the *chicana* and her *barrio* and the values of her mother, what has been most strongly emphasised, according to Margo Glantz, is the figure of la Malinche as *lengua* and *faraute*, go-between and interpreter, 'lanzadera entre dos culturas diferentes [...] intérprete de ambas culturas'.[7] In 1993, in 'Los hijos del conquistador' from *El naranjo, o los círculos del tiempo*, Martín the son of Marina, was still seen as an 'hijo de la chingada', reflecting an essentialist and perhaps misogynistic vision of La Malinche.[8] In *La frontera de cristal* we will see the figure of Malintzin more clearly, *en filigrana*, if we go back to another story from *El naranjo*, 'Las dos orillas'. The story 'La apuesta', from *La frontera de cristal*, can be read as a contemporaneous, demythifying reading of the earlier story. In 'Las dos orillas' we see the rivalry between Malintzin as the interpreter of Cortés and the Andalusian Jerónimo de Aguilar. The latter had been shipwrecked in Yucatán and, when he was rescued by the expedition of Cortés, had almost turned into a Mayan Indian and spoke their language well, but opted to follow Cortés. His companion Gonzalo de Guerrero, on the other hand, stays with his wife and helps to launch the Mayan conquest of Andalusia! According to later, unreliable sources Jerónimo de Aguilar even married Marina.[9] Jerónimo de Aguilar, almost assimilated into the indigenous culture of the South, has a counterpart or twin in Alvaro Núñez Cabeza de Vaca, who was shipwrecked and wandered for eight years in the swamps and deserts of the North. The account of his adventures, which he published in 1539

---

[7] 'La Malinche: La lengua en la mano', in Margo Glantz, ed., *La Malinche, sus padres y sus hijos* (México: Facultad de Filosofía y Letras, 1994), 81. See also Luis Leal and Manuel Martín Rodríguez, 'Chicano Literature', in Roberto González Echevarría and Enrique Pupo-Walker, eds., *The Cambridge History of Latin American Literature* (Cambridge: CUP, 1996), vol. 2, 579–80.
[8] *El naranjo, o los círculos del tiempo* (México: Alfaguara, 1993), 101.
[9] Diego Muñoz Camargo, cit. by Georges Baudot, in Glantz, 52.

as *Naufragios*, make him the first author of New Spain. It is the fantasies of his companions, the negro Estebanico and Fray Marcos de Niza, which launch the myth of the Siete Ciudades de Cíbola. According to Fuentes's version in 'Río Grande, río Bravo' Cabeza de Vaca misses the chance to be the interpreter of the Indian soul: 'se ha vuelto idéntico a [los indios], pero pierde la oportunidad de ser uno de ellos, es igual a ellos pero no comprende la ocasión que tiene de ser el único español que podía entender a los indios y traducir sus almas al castellano' (261–62).

With a little imagination, these three figures, Malintzin and the two Spaniards who had become half assimilated into the indigenous cultures of the North and the South, Jerónimo de Aguilar and Cabeza de Vaca, can be seen to come together in the pages of 'La apuesta'. This, the penultimate story of the novel, tells in counterpoint, rather in the style of Mario Vargas Llosa, two stories which take place in Mexico and Spain, and which literally collide at the end, eliminating all the characters in a motorway tunnel between Asturias and León. Right from the beginning the outlandish nature of the plot points to a bizarre pseudo-allegorical game which dismantles all the conventions of realism. In a scruffy tourist taxi the Mexican driver Leandro Reyes, resentful and raging, meets an outrageously stereotypical Spanish woman, Encarnación Cadalso, who is enjoying the holiday in Mexico that she had won by being voted the best cave guide in Asturias. As epigons, they are decidedly less gifted than their interpreter precursors: Leandro confines himself to playing a pre-recorded tape of tourist information on the car cassette for the randy *gringa* and the *naco* Latin Lover making out on the back seat; Encarnación in Spain, showing off the splendid cave paintings, confines herself to saying 'Muy primitivo. Esto es muy primitivo' (230). Where else but to the Palace of Cortés in Cuernavaca would he take Encarna-Malintzin? A Spanish Malinche she gets the better of Leandro-Jerónimo in Mexico with her unanswerable commentaries on the murals ('a ver por qué hablan castellano y no indio entonces, si tanto les duelen los indios' (221)) and her fierce stand against the Mexican *machos* at a filling station: '¡Ya deja de comportarte como un machito de mierda y ven a cumplir con tu obligación, hijo de puta!' But when he in turn visits Spain, he repeats the reverse Mayan conquest by being the one able to invite the Spaniard to Madrid to show her the *castizo* Cibeles fountain and the Calle de Alcalá.

While the two *farautes* of Cortés leave Asturias in the North of Spain, the cradle of the Reconquista, in the Mercedes of Leandro's explorer, let us return to the other story, which takes place in the South of Spain, in Extremadura, the birthplace of many conquistadors and frontier territory with the Arab empire: 'hombres de frontera, hombres de allende el Duero' (261). The young protagonist of this story lives in a stone vilage which suffocates him: 'País de piedra. Lengua de piedra. Sangre y memoria de piedra. Si no te escapas de aquí, tú mismo te convertirás en piedra. Vete pronto, cruza la frontera, sacúdete la piedra' (215). Some pages later, the identification with Cabeza de Vaca is confirmed: 'Alvar Núñez Cabeza de Vaca, extremeño en fuga de la piedra insomne como la mayoría de los conquistadores' (261). His companions are offended by the young Extremaduran's 'interés por las palabras' and the rage that he feels is expressed in the beating that, for a bet, he gives to the village idiot. A mysterious figure appears who could well be the father of both the idiot and the protagonist, and challenges him to a strange test (whch is however practised by some Spanish youths): both would cross a motorway tunnel in distant Asturias on the wrong side of the road. (The youth was in fact already going to Asturias to see the sea, thanks to the previous bet, like Marina the 'Malintzin de las maquilas'.)

The *extremeño*, the Mexican Leandro Reyes and the Asturian cave guide are all wiped out in a 'gran abrazo de piedra' (238) on the frontier between Asturias, the 'patria querida' and the rest of Spain, 'tierra conquistada de los moros'. I prefer to conclude that together with them dies any fully allegorical, totalising reading, any fixed or mythical interpretation of their story, and indeed of *La frontera de cristal*.

It is not easy to determine to what extent *La frontera de cristal* belongs to *chicano* literature. It constitutes a large, all-encompassing gesture, and as such is a gesture of power, but at the same time it is a demythifying gesture, as suggested in the reading of the last story. In a sense it is a meta-*chicano* piece, a compendium of its major themes and symbols, a synthesis of the history of the Border from *Los naufragios* of Cabeza de Vaca, through Villará, Tomás Rivera and Alurista to the José Francisco who appears in the final pages with his Harley Davidson (the writer Aguilar Melantzón), disseminating his language to the wind: 'arrojando manuscritos al aire, al río, a la luna, a las fronteras, convencido de que las palabras volarían hasta encontrar su destino, sus lectores, sus auditores, sus lenguas, sus ojos...' (282).[10]

[10] This image is reminiscent of *Una familia lejana*, where the words fly off the pages of Dumas's memoirs like migratory birds, and of *Gringo viejo*, when the Old Gringo burns the papers of Arroyo-Zapata, and their liberated words fly over the desert.

BIBLIOGRAPHY

Works by Carlos Fuentes mentioned in the text

The place of publication is Mexico City unless otherwise stated.

Narrative

1954	*Los días enmascaradas* (Era, 1982).
1958	*La región más transparente* (Fondo de Cultura Económica, 1972).
1959	*Las buenas conciencias* (Fondo de Cultura Económica, 1973).
1962	*Aura* (Era, 1976).
1962	*La muerte de Artemio Cruz* (Fondo de Cultura Económica, 1970).
1964	*Cantar de ciegos* (Joaquín Mortiz, 1978).
1967	*Cambio de piel* (Barcelona: Seix Barral, 1974).
1967	*Zona sagrada* (Siglo XXI, 1976).
1969	*Cumpleaños* (Joaquín Mortiz, 1976).
1975	*Terra Nostra* (Barcelona: Seix Barral, 1975).
1978	*La cabeza de la hidra* (Barcelona: Argos, 1978).
1980	*Una familia lejana* (Barcelona: Bruguera, 1980).
1981	*Agua quemada* (Fondo de Cultura Económica, 1981).
1985	*Gringo viejo* (Madrid: Fondo de Cultura Económica, 1985).
1987	*Cristóbal Nonato* (Fondo de Cultura Económica, 1987).
1989	*Constancia y otras novelas para vírgenes* (Madrid: Mondadori, 1989).
1990	*La campaña* (Buenos Aires: Fondo de Cultura Económica, 1990).
1993	*El naranjo o los círculos del tiempo* (Alfaguara, 1993).
1994	*Diana o la cazadora solitaria* (Alfaguara, 1994).
1995	*La frontera de cristal* (Alfaguara, 1995).
1999	*Los años con Laura Díaz* (Alfaguara, 1999).

Essay

1968	*París, la revolución de mayo* (Era, 1968).
1969	*La nueva novela hispanoamericana* (Joaquín Mortiz, 1972).
1970	*Casa con dos puertas* (Joaquín Mortiz, 1970).
1971	*Tiempo mexicano* (Joaquín Mortiz, 1978).
1976	*Cervantes o la crítica de la lectura* (Joaquín Mortiz, 1976).

1988	*Myself with Others* (London: André Deutsch, 1988).
1990	*Valiente mundo nuevo: épica, utopía y mito en la novela hispanomericana* (Fondo de Cultura Económica, 1990).
1992	*El espejo enterrado* (Fondo de Cultura Económica, 1992).
1993	*Geografía de la novela* (Alfaguara, 1993).
1993	*Tres discursos para dos aldeas* (Buenos Aires: Fondo de Cultura Económica, 1993).
1994	*Nuevo tiempo mexicano* (Aguilar, 1994).
1995	*Feliz año nuevo* (Aguilar, 1995).

Articles, etc.

'Cronología personal', in Julio Ortega, ed., *Retrato de Carlos Fuentes* (Barcelona: Círculo de Lectores/ Galería Gutenberg, 1995), 104-14.

'Cómo escribí algunos de mis libros' *Sábado*, suplemento de *Uno más Uno* (9 Oct. 1982), 1-3.

'Seis cartas de Carlos Fuentes a Octavio Paz', *Revista Iberoamericana*, 37:74 (1971), 17-27.

'Mi amigo Octavio Paz', *El País (Edición Internacional)*, (18 al 24 de mayo 1998), 7-8.

Interviews

Fuentes, Sylvia, 'Estos fueron los palacios', in Reina Roffé, ed., *Espejo de escritores* (Hanover N.H.: Ediciones de Norte, 1985), 81-103.

Harss, Luis, 'Carlos Fuentes, o la nueva herejía' in *Los nuestros* (Buenos Aires, 1973), 338-80.

King, John, 'Carlos Fuentes: An Interview', in his *Modern Latin American Fiction: A Survey* (London and Boston: Faber and Faber, 1987), 137-54.

Reyzábal, María Victoria, 'Mantener un lenguaje o sucumbir al silencio', in Julio Ortega, ed., *Retrato de Carlos Fuentes* (Barcelona: Galaxia Gutenberg / Círculo de Lectores, 1995), 81-89.

Rodríguez Monegal, Emir, 'Carlos Fuentes', in Giacoman, ed., *Homenaje a Carlos Fuentes: variaciones interpretativas en torno a su obra* (New York: Las Americas, 1971), 23-65.

Critical Studies on Fuentes

Allen, C., 'La correlación entre la filosofía de Jean-Paul Sartre y *La muerte de Artemio Cruz* de Carlos Fuentes', in Giacoman, *Homenaje*, 399–442.

Avellaneda, Andrés, 'Mito y negación de la historia en *Zona sagrada* de Carlos Fuentes', *Cuadernos americanos*, 37:75 (1971), 239–48.

Befumo Boschi, Liliana and Elisa Calabresi, *Nostalgia del futuro en la obra de Carlos Fuentes* (Buenos Aires: Fernando García Cambeiro, 1974).

Boldy, Steven, 'Una familia cercana: *Los años con Laura Díaz*', in *Hoja por Hoja*, monthly supplement of *Reforma* (5 June 1999), 2–3.

——, '*Valiente mundo nuevo, La campaña*: Se siempre un problema', *Nexos*, 14:163 (1991), 81–85.

——, 'Jorge Ruiz Basto, *De la modernidad y otras creencias*' (review), in *Literatura Mexicana*, 4:1 (1993), 236–9.

Brody, Robert and Charles Rossman (eds), *Carlos Fuentes: A Critical View* (Austin, Texas: University of Texas Press, 1982).

Chanady, Amaryll, 'La problematización del pasado en "Estos fueron los palacios"', in Ana María Hernández de López, ed., *La obra de Carlos Fuentes: una visión múltiple* (Madrid: Pliegos, 1988), 289–96.

Dauster, Frank, 'The Wounded Vision: *Aura, Zona sagrada*, and *Cumpleaños*', in Brody and Rossman, 106–20.

Durán, Gloria, *The Archetypes of Carlos Fuentes: From Witch to Androgyne* (Hamden, Conn.: Archon, 1980).

Durán, Manuel, *Tríptico mexicano: Juan Rulfo, Carlos Fuentes, Salvador Elizondo* (Mexico City: SEP, 1973).

Echeverría, Manuel, 'Prólogo' to Carlos Fuentes, *Las buenas conciencias*, in *Obras completas* (Madrid: Aguilar, 1972), I.

Écrire le Mexique, América (Cahiers du CRICCAL), 25 (1999), 5–161.

Faris, Wendy, *Carlos Fuentes* (New York: Frederick Ungar, 1983).

——, '"Proustitución": *Una familia lejana*', in Merlin Forster and Julio Ortega, eds., *De la crónica a la nueva narrativa mexicana. Coloquio sobre literatura mexicana* (Mexico City: Oasis, 1986), 369–82.

Feijoo, Gladys, *Lo fantástico en los relatos de Carlos Fuentes: aproximación teórica* (New York: Senda Nueva de Ediciones, 1985).

Fernández Retamar, Roberto, *Calibán* in José Enrique Rodo, *Ariel* and R.

Fernández Retamar, *Calibán* (Mexico City: SEP / UNAM, 1982).

García Gutiérrez, Georgina, *Los disfraces: la obra mestiza de Carlos Fuentes* (Mexico City: Colegio de México, 1981).

——, 'Post scriptum' in her edition of Carlos Fuentes, *La región más transparente* (Madrid: Cátedra, 1982), 62–9.

Giacoman, Helmy, ed., *Homenaje a Carlos Fuentes: variaciones interpretativas en torno a su obra* (New York: Las Americas, 1971).

Glantz, Margo, 'Cambio de piel: Fuentes y las fiestas imposibles', in *Repeticiones: ensayos sobre literatura mexicana* (Xalapa: Universidad Veracruzana, 1979), 35-46.

Gyurko Lanin, 'Carlos Fuentes', in William Luis, ed., *Modern Latin American Fiction Writers*, vol. 113 of the Bruccoli Clerk Layman Dictionary of Literary Biography (Detroit, 1992), 150-67.

——, 'The Myth of Ulysses in Fuentes' *Zona sagrada*', *Modern Language Review*, 69:2 (1974), 316-24.

González Boixo, José Carlos, 'Introducción' to his edition of *La muerte de Artemio Cruz* (Madrid: Cátedra, 1998).

Hernández de López, Ana María (ed.), *La obra de Carlos Fuentes: una visión múltiple* (Madrid: Pliegos, 1988).

Ibsen, Kristine, *Author, Text and Reader in the Novels of Carlos Fuentes* (New York: Peter Lang, 1993).

Jara, René, 'El mito y la nueva novela hispanoamericana: a propósito de *La muerte de Artemio Cruz*', in Giacoman (1971), 147-208.

Krauze, Enrique, 'La Comedia Mexicana de Carlos Fuentes', in *Vuelta*, 139 (junio 1980), 15-27.

Lewald, Ernest, 'El pensamiento cultural mexicano en *La región más transparente* de Carlos Fuentes', in *Revista Hispánica Moderna*, 33:4 (1967), 216-23.

Ministerio de Cultura, Spain, *Carlos Fuentes: Premio Miguel de Cervantes (1987)* (Madrid, 1988).

Montero, Óscar, 'The role of Ixca Cienfuegos in the thematic fabric of *La región más transparente*' in *Hispanófila*, 20:58 (1976), 61-83.

Olivier, Florence, 'Une littérature d'actualité légère et engagée: *La frontera de cristal* de Carlos Fuentes', in *Les nouveaux réalismes, América (Cahiers du CRICCAL)*, 25 (2000), 77-82.

Ortega, Julio, ed., *Retrato de Carlos Fuentes* (Barcelona: Galaxia Gutenberg / Círculo de Lectores, 1995).

Ramírez Mattei, Aida Elsa, *La narrativa de Carlos Fuentes* (Río Piedras: Universidad de Puerto Rico, 1983).

Reeve, R., 'Carlos Fuentes y el desarrollo del narrador en segunda persona: un ensayo exploratorio', in Giacoman (1971), 75-87.

Ruiz Basto, Jorge, *De la modernidad y otras creencias (en torno a 'Cambio de piel' de Carlos Fuentes)* (Mexico City: UNAM, 1992).

Salgado, María A., 'El mito azteca en *La región más transparente*', in Giacoman (1971), 229-40.

Sarduy, Severo, 'Un fetiche de cachemira', in Giacoman (1971), 261–73.
Tittler, Jonathan, 'Cambio de zona/ Piel sagrada: Transfiguration in Carlos Fuentes', in *World Literature Today*, 57:4 (1983), 359–380.
van Delden, Maarten, *Carlos Fuentes, Mexico and Modernity* (Nashville, Tenn.: Vanderbildt University Press, 1998).
—— 'The Banquets of Civilization: the Idea of Ancient Greece in Rodó, Reyes and Fuentes', in *Annals of Scholarship*, 7:3 (1990), 303–21.

Other

Adorno, Theodor, and Max Horkheimer, *Dialectic of Enlightenment*, trans. by John Cumming (London: Verso, 1986).
Anon., *Lazarillo de Tormes* (Madrid: Castalia, 1982).
Baedeker's Paris and its Environs (London: Dulau and Co., 1898).
Baudelaire, Charles, *Oeuvres complètes* (Paris: Robert Lafont, 1980).
Bethell, Leslie, ed., *Mexico since Independence* (Cambridge: CUP, 1991).
Bierce, Ambrose, *The Collected Writings* (London: Picador, 1974).
Blake, William, *The Marriage of Heaven and Hell*, in *Complete Writings* (Oxford: OUP, 1984).
Blanchot, Maurice, *Lautréamont et Sade* (Paris: Minuit, 1984).
Blanco Fombona, Rufino, *Bolívar*, 3 vols (Caracas: La Gran Pulpería del Libro Venezolano, 1984).
Bloom, Harold, *The Anxiety of Influence. A Theory of Poetry* (New York: OUP, 1975).
——, *A Map of Misreading* (New York, OUP, 1980).
Boldy, Steven, *The Novels of Julio Cortázar* (Cambridge: CUP, 1980).
——, 'Making Sense in Carpentier's *El acoso*', *The Modern Language Review*, 85 (July 1990), pp. 612–22.
Borges, Jorge Luis, *Obras completas* (Buenos Aires: Emecé, 1974).
Bretall, Robert, ed., *A Kierkegaard Anthology* (Princeton, Princeton University Press, 1973).
Burland, C.A., *The Gods of Mexico* (London: Eyre & Spottiswoode, 1967).
Butler, E.M., *The Tyranny of Greece over Germany* (Cambridge: CUP, 1935).
Carpentier, Alejo, *El reino de este mundo* (Barcelona: Seix Barral, 1967).
Caso, Antonio, *La religión de los aztecas* (Mexico City: Imprenta Mundial, 1936).

Cirlot, J.E., *A Dictionary of Symbols*, trans. by Jack Sage (London: Routledge & Kegan Paul, 1983).
Cortázar, Julio, *Rayuela* (Buenos Aires: Sudamericana, 1969).
——, *Último round* (Mexico City: Siglo XXI, 1969).
——, *Obra crítica*, ed. by Jaime Alazraki (Madrid: Alfaguara, 1994), II.
——, *Cuentos completos* (Madrid: Alfaguara, 1994).
Culler, Jonathan. *The Pursuit of Signs. Semiotics, Literature, Deconstruction* (London: Routledge & Kegan Paul, 1983).
Dante Alighieri, *La Divina Commedia* (Milano: Lucchi, 1967).
Darío, Rubén, *Poesías completas* (Madrid: Aguilar, 1968).
del Paso, Fernando, *Palinuro de México* (Mexico City: Joaquín Mortiz, 1977).
Derrida, Jacques, *De la grammatologie* (Paris: Minuit, 1985).
Díaz, Lomberto, *Heredia: primer romántico hispanoamericano* (Montevideo: Geminis, 1973).
Diderot, Denis, *Jacques le fataliste* (Paris: Garnier Flammarion, 1970).
——, *Le Neveu de Rameau* (Paris: Garnier Flammarion, 1967).
Dostoyevsky, Fyodor, *Crime and Punishment* (Oxford: OUP, 1990).
Dumas, Alexandre, *Le Comte de Monte-Cristo*, 3 vols (Paris: Le Livre de Poche, 1973).
——, *Mes mémoires*, 2 vols (Paris: Rober Lafont, 1989),.
Dumas *fils*, Alexandre, *La Dame aux camélias* (Paris: Gallimard, 1991).
Encyclopedia of Visual Art (London: Encyclopaedia Britannica International, 1989).
Encyclopaedia Britannica, fifteenth edition, 1992.
Euripides, *Medea and Other Plays* (Harmondsworth: Penguin, 1979).
Faulkner, William, *Absalom, Absalom!* (Harmondsworth: Penguin, 1987).
Feder, Lillian, *Madness in Literature* (Princeton: Princeton University Press, 1980).
Foucault, Michel, *Madness and Civilization. A History of Insanity in the Age of Reason*, trans. by Richard Howard (London: Tavistock, 1982).
——, *Histoire de la folie* (Paris: Gallimard, 1979).
——, *Les Mots et les choses* (Paris: Gallimard, 1984).
Freud, Sigmund, *On Sexuality*, The Pelican Freud Library (Harmondsworth: Penguin, 1977), VII.
——, *Totem and Taboo*, in *The Origins of Religion*, The Pelican Freud Library (Harmondsworth: Penguin, 1985), XIII.
——, 'The Uncanny', in *Art and Literature*, The Pelican Freud Library (Harmondsworth: Penguin, 1985), XIV.
Gallegos, Rómulo, *Canaima* (Madrid: Espasa-Calpe, 1977).

Gamboa, Federico, *Santa*, in *Novelas de Federico Gamboa* (Mexico City: Fondo de Cultura Económica, 1965).
García Cantú, Gastón, *Utopías mexicanas* (Mexico City: Fondo de Cultura Económica, 1987).
Glantz, Margo, ed., *La Malinche, sus padres y sus hijos* (Mexico City: Facultad de Filosofía y Letras, 1994).
Goldmann, Lucien, *Le Dieu caché* (Paris: Gallimard, 1979).
Gorostiza, José, *Muerte sin fin*, in Héctor Valdés, ed., *Los Contemporáneos: una antología general* (Mexico City: SEP/UNAM, 1982).
Guerlac, Othon, *Les Citations françaises* (Paris: A. Colin, 1961).
Gutiérrez Martínez-Conde, Juan, *Literatura y sociedad en el mundo chicano* (Madrid: Ediciones de la Torre, 1992).
Guzmán, Martín Luis, *El águila y la serpiente*, in *La novela de la Revolución Mexicana*, ed. by Antonio Castro Leal (Mexico City: Aguilar, 1974).
——, *Memorias de Pancho Villa* (Mexico City: Compañía General de Ediciones, 1981).
Heredia, José-Maria de, *Œuvres poétiques complètes* (Paris: Société d'Edition 'Les Belles Lettres', 1984).
——, *Les Trophées*, ed. by Anny Detalle (Paris: Gallimard, 1991).
Huizinga, Johan, *Homo ludens*, trans. by Eugenio Imaz (Madrid: Alianza-Emecé, 1972).
Huysmans, Joris-Karl, *À rebours* (Paris: Editions Fasquelle, 1968).
Kierkegaard Soren, in Robert Bretall, ed., *A Kierkegaard Anthology*.
Kracauer, Siegfried, *From Caligari to Hitler. A Psychological History of the German Film* (New York: Dennis Dobson, 1947).
Krauze, Enrique, *Mexico: Biography of Power. A History of Modern Mexico, 1810–1996*, translated by Hank Heifetz (New York: Harper Collins, 1997).
Lautréamont, Comte de (Isidore Ducasse), *Les Chants de Maldoror. Lettres. Poésies I et II* (Paris: Gallimard, 1973).
Larroyo, Franciso, *La filosofía iberoamericana* (Mexico City: Porrúa, 1978).
Lawrence, D.H., *Lady Chatterley's Lover* (Harmondsworth: Penguin, 1972).
Leal, Luis and Manuel Martín Rodríguez, 'Chicano Literature', in Roberto González Echevarría and Enrique Pupo Walker, eds., *The Cambridge History of Latin American Literature* (Cambridge: CUP, 1996), II.
Lévi-Strauss, Claude, *Anthropologie structurale* (Paris: Plon, 1984).

——, *The Savage Mind* (London: Weidenfeld & Nicolson, 1989).
López Velarde, Ramón, *Obras* (Mexico City: Fondo de Cultura Económica, 1972).
Mann, Thomas, *Doctor Faustus* (Harmondsworth: Penguin, 1985).
Marx, Karl, *Selected Writings*, ed., David McLellan (Oxford: OUP, 1977).
Michelet, Jules, *La Sorcière* (Paris: Librairie Marcel Didier, 1952).
Monsiváis, Carlos, 'Notas sobre la cultura mexicana en el siglo XX', in *Historia general de México* (Mexico City: Colegio de México, 1981), II, 5-548.
Mounier, Emmanuel, *L'Affrontement chrétien, Œuvres* (Paris: Seuil, 1962), III.
Mujica Láinez, Manuel, *Bomarzo* (Barcelona: Círculo de Lectores, 1973).
Neruda, Pablo, *Residencia en la tierra* (Buenos Aires: Losada, 1959).
——, *Canto general* (Buenos Aires: Losada, 1970).
Nerval, Gérard de, *Les Chimères*, Genève: Droz, 1966).
Nietzsche, Friedrich, *The Birth of Tragedy and The Genealogy of Morals* (New York: Doubleday, 1956).
——, *Ecco Homo* (Harmondsworth: Penguin, 1992).
——, *Untimely Meditations* (Cambridge: CUP, 1994).
O'Connor, Richard, *Ambrose Bierce. A Biography* (London: Victor Gollancz, 1968).
Orellana, Margarita de, *La mirada circular. El cine norteamericano de la Revolución Mexicana* (Mexico City: Joaquín Mortiz, 1991).
Ortega y Gasset, José, *La deshumanización del arte* (Madrid: Revista de Occidente/Alianza, 1983).
Paz, Octavio, *Poemas (1935-1975)* (Barcelona: Seix Barral, 1985).
——, *El laberinto de la soledad* (Mexico City: Fondo de Cultura Económica, 1973).
——, et al., *Poesía en movimiento: México 1915-1966* (Mexico City: Siglo XXI, 1975).
——, *Lévi-Strauss o el nuevo festín de Esopo* (Barcelona: Seix Barral, 1993).
——, *Conjunciones y disyunciones* (Mexico City: Joaquín Mortiz, 1978).
——, *Puertas al campo* (Barcelona: Seix Barral, 1981).
——, *Posdata* (Mexico City: Siglo XXI, 1982).
Pérez Galdós, Benito, *Fortunata y Jacinta* (Madrid: Hernando, 1971).
Poe, Edgar Allan, *Selected Writings* (Harmondsworth: Penguin, 1975).
Poniatowska, Elena, *¡Ay vida, no me mereces!* (Mexico City: Joaquín Mortiz, 1986).
——, *Fuerte es el silencio* (Mexico City: Era, 1987).

Prawer, S.S., *Caligari's Children. The Film as Tale of Terror* (New York: OUP, 1980).
Praz, Mario, *The Romantic Agony*, trans. by Angus Davidson (Oxford: OUP, 1985).
Proust, Marcel, *A la recherche du temps perdu* (Paris: Gallimard, 1999).
Roa Bastos, Augusto, *Yo el Supremo* (Buenos Aires: Siglo XXI, 1974).
——, 'Algunos núcleos generadores de un texto narrativo', in *L'Idéologique dans le texte (Textes hispaniques)* (Toulouse: Université de Toulouse-le Mirail, 1978).
Robbe-Grillet, Alain, *Pour un Nouveau Roman* (Paris: Gallimard, 1963).
Said, Edward, *Orientalism* (1978; Harmondsworth: Penguin, 1985).
Sayers, Dorothy L., in *The Comedy of Dante Alighieri the Florentine*, ed. and trans. by D. Sayers (Harmondsworth: Penguin, 1965).
Séjournée, Laurette, *Burnt Water. Thought and Religion in Ancient Mexico* (London: Thames and Hudson, 1957).
Silk, M.S. and J.P. Stern, *Nietzsche on Tragedy* (Cambridge: CUP, 1983).
Sinclair, John D. in Dante, *The Divine Comedy. Vol. 3: Paradiso*, trans. and ed. by J. Sinclair (New York: Oxford University Press, 1979).
Sontag, Susan, *Against Interpretation* (London: André Deutsch, 1987).
Steiner, George, *The Death of Tragedy* (London: Faber and Faber, 1982).
Stendhal (Henri Beyle), *Le Rouge et le noir* (Paris: Garnier-Flammarion, 1964).
Styron, William, *Lie Down in Darkness* (London: Black Swan, 1984).
Tanner, Tony, *Adultery in the Novel* (Baltimore: The Johns Hopkins University Press, 1979).
Todorov, Tzvetan, *La Conquête de l'Amérique. La Question de l'autre* (Paris: Seuil, 1982).
Unamuno, Miguel de, *Del sentimiento trágico de la vida* (Madrid: Austral. 1967).
Vallejo, César, *Los heraldos negros, Trilce* (Barcelona: El Bardo, 1972).
Weiss, Peter, *Marat/Sade* (London: Marion Boyars, 1978).
Womack, John, *Zapata and the Mexican Revolution* (Harmondsworth: Penguin, 1972).
Wilde, Oscar, *The Picture of Dorian Gray* (Harmondsworth: Penguin, 1971).
Williams, Charles, *The Figure of Beatrice. A Study in Dante* (London: Faber and Faber, 1950).
Worton, Michael and Judith Still, eds., *Intertextuality. Theories and Practices* (Manchester, Manchester University Press, 1990).
Yates, Frances, *The Art of Memory* (Harmondsworth: Penguin, 1978).

EU authorised representative for GPSR:
Easy Access System Europe, Mustamäe tee 50,
10621 Tallinn, Estonia
gpsr.requests@easproject.com

www.ingramcontent.com/pod-product-compliance
Ingram Content Group UK Ltd.
Pitfield, Milton Keynes, MK11 3LW, UK
UKHW041914140426

5217IPUK00013B/155